Lubna Tarabey is a Lecturer of Sociology at the American University of Beirut and an Assistant Professor of Sociology at the Lebanese University. She holds a PhD in Sociology from the Lebanese University.

FAMILY LAW IN LEBANON

Marriage and Divorce among the Druze

LUBNA TARABEY

I.B.TAURIS
LONDON · NEW YORK

Published in 2013 by I.B.Tauris & Co Ltd
6 Salem Road, London W2 4BU
175 Fifth Avenue, New York NY 10010
www.ibtauris.com

Library of Modern Middle East Studies 142

ISBN 978 1 78076 562 4

A full CIP record for this book is available from the British Library
A full CIP record for this book is available from the Library of Congress

Library of Congress catalog card: available

Typeset by Newgen Publishers, Chennai

To Wahib and May Tarabey

CONTENTS

List of Tables and Figures ix
Acknowledgements xii

1. Introduction 1
   Theoretical Framework 4
   Scope and Methodology 9
   Structure of this Book 15
2. The Druze 18
   Historical Background 18
   Druze Beliefs, Values and Perspectives 21
   Structures of the Druze Community 28
   Druze Socio-political Presence in Lebanon 31
   Change among the Druze 34
3. Marriage Among the Druze 39
   The *Tolbeh* 39
   The Official Engagement Celebration 40
   Signing of the Marriage Contract 43
   Wedding Party 44
   Legal Background 47
   Analysis of Marriage Practices 51
   Concluding Remarks 94

4. Divorce among the Druze 97
Legal Background 100
Analysis of Divorce Practices 102
Change: Case Studies 156
General Findings 162
Pseudo-divorce 166
Concluding Remarks 172
5. Marriage and Divorce: A Comparative Approach 175
Divorce Rates 175
Marriage and Divorce: A Comparison 179
Limitations of the Comparative Study 194
6. The Druze: Peripheral Change 196
Peripheral Change 199
The Legal Setting 201
Social Change and Solidarity 202
Appendix A: Personal Status Laws of the Druze Sect in Lebanon 205
Appendix B: Sample of Marriage Contract 227
Appendix C: Role of the Adjudicator 231
Appendix D: Divorce Case of Man Marrying a non-Druze 233
Appendix E: Divorce Case Involving a Social Worker Appointed by Court to Help Spouses 241
Appendix F: Divorce Case Brought Before the Court by Husband 249
Appendix G: Marriage Ceremonies among the *Ajaweed* 256
Appendix H: Description of the Court 258
Appendix I: Other Causes for Divorce Mentioned in Court Records 260

Glossary 262
Notes 265
Bibliography 286
Index 292

LIST OF TABLES AND FIGURES

Tables

3.1 Distribution of Marriage Contracts per Year 52
3.2 Frequency Distribution of Husband's Age at Marriage (1970–2003) 55
3.3 Age of Husband vs. Selected Time Intervals 56
3.4 Husband's Age vs. Date of Marriage 57
3.5 Frequency Distribution of Female's Age at Marriage 61
3.6 Age of Female at Marriage vs. Date of Marriage 62
3.7 Age of Female's Marriage vs. Date of Marriage 63
3.8 Age at Marriage vs. Husband's Residence 65
3.9 Wife's Residence vs. Age at Marriage 67
3.10 Frequency Distribution of Husband–Wife Age Difference 69
3.11 Date of Marriage vs. Husband–Wife Age Difference 70
3.12 Husband's Residence vs. Husband–Wife Age Difference 71
3.13 Wife's Residence vs. Husband–Wife Age Difference 72
3.14 Frequency Distribution of Husband–Wife Relationship 74
3.15 Husband–Wife Relationship vs. Date of Marriage 75

3.16	Parent's Relationship vs. Husband–Wife Marriage Date	76
3.17	Husband's Residence vs. Husband–Wife as Relatives	77
3.18	Wife's Residence vs. Husband–Wife as Related	77
3.19	Date of Marriage vs. Husband–Wife Residence	79
3.20	Marriage Date vs. Sewing Machine's Presence	82
3.21	Date of Marriage vs. Bedroom Mentioned in *Mahr*	84
3.22	Paid *Mahr* vs. Date of Marriage	88
3.23	Date of Marriage vs. Kind of Delayed *Mahr*	93
4.1	Type of Divorce vs. Time Intervals	115
4.2	Type of Divorce vs. Husband's Residence	119
4.3	Residence of Wife vs. Type of Divorce	121
4.4	Type of Divorce vs. Who Filed for Divorce	126
4.5	Number of Cases per Year	127
4.6	Person Who Brought Contested Divorce before Court vs. Time Interval	129
4.7	Elements of Court Decision vs. Time Interval	131
4.8	Wife's Causes for Divorce vs. Time Interval	136
4.9	Husband's Causes for Divorce vs. Time Interval	143
4.10	Wife's Place of Residence vs. Causes for Divorce According to Wife	145
4.11	Wife's Place of Residence vs. Causes for Divorce	146
4.12	Who Brings the Case Before Court vs. Wife's Place of Residence	147
4.13	Husband's Place of Residence vs. Husband's Causes for Divorce	148
4.14	Husband's Place of Residence vs. Who Brought the Case before the Court	150
4.15	Emigrant Status of Husband vs. Years of Marriage	151
4.16	Immigrant Status of Wife vs. Years of Marriage	152
4.17	Time Spent in Court vs. Type of Divorce	163
5.1	Rates of Divorce by Five-Year Intervals	177
5.2	Husband's Age by Year-Intervals in Marriage Contracts and Divorce Cases	180

5.3 Wife's Age by Year-Intervals in Both Marriage Contracts and Divorce Cases 185
5.4 Spouses' Age Difference Reported in Marriage Contracts and Divorce Cases 188
5.5 Percentages of Spouses Coming from the Same, Neighbouring or Different Places of Residence in Marriage Contracts and Divorce Cases 191
5.6 Percentage of Patriarchally Related Spouses in Marriage Contracts and Divorce Cases 192
5.7 Percentages of Maternally-Related Spouses Reported in Marriage Contracts and Divorce Cases 193

Figure

A Type of Divorce 105

Graph

1 Number of Cases per Five-Year Time Interval 128

ACKNOWLEDGEMENTS

A number of people whose support and assistance were crucial for the completion of this work accordingly deserve my acknowledgement.

I have to start with a word of remembrance to the late Judge of the Druze Court of Appeal, Nouhad Hariz who, along with Judge Nassouh Haydar granted me permission and access to the court records without which this research would not have been possible. Thanks are also due to all the court employees who also facilitated my work and were very helpful. I would also like to acknowledge all my informants and all the people who trusted me enough to tell their stories.

I shall forever be grateful to Sarah Vincent-Grosso who read and commented on the whole manuscript offering much appreciated advice.

I am also very appreciative of the hard work done by Ms Susan Kennedy in editing the manuscript and suggesting enlightening comments. Nadine El-Hadi at I.B.Tauris also offered helpful suggestions.

Thanks are also due to Dr Fredrick Maatouk and Dr Martha Mundy.

Last but not least, I am thankful to all my family members for their help and support. I would like to thank my grandmother, Ahsan Al-Halabi, and my late grandfather, 'Adel Al-Halabi, for the picture on the cover of the book. Thanks are also due to Maha Tarabey for her help. My biggest thank you goes to my two boys, Makram and Firas for appreciating that their mom had to work for very long hours.

This book is dedicated to my loving parents, Wahib and May Tarabey. Thank you for your constant encouragement.

CHAPTER ONE

INTRODUCTION

> 'The rate of divorce has increased drastically over the past years.'
> 'Women are asking for divorce because they are becoming more demanding. Nothing seems to be enough. They always want more.'
> 'The family is breaking down.'
> 'No one is willing to make sacrifices for the well being of the family. Whenever faced with a problem, the easiest way out is divorce.'
> 'Family values and morals are on the decline.'
> 'Young men and women think they know everything because they have attended schools. They no longer listen to the wise experienced elders.'

It was comments like these, heard every day in conversations among members of the Druze community, that motivated me to study family life and its supposed 'breakdown' among the Druze, only to find there is very limited research that tackles this topic. This led me to choose the topic of change among the Druze as the subject matter of my research. While it is certainly true that this research stems from personal interest in my own community, being a Druze, which might elicit criticism from scholars who prefer more impersonal socio-anthropological research, I find myself more inclined to agree with

Maxwell (2005) when he points out that incorporating personal interests is not something one should try to avoid:

> Attempting to exclude your personal goals and concerns from the design of your research is neither possible nor necessary. What is necessary is to be aware of these goals ... And think of how best to deal with their influence. In addition, recognizing personal ties to the study can provide you with a valuable source of insight. (Maxwell, 2005: 19)

Nicolas (2001) agrees and clearly states that when attempting any research, a number of key features must be taken into account, first of which is that the research problem should be of interest to the researcher.[1] Personal goals are thus a legitimate part of research, but they are not in themselves a sufficient condition for research (Nicolas, 2001: 21).

The limited nature of existing research into family change among the Druze community allows the study to meet Maxwell's (2005) two other goals/categories – namely the practical goal and the intellectual goal. On the practical level, research on family change among the Lebanese Druze would, if not alter, at least offer some insights into a certain 'problematic' situation – and if allowed some scope may serve as a basis for a reconsideration of laws and social practices by the Druze. While acknowledging the importance of the above factor, the most important goal of the research remains the attempt to understand certain social phenomena that give an insight into the mechanisms at play within the Druze family as revealed through a study of marriage practices and divorce choices among the Druze community – the two processes being legally restricted to and structured within the Druze personal status court.

At the basis of the research lies the assumption that over recent decades the Druze way of life has not remained the same but has been challenged by ongoing changes in the Lebanese society as a whole. Over the past decade huge changes have occurred in the mass media and means of communication, and will evidently continue to do so. The increase in industrialization, urbanization (as a mental attitude, not just as a physical reality), modernization and exposure to Western ideas resulting from the rise in education and the strong pull of urbanization may be expected to have left their influence on family life. In addition, one cannot ignore the fact that the extended Lebanese civil war has also had an impact on people's lives and choices, evident in the ever-growing trend towards migration, both temporary and permanent. This trend, while triggered by the war, has been sustained by an increased aspiration for a better standard of living.

The influence of the extended Lebanese civil war was not restricted to the economical aspect of migration. As well as destroying the physical structure of the country, it had a detrimental effect on the social fabric of Lebanon both by dividing people of different sectarian affiliations and by strengthening the sectarian identity of each group. The Druze people strongly held the common belief that they were fighting a war of existence and could not trust any other sectarian group. This feeling was shared by other groups that consequently led to a weakening of national feeling, an increase in dissent and the predominance of religious identity. The internal cohesion and solidarity of the religious group became ever more sacred and was not to be jeopardized. Although the war ended in the early 1990s, the feelings did not. They continue to shape the community and people's emotions, as became evident during the incidents of 8 May 2008 in Lebanon.[2]

All the above factors challenge people's ways of life, customs and traditions. A social group that undergoes such a process must change to cope with current realities. The challenge is perhaps most strongly felt by traditional groups who try to maintain a particular way of life. For generations, the Druze way of life was characterized by a high degree of 'traditional' practices and customs, so these changes might be expected to weigh heavily upon their traditional family life, changing it from one that was predominantly patriarchal and kin-oriented to one that is more individualistic and cognitive.[3] In a nutshell, this study sets out to analyse whether or not such individualism reveals itself in the marriage choices and divorce decisions that are being made or taken with limited, or at least less, consideration to previous 'traditionally accepted' norms or modes of conduct. Furthermore, the research will also shed light on any distinct trend in marriage choices and grounds for divorce as analysed through the court records.

Among the Lebanese Druze, the two aspects of family life – marriage and divorce – are regulated by application to the Druze court. A Druze person cannot, by law, marry or divorce outside the court except under special conditions and with a special permission granted by the Druze religious court – namely the judge. Even after the permission is granted, the matter remains pending until proper legal registration takes place in court. Article 16, as modified by the law issued on 2 July 1959, clearly stipulates that the marriage contract is not legally binding unless it was carried out by the Sheikh al-'Aql,[4] a judge or a person who has acquired, from either the Sheikh al-'Aql or the judge, the permission to do so (Awar, 1983: 178).[5] Similarly, divorce cannot be performed outside of court. Article 37 of the Druze personal status law stipulates that no marriage contract can be dissolved without a ruling issued by the judge (Awar, 1983: 181). Thus, any study of social change cannot be achieved without a consideration of the law and the influence of the law and the people involved in the legal process, such as the judge.

Theoretical Framework

The research focus will be on two interconnected trajectories – one that considers change in the overall family patterns as revealed in marriage and divorce records and another that places these changes within the legal context in which they occur, focusing on the interplay between the social and the legal. Although these are theoretically dealt with separately, yet, they overlap analytically and practically in the manner through which the legal process deals with, formulates, but is also formulated by, the social. The legal and the social become one 'field' that is shaped by and shapes the changes and the continuities experienced by the community at large, without the people being necessarily conscious of this reality. Bourdieu (1990) comments:

> The conditioning associated with a particular class of conditions of existence produces habitus, systems of durable, transportable

> dispositions, structured structures predisposed to function as structuring structures, that is as principles which generate and organize practices and representations that can be objectively adapted to their outcomes without presupposing a consciousness aiming at ends, or an express mastery of the operations necessary in order to attain them. (Bourdieu, 1990: 3)

Thus taking the habitus a step forward and considering marriage and divorce practices as belonging to one habitus, then these 'can only be accounted for by relating the social conditions in which the habitus that generated them was constituted, to the social conditions in which it is implemented' (Bourdieu, 1990: 56). This brings together the social and the legal, the family and the law.

Family Change: A Model

This research is concerned with analysing and understanding the change that had occurred within the structural values of the family as a basic social unit and the variables controlling its formation or disintegration. To explain and understand the contemporary Druze family, I have used the model of Gemeinschaft vs. Gesellschaft offered by the German philosopher Ferdinand Tonnies as a general guideline for my research. The model proposes that family values have undergone a change from traditional, kin-oriented values to more modern, individualistic ones.[6]

A group may change from Gemeinschaft to Gesellschaft when it is confronted by the emergence of motivations, ties and incentives that are of a more individualistic nature. Goode (1993) is very approving of Tonnie's model and claims that societies change from the first to the second with increasing levels of industrialization, urbanization and bureaucratization (Goode, 1993: 13). When these processes occur, there will be a change from face-to-face communication and familiar patterns to more objective and rational relationships. Many of the traditional rules of behaviour weaken and so does the control of elder family members over the choices made by the urbanized and 'industrialized' youth. Thus, the change from Gemeinschaft to

Gesellschaft occurs under the influences of increased education, urbanization and sustained migration, aided by the increased spread of mass media.[7]

Anderson (1964) associated the process of urbanization with the change from an agricultural-based family economy to a work-based individualistic economy that entails some considerable change for both the individual and the community. He comments that 'modern urbanization tends to become much less urban confined than ever before, becoming more globalized than was ever possible. One can no longer escape its influence by living in a village' (Anderson, 1964: 102).

Lois Wirth, a key figure in the development of the Chicago School theory of urbanization, claimed that the city led to the development of 'a loosening of community ties, increased social competitions, anonymity and a multiplication of interactions, often at low levels of intensity and trust' (Cohen and Kennedy, 2000: 268).[8]

Urban anthropologists uphold a somewhat different perspective of cities. While it is true that the spread of cities brings with it a movement from the countryside – the village – to the city, they maintain that traditions and kinship ties are sustained (Keesing and Strathern, 1998: 453–4). The ethos of the village or the community is brought into the city and often members of the same community tend to live in close proximity and maintain a way of life similar to the one they had left behind. This anthropological perspective is certainly observable among Druze migrating communities, which tend to live close to one another. However, the effect of city life even on these 'village-extensions' cannot be denied or underestimated. This effect is most likely to be felt within the family as a social unit as it comes under the direct influence of the city – way of life, characterized by mobilization, individualism and formal ties.

On a legal level, a change also occurs in a society as it is transformed from Gemeinschaft to Gesellschaft whereby the emergence of a state dominated legal system is noted. Matters related to citizens become the concern of the state and the law itself becomes a 'prominent tool for modernization in third world countries' (Engle Merry, 1988: 879) influencing and reflecting change in society.

Law and Society

In the fields of sociology and anthropology, the perspective that has dominated the discourse on law has been that of legal pluralism which proposes that within any society a number of normative agencies are at play simultaneously. In this sense, the state does not have a monopoly over the normative (Dupret, Berger and al-Zwain, 1999: xii). Legal pluralism further entails the presence within a single state of more than just one body of law before which all citizens of the state are held equally accountable. Woodman comments that

> many state laws contain several distinct sets of marriage laws, derived from different customs and religious laws. Each set may be regarded as a body of law, in the sense that it contains a number of interrelated norms, but is complete in itself. According to the law of the state, each set of norms is constituted part of state law through endorsement by the state authority. But it can still be said that each is a distinct body of law. Thus legal pluralism exists within this state law of marriage. (Woodman, 1999: 14)

In Lebanon, legal pluralism is characteristic of the state law. In all personal status matters, including marriage, divorce, inheritance, custody of children and so on, each religious sect in Lebanon has its own legal institutions and follows its own set of laws. These laws reflect each sect's own religious values and traditions and the norms that guide the behaviour of each group. These religious norms, derived from traditions, remain active in society and form part of the pluralistic order of the legal process, and since these norms are upheld even when they contradict any state legal principle, they tend to come out victorious. The personal status law in Lebanon was formulated in line with the particularities of each religious sect and could be understood in the framework of the diffusive approach that proposed that 'At the very basis of state law was a prior "social law" or "living law"... state law is subordinate to "living law". In the event of a conflict between the two, it would be ineffective' (Fitzpatrick, 2002: 4).

In fact, Ferrie considers that it is quite impossible to consider norms, laws and practices as three distinct categories. They simply cannot be separated. 'Norms, laws, and practices are in fact nothing more than different points in the same process' (Ferrie, 1999: 21). To achieve a better understanding of the function and nature of law, Dupret claims that it is best to have law 'stripped of its conceptual status and returned to the fold of general normality, so that there is no longer an ex post facto distinction between it and other types of norms such as moral injunctions, political rules, traditions, habits, etiquette and even table manners' (Dupret, 1999: 31).

This pluralistic approach to law in no way undermines the importance of law and the legal process. When a law is established, it brings about a change in the way people perceive social relationships and in the way they interact. Bourdieu (2002) describes the process through which law is formulated as a 'true social modification' whereby 'by eliminating exceptions and the vagueness of uncertain groupings, and by imposing clear discontinuities and strict borders into the continuum of statistical limits, juridical formalization introduces into social realities a clarity and predictability. It thus institutes a rationality that can never be fully guaranteed by the practical principles of habitus or the sanctions of custom by which these unformulated principles are directly applied to particular cases' (Bourdieu, 2002: 153). Writing a legal code that allows legislators and citizens the possibility of clearly studying, comprehending and acting in accordance with the legally stipulated rules, is something that is very essential (Messick, 2002: 273). To be able to comprehend fully the role of law in society, we must first understand the power that law has in society. Bourdieu (2002: 118–57) makes clear that we must understand the power of the law, the mechanisms that are at play within the legal system, the relationship between court personnel, litigants, lawyers and judges, if we want to understand the whole legal system with all its social ramifications. All these influence the manner in which this system operates in society but they also reflect the society in which it operates.

Put in theoretical terms, the research examines the change from Gemeinschaft to Gesellschaft in the practices of marriage and divorce and their unfolding within the legal framework of the court, focusing on the interaction between all those involved in the process including the individuals concerned and the legal personnel. These practices and socio-legal interactions are further framed by the religious values and norms of the Druze community and its historical and cultural experiences.

Scope and Methodology

Since the two aspects of family life, marriage and divorce, are regulated by the religious court and cannot be held anywhere else, the most suitable place to study them seems evidently to be through the study of the court records – the archives of the court. Analysis of court documents constitute the main method utilized in this study.[9] Kelly, in a different context, reflects on the importance of documents pointing out that

> documents should not be taken as abstract entities but must be understood in the wider institutional and political context in which they are produced, verified and take effect. This means looking directly at documents in order to analyze how they are experienced by their subjects and used to mediate social and political relationships. It also means looking beyond documents to examine conditions of their production and reception in a very particular historical context. (Kelly, 2006: 92)

The analysis of court documents should reflect the social circumstances in which they were produced, and hence constitute the dominant research method for this study. However, it would fail to reflect completely the nature of the lived realities of the people concerned with these documents – their experiences, perceptions and evaluations of marriage and divorce. To realize this purpose, other methods were utilized. These included semi-structured interviews with legal personnel and members of the community, an expository questionnaire and observation of court sessions and ethnographic analysis of my experiences in the community.

Sample and Data Gathering

There are six Druze Personal Status Courts in Lebanon and one court of appeal, located in Beirut. The six courts are distributed in the following manner: one each in Beirut, Aley, Matn,[10] Baaqlin, Rashaya and Hasbaya. In an attempt to make the research as representative as possible of the Druze community, the Beirut district court was chosen as the most suitable location for data collection, the reason being that it has legal jurisdiction over a wide area of Lebanon including parts of the Chouf district, the Matn, Aley district, and the Gharb, as well as, coastal areas.[11] The court, therefore, provides a diverse sample that includes people from both rural and urban areas.

Consultation of the divorce court records in Beirut showed that the earliest complete records date to the beginning of 1970; some cases from the 1960s are available but they are spread over the whole year with some months totally lacking. Therefore, 1970 was chosen as the starting date for the research, and as the aim was to study divorce over a large time interval, 2003 – the last year archived before the initiation of the research – was decided upon as the concluding year. The same time interval, 1970 to 2003, was also selected for the research into marriage contracts in the court's archive. This was done for comparative purposes. The period covered is 33 years – long enough to reveal any change – although, in reality, the time interval was imposed by the availability of court records.

Having settled the time interval to be covered, the sampling had to be dealt with. After completing the pilot study, it was decided to put aside any sampling technique and simply collect all data available. This was mainly for two reasons: First, no one so far has done any research remotely similar to this one. Prothro and Diab's research in the 1970s, which covered marriage and divorce in the Middle East, included a section on the Druze. However, the information was gathered through interviews with members of the community. Adel Hamdan Taqqi Ed-Dine (2004) has published on the subject of Druze women; however, the information was merely expository in nature, being an overview of well known women from the community. Another study that approached the topic was carried out by Alamuddine and

Starr (1980). However, their research only dealt with marriage before the 1970s. This analysis is the first that attempts to study both divorce and marriage in Lebanon using court records. The second reason for including all cases was the fear that certain important cases, especially those of divorce, might be sorted out in the sampling procedures. Therefore, it was impermissible for such cases to be sampled out if the possible loss of essential change variables was to be prevented.

Since it was decided that no sampling would be attempted with the divorce cases, it was imperative to include all marriage contracts so as not to compromise any comparative studies. Therefore, all marriage contracts and all divorce cases brought before the Beirut court were included in this study. The basic method of collecting the information to be utilized in this research was that of documentary research. However, the nature of the topic and the nature of the court imposed certain restrictions on the data-gathering process.

The nature of divorce, and the personal considerations that accompanied dealing with such intimate topics, limited data gathering to some extent. As it proved impossible to photocopy the records, all the divorce cases (a total of 1,066 in 33 years) were copied by hand.[12] The process was undoubtedly laborious and time consuming but could not be avoided.

With respect to marriage cases, the situation was a bit different. Marriage among the Druze is considered a legal agreement – a contract – between two people. No stigma or negative consideration is attached to marriage contracts being made open, and thus permission to photograph them was granted.[13] The photographs were downloaded to the computer and later printed out. This was done for all contracts drawn up between 1983 and 2003, while those before 1983 were hand copied.

With respect to marriage contracts, the documents included the following information, all of which were transformed into variables that were subject to statistical manipulation:

1. the date of marriage;
2. full names of each spouse (including father's name);
3. names of each spouse's mother;

4. place of birth of each spouse;
5. date of birth of each spouse;
6. place of residence of each spouse;
7. the name, place of birth, place of residence and the date of birth of the *wakeel* (person granted power-of-attorney) if present;
8. names of the husband's two witnesses and the wife's two witnesses and their birth date, birth place and place of residence;
9. detailed dowry in both its prompt and deferred forms.

With respect to divorce cases, the information provided in each case was quite abundant. This is due to the nature of a legal case brought before the court. These cases included the following documents, all of which were hand copied except when a document was missing or displaced. The documents were:

1. A personal particular (Ikhraj Qayd Fardi) and/or family particular (Ikhraj Qayd 'Aeleh) of each contending party. These offer information regarding the person's place and date of birth, any change in place of residence (of females) normally due to marriage, the number of children of the household including those of the husband's from a previous marriage.[14]
2. The marriage contract.[15]
3. The name of the person who filed for the divorce (which could be the husband, the wife, or any official representative on their behalf and this may be any person – not necessarily a lawyer).
4. The documents or legal claims of each party or his/her lawyer regarding their claims as to the reasons for filing for divorce. These are normally exaggerated and have to be treated with care, which was done by comparing the claims of each party.
5. In some cases, the judge appoints two people to act as adjudicator from the family of each contending party; if no reliable person can be found, the judge appoints a person from the family's residential area. That person must be a well-known, trustworthy individual who has direct knowledge of the particularities of the contending party. The adjudicators, known as *muhakkem*, are asked to try to amend matters between the spouses. At the end of their attempts,

they are required to submit a written report to the judge. The report must include a summary of what was done and what resolution if any has been reached. These documents provide in-depth information of the causes of the divorce and a case history of the conflict between the two parties.[16]

6. The judge's summary and the ruling issued: This includes a summary of the claims of each party, the terms of the agreement when reached, and the decision reached by the judge. In some cases, the direct ramifications of the divorce are also included detailing the dowry to be paid, child custody in most cases, visitation rights and payment of *nafaqa* (support money for wife and children).

As mentioned previously, other additional and secondary resources were utilized. These included nine semi-structured informal interviews with members of the community; five divorcees were questioned as to their opinion regarding their own divorce procedures; 20 people were also asked about their opinion regarding the marriage contract and the way they are formulated and carried out. In addition to these informal interviews, interviews with five legal experts were also carried out in order to obtain an objective opinion as to the nature of the legal process: these included three lawyers and two court employees.

While conducting my research a number of divorce cases were brought before the court. I made it a point to attend the court sessions over a period of three months and observe the legal process at first hand. I also participated in one such session, upon the request of the judge.[17] These observations offered illuminating information as to the legal process itself and the role that the judge plays in regulating divorce procedures.

A number of divorce cases brought before the court during the course of the research, and included in it, were of a special nature that called for further particular research. These were divorce cases brought before the court to seek dissolution of a marriage in which the couples were not, in reality, married, which in the Druze community entails co-residence and sexual intercourse. They had never resided together and had not consummated the marriage. Although legally they were married, as they had signed the marriage contract, they are not treated so socially. Moreover, legally the females were allowed to file for the return of their status as unmarried. These cases were either contested or brought before the court by common consent with an explanation that the marriage had not been consummated and that both parties wished to end the legal commitment. A number of questions formulated themselves: Why had these couples signed the marriage contract but had not consummated the marriage? What drove individuals to make a legal commitment before being actually ready or serious enough to go through with the marriage? To answer the questions, a questionnaire was prepared and put to 125 members of the community. Since the aim of the questionnaire was simply to gain an understanding of this phenomenon and not to carry out 'complete sociological research', it was decided to bypass any sampling procedure and rely upon the researcher's personal contacts. A diversified sample was attempted to include high school students, university students, housewives and working adults.

Being a Druze, I could in my analysis rely on my reflections as a member of the community, living among the Druze and observing at first hand social life as it unfolds around me. Weddings, the signing of marriage contracts and divorce negotiations were events that I witnessed and experienced. These gave me the background against which I was able to place the different information I gathered and the observation I conducted.

To conclude, the basic methods of data gathering relied on the study of 1,066 divorce cases brought before the court over a period of 33 years, and of 2,986 marriage contracts made during the same time period. These were supported by some semi-formal and informal interviews and an exploratory questionnaire. The main research method used was documentary research, perceived as being the most suitable to answer the research questions.

Ethical Questions

Any sociological research involves certain ethical considerations that must be dealt with appropriately. The overwhelming part of this research relied on information derived from archives. Such research is unobtrusive in nature since it 'does not have an effect on the subjects' being studied (Babbie, 1992: 309). Thus, the ethical question often involved in any sociological research – namely the influence the researcher might leave on the subjects – does not apply here.

To further deal with ethical issues of confidentiality, the consulted documents were assigned numbers without any mention being made of a subject's name or of any information that might compromise the identity of any person involved in the cases brought before the court. Similar precautions were taken with the interviewed informants.

In certain instances, case studies were relied upon so as to provide a personal viewpoint and lend supporting details to the statistics provided. Here, names were changed or avoided altogether to maintain confidentiality. The same precautions were taken for the evaluation and analysis of the questionnaires and interviews except when the person involved allowed otherwise.

One ethical question that poses itself and with which I chose to introduce this chapter is the fact that I am doing research in my community. Acknowledging that this might be problematic for a number of scholars who object to 'research at home', however, I think that the advantages of my situation outshine any negative aspect. Any non-Druze studying the Druze cannot fully understand the community, simply because the Druze do not allow any outsider into the 'secrets' of their faith. Many people are intentionally misinformed by the Druze about the socio-religious organization of the community. Only a Druze, and even then within limitations,[18] can understand the nature of the relationships that bind the 'religious' and the 'non-religious' groups within the community and the importance of Druze identity and solidarity which is a lived reality rather than one that can be objectively described. Another important point is that a non-Druze would not have access to the court records and to the lives of the people. Being a Druze allowed me such access.

Structure of this Book

Chapter 2 offers an overview of the Druze, including a historical background of the Druze religion – the Tawheed – offering a brief account of how, where and when the religion started and spread, along with the many upheavals and persecutions that befell the faith's adherents. Persecution continued until the call for the new religion came to an end, closing the religion to outsiders. The second part offers a general overview of the particular beliefs upheld in the community that give the Druze people their distinct and separate identity that established a strong sense of internal solidarity and group unity. These beliefs included reincarnation, freedom, equality and secrecy. A discussion of the Druze perception of women, as revealed in their religious history, is also provided. An overview of the Druze's presence in Lebanon including their legal organization, social structure, and group relationships follows, pointing out the control that the religious strata of *Ajaweed* play in society.

Chapter 3 provides a summary of the findings of the research pertaining to marriage among the Druze as revealed in the marriage contracts studied over a period of 33 years from 1970 to 2003. The chapter begins with a general idea of the legal system controlling marriage among the Druze. The next part deals with the findings of the study concerning a multitude of variables that were considered so as to interpret any change. Changes pertaining to certain variables such as age at marriage and mate selection were clearly noted; however, a number of other practices remained constant. These are supported by detailed discussion with certain Druze individuals as to the importance of the *mahr*, the whole nature of the legal process of marriage, and of their choice of spouses.

Chapter 4 deals with the research's findings pertaining to divorce among the Druze. The chapter starts with a legal part offering a summary of divorce laws applicable in the Druze court. After that, the findings are reported. Alongside the changes across time that were identified in relation to some aspects of the divorce process, a remarkable consistency in certain other aspects was observed. Case studies and opinions of community members are included so as to provide a more nuanced perspective of the experience of the people involved. The chapter also provides some general findings associated with divorce and ends with a section entitled 'Pseudo-Divorce' which portrays a particular phenomenon related to divorce whereby the individuals divorce before the marriage has actually been consummated.

Chapter 5 offers a comparison of marriage contracts and divorce cases. The first part attempts to calculate divorce rates over the 33-year period of study. Some fluctuations in divorce rates were revealed, and these were analysed and an explanation offered. The second part compares certain aspects of marriage choices with these same aspects in divorce cases, with the aim of trying to predict divorce. Certain generalities were detected such as the influence of in-kin marriages on the possibility of divorce, while acknowledging the limitations of the comparative analysis of rates of marriage and divorce in light of the lack of a general population census.

Chapter 6, titled 'Peripheral Change', concludes with a perspective of change and continuity and how the two were expressed in the Druze community during the period of study. The 'changes' reported in the research are explained in light of the values upheld in the Druze society – as are stability and consistency that were also revealed.

CHAPTER TWO
THE DRUZE

A study of Druze family life in Lebanon can only be fully comprehended when perceived within the wider context of the Druze people and their presence in the Middle East. Some knowledge of the general beliefs and traditions of the Druze people is essential to understand better the inner forces that shape their internal relationships, and especially the relationship of individuals within a family. This chapter therefore opens with a brief historical background of the Druze people. Then follows a section dealing with the general beliefs and traditions that guide their life and it concludes with a discussion of the social organization of the Druze.

Historical Background

The *Tawheed* faith, commonly recognized as the Druze, originated in Egypt from Shi'i Islam under the guidance of the sixth Fatimid Caliph Abu Ali Al-Mansur Al-Aziz Bi-Allah – more commonly known as Al-Hakim Bi-Amr Allah (Khuri, 1988: 180). Al-Hakim was a caliph of great wisdom and knowledge. He supported education and established the University of Dar Al-Hikma (house of knowledge) in 1005, thereby transforming Cairo into an intellectual capital sought out by philosophers and men of knowledge (Atashe, 1995: 11). It was amid this climate of intellectual fervour that the *Tawheed* movement was publicly declared in 1017. For 21 years prior to the public announcement of the faith, heralds prepared the ground[1] by gathering supporters. The 21 years were divided into three seven-year intervals, each led by a specific herald – the first Salama ibn Abd Al-Wahab, the second Mohammad ibn Wahab, and the third Ismael ibn Muhammad – all chosen by Al-Hakim himself to prepare the people for the new faith. These are among the five *Hodoud*[2] that the *Muwahhiddeen* – the Druze believers in *Tawheed* – believe in. At the end of 21 years, Al-Hakim summoned all his followers along with the three *Da'is* (the heralds) to Cairo where they gathered at sunset on Thursday, 30 May 1017 (the first day of Muharam 408) to hear Al-Hakim declare the new faith. On the same day, Al-Hakim appointed Hamza Bin Ali as Imam or leader of the faith (Makarem, 2005: 2–16).

Hamza bin Ali bin Ahmad was born in Zawzan in Iran in 985 but came to Cairo and associated himself with Al-Hakim. He was in fact the first believer in *Tawheed* and as such was appointed by Al-Hakim as the Imam of the faith. On becoming Imam, he began to send missionaries to different parts of the world to spread the teachings of the new faith. Those who accepted the teachings were required to write an individual *mithaq* – a covenant or a vow of affirmation. These covenants were collected by the missionaries and taken back to Hamza (Mukassa, 2004: 100). The Druze believe that the *mithaq* is what unites the Druze. For them, it is a covenant made by the Druze soul or spirit that binds the individuals in each and every reincarnation – which is why they believe you cannot chose to be or not to be a Druze. The *mithaq* that every Druze (soul) wrote upon him or herself does not perish with the death of the body but is 'inherited' in each subsequent life.

The call of the *Da'wa* did not progress calmly or without conflict. It suffered from a number of setbacks that had a negative impact on the spread of the faith. The first came from within, at the hands of one of the *Da'is*, Nashtakine Ad-Darazi. His fervent acceptance of the call for *Tawheed* won him Al-Hakim's approval but he misinterpreted the favours shown him by Al-Hakim and declared himself Imam. Al-Hakim did not approve his undermining of Hamza Bin Ali (Atashe, 1995: 12), and as a result Ad-Darazi became an outcast;

he was persecuted by followers of the faith and later killed. Ironically, the followers of the new faith became known by the name of this *Da'i* (Abu-Tourabi, 1988: 83), acquiring the name Druze (from Ad-Darazi) rather than the name given them by Al-Hakim – *Muwahhideen.* This is the term used in the Druze scriptures (where the name Druze never appears) and that is why many Druze writers always use the term *Muwahhideen* in preference to Druze. The turmoil that Ad-Darazi had caused within the new faith was so huge that 'the call to the movement was suspended at the end of AH 408 (19 May 1018)' (Makarem, 1974: 22), resuming a year later when the damage had been brought under control.

The next setback to the call occurred after the absence of al-Hakim. It is believed that on the night of 12–13 February 1021, Al-Hakim went on one of his regular trips to Al-Muqattam Mountain where he used to seek solitude but this time he did not return and no trace of his body was found. He went into what the Druze call *alghaiba* meaning the absence or missing. Hamza Bin Ali along with the three heralds Ismael ibn Muhammad, Muhammad ibn Wahab and Salama ibn Abd Al-Wahab also went into retreat at this time, leaving the call to the sole guidance of Bahauddine Al-Samuqi (Makarem, 1974: 24–6). The Druze view this period as a period of testing – *al tajruba* – aimed at distinguishing true believers from non-believers.

Left without the guidance and protection of the Caliph Al-Hakim, it was under the rule of his successor, the Fatimid Caliph Al-Daher Ad-Din Allah, that the faith suffered its worst blow. Within only 40 days of becoming caliph, he had broken the 40 oaths he had taken not to harm the followers of the new faith, claiming that each oath held only for a day, and for the next six and a half years he ruthlessly hunted down and killed believers (Atashe, 1995: 13). The effect of his persecution was that for the second time in history the call to the new faith was suspended. In 1026, Bahauddine received a letter from Hamza in his retreat, instructing him to resume the call. Emissaries were sent out to preach the faith and to gather believers under his guidance from Cairo. This continued until 1043 when Bahauddine himself departed, announcing that the divine call had fulfilled its purpose (Makarem, 1974: 38). Bahauddine left behind his writings and those of Hamza and Al-Hakim to guide followers. Written in the form of letters or epistles, they make up the Druze religious books known as *Kutub Al-Hikma*, or Books of Wisdom.

The above constitute a brief overview of the historical development of the Druze. The next part offers an overview of the basic beliefs of the Druze – what constitutes their habitus. A study of a community's practices cannot be understood except against the background of what constitutes the beliefs, values and norms of that community. It is within this framework that changes or continuities of behaviour can be explained. Practices can

> be accounted for by relating the social conditions in which the habitus that generated them was constituted, to the social conditions in which it is implemented, that is, through the scientific work of performing the interrelationship of these two states of the social world that the habitus performs while concealing it, in and through practice. (Bourdieu, 1990: 56)

Among the Druze, a large aspect of what constitutes their habitus lies within the religious – the beliefs that they hold dear and that shape their social and legal structure.

Druze Beliefs, Values and Practices

The Druze beliefs and understanding of God and the universe included in the Books of Wisdom are derived from the intellectual discourse of Islam's many schools of thought and religious interpretations[3], together with an assimilation of Greek thought and philosophy, among other ideas. All the intellectual and theological processes that came before it played a critical role in preparing the ground for *Tawheed*, the revelation of God's true entity and reality, which is the ultimate purpose of all knowledge (Makarem, 1974: 12–13). *Tawheed* is basically the knowledge and belief that all creation and God are one – a unity: 'From his light originated all things' (Makarem, 1974: 41). God is existence and all things that exist in the world, including humans, are but an expression of God.

The Druze do not believe that God is in heaven because, according to their interpretation, this would limit him to a place – heaven. According to *Tawheed*, God is everywhere without being anywhere. Further, knowledge of God comes through belief and faith, not through human or other intermediaries – that is to say, by practising *Tawheed* (Atashe, 1995: 17).

The above should not be taken to mean that God equals existence for, according to the Druze, God cannot be limited to an existence. Yet, removing him from existence is also a limitation that cannot be attributed to God since He is not limited to, nor is, outside existence.

> For the Druze, God is absolute existence consequently; he is not a creator in that he created the universe 'ex nihilo'. Since God is absolute, he has not created the world outside of him, for, as absolute, He has no limit: Similarly the world did not emanate from him in time. He is the one: there is none other than God: He is the only existence. The world is a constant projection from him, by him, within him and to him. (Makarem, 2005: 3)

These words of Makarem, a frequently quoted authority on the *Tawheed* faith, offer the best explanation of what the Druze believe about God. The role and duty of man is to realize the true meaning of God, which can only be achieved through a gradual process of spiritual experience whereby the human being – the soul – can achieve actualization and self-realization. For this to come about, a single lifetime is self-evidently not sufficient since realization of God is a process of spiritual experience and since realizing unity, as much as humanly possible, with God is only achieved through knowledge and faith. Hence, the Druze's (*Muwahhiddeens*') belief in *taqamous* or reincarnation.

According to Makarem (2005), reincarnation is necessary since the human being must be intellectually and spiritually prepared to achieve self-realization in the One. This is done through the process of acquiring knowledge and understanding, which allows for the true discovery of the self, which in its turn enables humans to behold God – only as much as a human (soul) is prepared to understand or behold God (Makarem, 2005: 6). Since God is just and since not all humans are endowed with the same degree of preparedness to acquire knowledge, then reincarnation is necessary. The Druze believe that the true Muwahhid's (a believer in Tawhid) soul reincarnates successively until it eventually unites with the Cosmic Mind, which is nothing but God's will through which the universe came into existence (Makarem, 2005: 101–2).

Reincarnation[4] allows the soul to acquire all necessary knowledge needed for self-realization. Knowledge is acquired through experience and reincarnation allows for extensive experience. However, what the human being experiences in each reincarnated life is nothing but the product of his or her choice and free will. In each life, the human being makes free choices that in turn guide his or her next reincarnation. Free will is basic to the *Tawheed* faith. Hamza Ibn Ali is quoted as saying 'Truly, it is your deeds that return to you. Any difficulty you meet in your life is the result of your wrong deeds' (Makarem, 1974: 113). How can you be held accountable if you do not have free will? Thus, free will and the freedom of choice in acquiring knowledge, aimed at self-realization, are of central importance in the teaching of *Tawheed*.[5]

Because freedom and free choice are thus basic to the faith, the Al-Du'a and callers to the faith never used any form of force to gather believers. When the *Tawheed* religion was announced, the people who joined the religion were those who truly believed, freely and without coercion. They wrote the *mihtaq*[6] upon themselves (their souls in all reincarnations) freely and willingly. Such freedom is mirrored in the rites and rituals of the Druze or, rather, in the lack of these. The Druze perform no public prayers, no structured prayers and no other form of religious ritual.[7] The assumption is that if these can be monitored, then freedom is abolished. Khuri maintains that the underlying reason for the secretive observance of the pillars of religion of Islam as understood by the Druze is Freedom itself:

> [if] Religion is taken to be primarily a moral reference and a way of attaining spirituality, as it is among the Druze, it has to be dealt with privately both in terms of behavioural choices and in terms of worship. (Khuri, 2004: 2)

Public practices involve a degree of coercion and thus offer no choice or freedom, which is contrary to religion. Thus, a Druze enjoys freedom in his or her practice of faith. He or she is totally free – except, that is, in being a Druze. According to this belief, a Druze shall always be a Druze, in this and later lives.

The above mentioned freedom, free will and choice entail the concept of equality. The equality of all mankind is a prerequisite of the *Tawheed* faith. Khuri maintains that 'equality' is as central a theme to the Druze as 'love' is to Christians and 'justice' to Muslims (Khuri, 2004: 63). A human's role, according to the *Taweed* faith, is to seek knowledge and oneness with God. This cannot be achieved without equality between all humans. That is why the Druze scriptures ordain equality among men and between men and women. Epistle 25 of the Druze scriptures, which deals with domestic relationships, stipulates that when a *Muwahhid* (Druze man) takes a *Muwahhida* (Druze woman) as his wife, he should treat her as his equal and share with her all his worldly possessions as well as all his knowledge. Makarem asserts that this equality between males and females was quite strong during the establishment of the Druze faith (Makarem, 1974: 112–13). However, it grew weaker as the Druze were absorbed into other more oppressive Islamic political regimes that suppressed these kinds of thoughts or movements.

This equality is reflected in the history of *Tawheed*. Druze history abounds with pious women who were sent out as fighters against misled *Da'is* and as messengers to spread the religion. For example, Sitt Sarah (Abu Tourabi, 1988: 31) was ordained by her uncle Al-Muqtana Bahauddine to lead a group of men on a religious mission from Egypt to Wadi Al-Taym (the Hasbaya region of Lebanon). Her role was to spread religious teachings and correct the deeds of the *Da'is* who had gone astray. Among the group of men she headed was her father. Her uncle could have chosen her father as a leader, but he picked her for her strong personality, intelligence and skill in argument (Taqi Eddine, 2004: 97). Equality is basic to the Druze and this is reflected in their laws concerning marriage, divorce and inheritance.

At a time when women were considered inferior to men and treated as such, the *Tawheed* faith came to reassert the role of women and their equality with men. It is true that Islam allowed women certain rights that they had not enjoyed before the Qur'an, especially with regard to property ownership; however, whatever equality this bestowed was undermined by the fact that Islam permitted polygamy. When Al-Hakim announced the *Tawheed* faith he abolished polygamy, so giving female believers a sense of equality and self-worth that some argue Islam had never fully provided. It is against the teachings of the *Tawheed* faith for a man to have more than one wife. This is reflected in the Druze laws in Lebanon, which consider any second marriage to be illegal and automatically revocable.

Marriage, moreover, cannot be forced on a female. The religion stipulates that consent to a marriage must be clearly given for that marriage to be considered lawful. This consent must be made by both parties to the marriage, equally and freely.

Another important aspect of the Druze scriptures is that men and women are referred to together. Azzam points out that even in the 'four epistles that are addressed specifically to girls and women, it is specified and reiterated that women and men are equally accountable for their moral actions and behaviour, and both sexes are cautioned against deviance from *Tawheed* (Azzam, 2005: 96–7). This equality in reference to males and females clearly shows that the *Tawheed* faith does not differentiate gender-wise between believers. Equality between males and females, and the high esteem that *Tawheed* bestowed upon females was significant at that time.[8]

Another important feature of the *Tawheed* faith is the secrecy associated both with the religion itself, and with the way of life of its adherents. This secrecy has two aspects: one related to the social environment in which the faith was declared and the other to the teachings of the faith itself. The first factor to impose a secretive nature on the adherents of the new faith was the practice of what is generally termed as *Taqiya*. Briefly, *Taqiya* – concealment behind the accepted forms – was forced upon members of the new faith during the years of political turmoil and severe political persecution following the disappearance of their protector Al-Hakim. According to Azzam, the religious scriptures even 'encourage *Al-Estitar Bilma'louf* – behaviour in accordance with the prevailing or conventional codes or outward assimilation to avoid harmful curiosity' (Azzam, 1997: 27–8). Believers were compelled to keep their teachings to themselves and act in compliance with the prevailing Islamic religion. This gave the faith a somewhat esoteric nature that has led to the creation of many misconceptions surrounding the religious traditions and beliefs of the Druze. What began as a necessary policy of survival continued as a way of life. Although the Druze are not under any kind of politically structured exploitation or persecution in Lebanon today, the practice of secrecy remains intact.

The Druze continue to keep their religion secret and do not provide answers to those seeking religious information of any kind.[9] Moreover, they continually attempt to avoid 'confrontation or contact with the members of the dominant religions in their areas' (Mukasa, 2004: 1001). This idea of secrecy, and the need to practise *Taqiya* so as to safeguard their existence in a hostile environment, has left a lasting mark on members of the community. Sayings such as 'We can't rely on anyone but ourselves', 'A Druze can only trust a Druze', and 'We can't survive in the Arab world if we do not continuously watch our backs' are words of wisdom constantly repeated by the community elders. Khuri notes that this feeling of being under constant persecution, reinforcing the need for unity, may be the root cause of why, throughout the civil war in Lebanon, the Druze community remained the only religious sect that did not undergo any major internal conflict (Khuri, 2004: 102).

The second factor affecting the secretive nature of the Druze stems from the nature of the religious teachings themselves. The knowledge revealed in the Books of Wisdom is assumed to be beyond the comprehension of ordinary people without guidance and instruction. The texts are written in esoteric and elaborate language and should not be read by people unqualified to do so as they will be sure to misinterpret them. On another level, all people were given a chance at the beginning to respond to the call to *Tawheed*, and those who did not should not be allowed access into the secrets of the faith but must remain in ignorance as the price of their rejection of its teachings.

The above beliefs, that formulate part of the Druze habitus, are indoctrinated within the Druze and shape their lives in ways that are unique to this sect. To begin with, if we examine the influence of reincarnation we find that, because the Druze believe in reincarnation as God's way of imposing justice, they rarely seem to complain about their lot. Druze people are accepting of what occurs to them because they believe that 'their soul' is paying amends in this life for a sin committed in a previous life. Moreover, it is God's way of testing their belief and of judging them. It is common to hear a Druze say, 'This is what God ordains', or 'God knows how to punish and when.' At the sight of a disabled person, a Druze will say, 'God knows what he or she did in a previous life.' The lengthy suffering of an individual, especially a child, may evoke the comment, 'His soul is paying amends for wrongs done in all his previous reincarnations.' This acceptance has bred a community that rarely views any misfortune with extreme resentment. Acceptance and forbearance broadly characterize the Druze people.

However, this does not mean that the Druze people are content to remain in one place and not try to change their lot – quite the contrary. If they do not attempt to improve their life they will be held accountable for 'not making an effort' in their next reincarnation. Therefore, reincarnation fulfils a double purpose: on the one hand, the Druze are accepting of their fate, but on the other, they strive to build a better life for themselves.

Moreover, since the Druze believe that a Druze always reincarnates as a Druze, they should always rush to each other's aid because they believe that their souls are reincarnated in each other's households, thereby strengthening the internal cohesion of the group. Druze people often express this belief in words like, 'We are born to each other' or 'He or she might have been my parent in a previous life.' The internal cohesion produced by belief in reincarnation is further promoted by the secrecy imposed by the teachings of the faith. A group that considers its religious teachings as secrets not to be divulged to outsiders would certainly be singled out for their internal solidarity and strong sense of group unity. A Druze rushes to the aid of another Druze simply because he or she is a 'brother' or 'sister' in need. This is seen very markedly in the tendency of Druze immigrants in other countries to form associations and support groups. A visit to the ADS (American Druze Association) website shows very clearly the extent to which the Druze are characterized by a strongly binding religious unity.[10]

The internal solidarity of the Druze is further strengthened by their belief in freedom and equality. A person who truly believes that he/she enjoys complete freedom will understandably be less willing to break the rules of the group. The only element of personal freedom an individual is sacrificing is being defined as Druze. This is a reasonable price to pay for freedom at all other levels. The psychological value of feeling free is so high that it surpasses the actual freedom a person enjoys. A Druze individual is bound by the limits of being a Druze, yet because the religion does not impose any form of structured worship, the feeling of being free it affords the individual dissuades even the mere thought of breaking the internal solidarity of the group. This is especially so since the Druze believe that their souls had freely and willingly made the decision to join the *Tawheed* faith at the beginning of the *Da'wa* – a very high privilege if one truly thinks about the matter. Furthermore, the Druze belief in equality at all levels – that men are equal to women and the poor are 'religiously speaking' equal to the rich – has bred an internal sense of strength and invulnerability, especially when associated with the belief in reincarnation: 'In my next life, I might be very rich' or 'I was very wealthy in a previous life.' Acting together, these beliefs promote the separate identity and solidarity of the Druze, which is why it is worth studying any element of change that might have worked its way into such a self-enclosed group.

Structure of the Druze Community

A Druze belongs to one of two categories, the *Ajaweed* or the *Jismani*. The *Ajaweed* stratum consists of individuals who have willingly and freely chosen a religious life, and includes both men and women. Joining this group, however, is not a simple process. Those who wish to join may ask to do so, but they must undergo considerable scrutiny by other members of the *Ajaweed* stratum before gaining acceptance, and this may take several months, and in some instances years.[11]

Many things distinguish the *Ajaweed* from the rest. First of all, they dress distinctly. Men wear dark (usually black) baggy trousers called *Shirwal* and a head cover. This might be a simple white hat called a *Kalousah*, a white and red fez or a white turban, this last denoting a high rank of religious knowledge.[12] Women are required to wear special unrevealing long-sleeved shirts or blouses and long skirts, normally black or dark blue in colour; they cover their heads with a thick white veil called a *mandeel*. Secondly, the *Ajaweed* follow an austere way of life: they are forbidden to smoke, drink alcohol or eat extravagantly. They do not attend wedding parties, listen to music or watch television.[13] But the most important feature that sets them apart is their religious practices. They gather every Thursday evening for prayer at the *Khalweh*, a simple room or hall, where they pray and read the scriptures, most often memorizing the epistles and explaining the religion to new initiates. Only members of the *Ajaweed* stratum are allowed to read the Books of Wisdom and the writings of Al-Sayed Abdallah, a prominent religious figure among the Druze who took it upon himself to compile and explain the religious scriptures. The *Ajaweed* are considered the keepers of the faith and the protectors of the religion. The *Jismani* dress as they wish, do not abide by any religious practice and may eat or drink whatever they want, but they are not allowed access into the secrets of the faith.

Although divided into two distinct groups this does not in any sense mean that the *Ajaweed* and *Jismani* live apart from each other, nor that the *Ajaweed* are aloof from the general Druze community.

> Although the *Ajawid* live differently from the *Jismani*, the two communities are not in opposition. Any family may have members belonging to both categories. Moreover, the *Ajawid* are obliged to guide the *Jismani* in the attainment of religious knowledge. (Azzam, 2007: 132)

It is true that the *Ajaweed* do not mix with *Jismani* in social gatherings that may involve drinking, smoking and 'inappropriate' dress, yet their presence is constantly felt and given significance in Druze society – especially in matters relating directly to the family. For example, the presence of a *Jwayid* (a sheikh) at the *tolbeh* (the visit that the groom's family makes to the house of the bride's family to ask for her hand in marriage) is considered a blessing and if there is none in the family, then a *Jwayid* from the village is often invited to grace the occasion with his presence. It is true that the *Ajaweed* do not attend weddings (although some may offer their congratulations at a specified time the same day or later); however, their presence at funerals is highly valued. The more *Ajaweed* present at a person's funeral, the greater the merit to be accorded to the deceased. The following is often heard at funerals.[14]

> He/She was a very good person and his/her soul deserving of the *Rahma* (blessing upon death). Did you notice the large number of *Ajaweed* attending the funeral?

Most Druze pay attention to this during their lives and try as hard as possible not to offend the *Ajaweed*. If, for any reason, the *Ajaweed* choose to boycott a funeral, it is shunned by all members of the community and the stigma attaches itself not only to the deceased but to his descendants for generations to come.

Another way in which the *Ajaweed* have power over the Druze community is by abstaining from visiting, or even talking to, someone who is known to be an alcoholic, drug addict, thief or wrong-doer. Other members of the community, including direct relatives, will often follow the example of the *Ajaweed*, and so the individual becomes a social outcast. Therefore, anyone who may be thinking of breaking a moral or social code is consequently forced to think a lot about their decision since the costs of their actions will be high.

> The Ajaweed are even concerned with preserving the values and morals of the society, setting the believers on the right track and holding them accountable for their behaviour through different social punishments such as not attending funerals. (translated from Khuri, 1988: 296)

All the functions of the *Ajaweed* outlined above aim at preserving the group and the religion. The *Ajaweed* act as mentors for the Druze community, keeping people's behaviour in line with the accepted codes of behaviour, and safe guarding the internal morality of the group. However, they play a further role related to preserving the solidarity of the group and limiting conflicts within it. Even though the meetings that the religious *Ajaweed* hold every Thursday evening are devoted to prayers and religious readings, they are not restricted to that. It is a common practice for the religious *Ajaweed* to discuss matters relating to their society and to intervene to resolve any conflict, whether between members of the same family or between different families (Khuri, 1988: 298). Such mediating efforts even extend to resolving conflicts across villages. Almost every Druze village contains one or more well-known and respected *Jwayid* who is often approached to solve conflict, including family feuds, conflicts over inheritance and divorces. The conciliatory function of the *Ajaweed* is important not only to the Druze themselves but also extends to attempts at conflict resolution made across the sect's borders. *Ajaweed*, for instance, are present whenever the Druze political leader Walid Junblat holds 'reconciliation' discussions with other religious groups such as the Maronites. Their presence is expected and valued as bestowing a seal of approval or blessing on any conciliatory attempt.

The above clearly shows that the *Ajaweed* play two roles, the first of a religious nature, the second of a social nature. They are the keepers of the religion and the guardians of divine knowledge. At the same time, they guide the Druze in the rules of proper moral and religious conduct, and limit any internal conflict that might erupt within the Druze community. All these functions basically result in one end – maintaining the solidarity and unity of the group.

Druze Socio-Political Presence in Lebanon

All of the above beliefs are basic to the Druze faith although not all of them are as strongly held and espoused as reincarnation. For example, gender equality is a basic religious value among the Druze, yet is not fully reflected in the Druze community on the socio-legal level.[15] Socially, patriarchal authority is dominant in Lebanon and among the Druze the case is not different. The father, elder brother or the husband is considered the main authority figure in the family. Legally, the husband is the head of the family, responsible for sustaining the family and considered the legal custodian over the children. Laws of inheritance further reflect gender inequality whereby, in accordance with the dominant Islamic tradition, a male is entitled to inherit twice the amount of the female's inheritance. Nevertheless, ideas of freedom and equality find expression within the community, tacitly in the relationship between members of the community or more openly in the legal system. Objectively considered, the Druze personal status law appears quite progressive by contemporary legal standards, emphasizing as it does equality between men and women in rights of testation (disposal of property after death through a will) and divorce. Nevertheless the Druze's existence as a numerical minority and their constant persecution at the hands of dominant majorities had left their impact on the group. That persecution forced the Druze to practise *Taqiya* and this was incorporated into the legal system, which is a form of the Hanafi legal code modified to meet the Druze's basic beliefs.[16]

Although there are Druze in Palestine, Syria and Jordan, their presence in the Middle East is greatest in Lebanon, where they are politically recognized as a minority and possess certain political rights such as parliamentary representation and an independent legal jurisprudence over their personal status matters. Historically speaking, when Lebanon was under the Ottoman rule, the law that was applied was that of the Hanafi Islamic sect.[17] This law remained in force until 1926 when the French colonial powers decided to modify it so as to give separate legal standing to the Shi'i sect. On 9 December 1926, the French similarly acknowledged the Druze sect, but it was not until 1948 that the Druze Personal Status Law was issued. Laws guiding the special organization of the Druze courts were subsequently issued on 5 March 1960.

These laws regulate all personal matters affecting the Druze people. However, when a situation that has no legal ruling within the legal stipulations of the sect's laws raises itself, the judge is required to rely on the Islamic Shi'i and Hanafi codes applied in Lebanon, as well as on Druze traditions, customs and the principles of justice and equality, the nature of which is left to the judge to evaluate[18] (Al-Awar, 1983: 13).

Hence the judge takes up an active role and becomes an agent in determining justice. Dupret claims: 'legal rules interact with moral principles within the judge's work and that many standards, including that of Islamic normativity, emerge in the course of the adjudicative process. It is up to the professional jurist to interpret the context of these moral principles, and as a result, legal actors have the final word with regard to their definition and implementation' (Dupret, 2002: 42). The judge among the Druze plays such an active role as it is up to him, for example, to enunciate divorce, allocate and define harm and sign marriage contracts.[19]

Before 1948, the affairs of the Druze community were settled in accordance with the prevailing Islamic law but Druze practices that deviated from Islamic practices were upheld by the community, and the people abided by their customs when the Islamic law ran contrary to them, even when this meant acting against the law operating within society. The values of the Druze community were perceived as more important than the legal stipulations. Therefore, when the law came to be written, the legal stipulations took into account these social particularities, especially with regard to matters relating to marriage, divorce and inheritance.[20] In fact the law was formulated in accordance with the modifications and suggestions presented by a committee referred to as the 'spiritual committee of the sheikhs of *al-bayada*[21] and others from all over Lebanon in association with sheikhs from Syria and Palestine' (Taqi el-Dine and Abu Shakra, 2000: 8).[22]

The Druze's existence as an independent sect – and not a major one – has imposed a particular way of life on the Lebanese Druze. Historically they lived in distinct areas at a distance from the centre of authority and thus away from the major cities. Khuri uses the term 'territoriality' (Khuri, 1988: 71) to describe a group that perceives itself as an independent community with its own organizational and economic structure and is often semi-dominant within its territory of existence. Territories of existence may often be transformed into semi-sacred landscapes if they contain shrines and holy places (Khuri, 1988: 83–4). The Druze territories are abundant with sacred sites that people visit for blessings and prayer. They consider themselves to be the owners and protectors of the land. Even in more recent times, the

Druze have frowned on the selling of land and you often find conditions in Druze wills to prevent a certain piece of land from being sold outside the family.

The specific traits that are particular to the Druze in Lebanon (their status as a sectarian minority) play an important role in strengthening internal solidarity. This becomes more strongly pronounced when confronted by an outside force that might change – intentionally or not – the structure of the group and even its existence. It gives rise to what might be termed as 'minority feeling' – the sensation of being under continuous persecution and thus in danger, which builds up still further the group's solidarity and internal cohesion. Solidarity is further enhanced by certain religious teachings that are considered the pillars of the Druze faith. The most important of these is the pillar of *Hofz al Ikhwan*, which literally means the protection and aid of brothers in the faith and imposes on individual Druze a religious obligation to help any fellow believer in trouble.

Change Among the Druze

The Druze community was, historically speaking, characterized by endogamous relationships rendering the community self-enclosed from surrounding communities. Physically speaking, the Druze concentrated in certain areas, generally rural and mountainous in nature, performing their distinctive rituals and traditions.[23] This has created a meticulous kind of solidarity within the community – one that has been, and some argue still is, nurtured in different ways, particularly through the practice of endogamy, as well as particular religious and cultural practices. This solidarity is a simple mirror of their much-felt ethno-religious identity[24] – the sense of belonging to the 'Druze'. Khuri maintains that 'except for some brief interruptions, the Druze had displayed throughout their history a clear internal cohesion and a strong attachment to ethnic identity' (Khuri, 2005: 61). This strong ethnic identity and internal cohesion leaves a heavy toll on members of the community since every kind of behaviour either increases or breaks it down. Nowhere is this cohesion felt more powerfully than within the internal circle of the family and the formation of relations within it. Marriage and divorce are the most obvious processes to be influenced by such manifestations of the community's internal cohesion.

The only way to enrich and sustain such internal cohesion is by preserving a traditional way of life and maintaining traditional relationships. Endogamy[25] represents the strongest method for preserving ethnic identity and a high level of cohesion. Marriage among the Druze was expected of any girl who came of age and the marriage partner normally belonged to her village or family. Change regarding marriage choices was indeed very slow.

> Few young Druze question the role of their family in arranging[26] (or at least helping to arrange) suitable matches and deviation from the family choice is relatively rare. As Nura Alamuddine has noted 'given the massive socio-economic transformation which has taken place in Lebanon... the basic nature of Druze marriage pattern shows a truly remarkable resilience'. (Betts, 1988: 48)

Historically speaking, the Druze people practised (and still do practise) endogamy in the strictest sense. Marriage outside the group is simply not tolerated – it is considered illegal. A Druze who opts to marry outside the group loses his/her Druze privilege[27] and is shunned by family, society and religion. Marriage outside the sect is considered to be 'contrary to *'Aqida* (belief), *Shari'a* (law) and *Taqlid* (tradition)' (Azzam, 1977: 42). Khuri writes, 'What is unique to the Druze is not the practice of endogamy per se, but the frequency and the level at which it is maintained. When conditions allow, the Druze marry endogamously within the lineage or the clan at a very high rate' (Khuri, 2004: 234).

These two factors – ethno-religious identity and endogamy – have continuously shaped the Druze community. However, the community could not remain immune to the ever-increasing 'Westernization' of the younger generation's outlooks and perceptions arising from a number of factors that influence the society and bring about change.

The past century was characterized by the spread of education all over Lebanon. The building of public schools in every part of Lebanon, however remote, has made education available to all – at least at elementary and intermediate levels. Moreover, universities now exist all over the country. Education is no longer limited to the large urban cities. Rural areas were being educationalized and the effect of education on the younger generation was noticeable. Educated Druze youth exposed to the idea of freedom of choice began to challenge the traditions and role of the older generation – namely the father or grandfather. Patriarchal authority was being undermined and started to be challenged as the origin of all decisions. This challenge was bound to be felt inside the family and might be expected to reveal itself in marriage choices and divorce decisions. The Druze traditional way of doing things will inevitably have undergone certain changes. For example, as noted above, endogamy in its closest sense – first cousin marriage – was a predominant practice among the Lebanese Druze, especially between patrilineal parallel cousins.[28] Endogamy – marriage within the family – accounted for about 35.5 per cent of all Druze marriages recorded in the Druze Beirut Personal Status court from 1931 to 1940 and from 1971 to 1974 (Alamuddine and Starr, 1980: 77). Such a percentage is quite high and shows the extent to which the Druze have favoured family marriage. A young Druze who has been educated to the fact that cousin marriage is not advisable for reasons of consanguinity may be expected to begin questioning the tradition of cousin marriage – challenging accepted modes of behaviour and asserting an ever increasing sense of individualism.

As well as increased education, the spread of urbanization has also challenged the traditional way of life among the Druze. Before the twentieth century, the Druze of Lebanon's mountain areas, mainly subsisted on agriculture. They were concentrated in villages, engaged in a rural way of life. However, with the increase in educational awareness came the realization of life outside the village and the trend towards migration to the city in search of a better life. The Druze youth – mainly males – who left their villages to live in urban areas, or at least worked there and commuted to their village, were introduced to new ideas – ideas that opposed the traditional patriarchal values of the village community.

Over the past decade, the boundaries of urbanization have been extending dramatically and the effect of this process continues to be felt on the Druze way of life. The indoctrination of Druze youth into the mentality of the city (of freedom, choice and individualism as personal values) is bound to have impacted on family life, and is likely to be revealed in marriage and divorce. The effect of urbanization was further strengthened by the changes brought about by the mechanization of agriculture, which reduced the need for manual labour to work the land, thereby creating unemployment in rural communities. This surplus labour sought employment in cities, focused in Lebanon on the service sector, including tourism and banking. As the family, as an institution, ceased to be the productive unit, the increased involvement of young people, especially young women, in work outside the household weakened extended family ties and patriarchal authority. Individualism as a way of life began to replace communalism or the extended family.

A third factor that definitely played an important role in bringing about change was the increase in the scope and spread of means of communication, mainly the mass media[29] and the internet. Over a period of 30 years (1970 to 2003), the Lebanese village has changed from one that was lucky to have a single TV or radio set to one where every household owns at least one TV set, mostly connected to a cable service. It is quite rare to find a village, no matter how distant from the capital, that does not have an internet shop. The effect of these huge changes in communication technology is bound to be felt most deeply in traditional societies, not just in Lebanon but worldwide. Individual Druze, living in the once enclosed, self-sustained community, was increasingly bombarded with new ideas. Family values upheld over many decades were challenged. The authority of the father was questioned and social values and traditions consequently scrutinized. Influenced by the mass media, young Druze males began to take more initiative in making decisions and choices concerning their own lives. Over time and with increased exposure to new ideas either through work outside the village, the mass media or education, the direct influence of family, tradition and religion tends to diminish which is projected on to marriage and divorce.

Ever since Lebanon's independence, elements of change have found their way into Lebanese society, and in relation to the Druze community this has been particularly affected in their legal system. The Druze have enjoyed legal independence since 1948, and their legislative system contains many modern elements in matters relating to marriage and divorce (Azzam, 2007: 103). Before that date, all family matters relating to marriage, divorce, child custody, inheritance and all personal issues were dealt with within the family. In general, the patriarchal head of the family was the sole decision maker. After 1948, the patriarchal head of the Druze family lost this power to the legislative system in the person of the judge. This change promoted an increase in individualism and a lesser concern for the traditional aspects of family life – mainly the extended family, patriarchal authority and general community values.

CHAPTER THREE

MARRIAGE AMONG THE DRUZE

Ahmad, under a lot of pressure from his family, decided at the age of 32 to get married. A Druze working in one of the United Arab Emirates states, he was not in love with any girl so he asked his parents in Lebanon to carry out the traditional 'bride searching' procedure. This entailed his parents, mainly his mother, asking relatives, friends and members of the community about suitable 'brides'. Ahmad's parents accordingly accumulated a list of suitable names and accompanying details. Whenever Ahmad could take time from his job, he returned to Lebanon and accompanied his parents on visits to the houses of those on the list. He visited more than 20 houses over a period of two years until he found a girl he liked – Samia. He proposed and Samia accepted. This proclaimed the start of Ahmad's journey along the route of traditional ceremonies.

The *Tolbeh*

The word *tolbeh* etymologically means 'the asking'. The groom, along with his family members including paternal and maternal uncles, aunts and cousins, goes to the bride's house to ask officially for her hand in marriage. An elder person, if possible a religious sheikh, preferably not closely related to the groom, speaks on behalf of the groom. The elder, in Ahmad's case a distant relative, enumerated the good qualities of Ahmad and his family, pointing out his good conduct, educational background and economic reliability and ended his speech by asking Samia's father to accept Ahmad and Ahmad's family's request, or marriage proposal. Samia's father stood up and officially accepted the request, adding that such a relationship would honour his family and remarking 'Ahmad is now our son'. Ahmad's family had brought with them sweets and chocolate which they offered to all those present once Samia's father had given his approval.[1] Ahmad was accompanied to the *tolbeh* by 40 people and the number of people present on the bride's side was 30.[2] As is customary, Ahmad's parents left more sweets and chocolate at Samia's house for the guests who were expected to come to offer their congratulations on the *tolbeh*. The receiving of guests would continue for about a month at both Ahmad's and Samia's houses, and enough sweets and chocolate must be on hand to be offered to them all – otherwise the groom and his family would be labelled 'stingy'.

The Official Engagement Celebration

The *tolbeh*, or engagement party, is a traditional public occasion among the Druze that officially proclaims the betrothal of the two individuals. Although some younger Druze in recent years have begun to do without it,[3] the majority of the Druze still have one, especially when the couple met in the traditional manner. Ahmad and Samia held a *tolbeh* upon the request of Samia's parents.

Ahmad's Side

For the engagement party, Ahmad's parents personally visited and invited immediate and extended family members, both paternal and maternal, and a number of people from the village,[4] in addition to a few friends, amounting to 150 people in all. On the day of the celebration, all the guests gathered at the house of the groom's parents, where they were offered coffee and chocolates. At 2.30 they got into their cars and followed the groom's car, decorated with flowers for the occasion, driving for 45 minutes until they reached Samia's village.

Samia's Side

Samia's parents similarly invited family members, villagers and friends to their family's *khalieh*.[5] The number of invitees amounted to 250 people. On the day of the engagement, Samia, wearing a fashionable evening gown, sat on one of two armchairs placed along one wall and surrounded by floral decorations. In front, on either side of the hall, were two lines of chairs. As the guests invited by Samia's parents started arriving, the women would walk up to Samia, greet her and sit on the chairs closest to her. The men, on the other hand, confined themselves to greeting Samia's father and male relatives before placing themselves on the chairs nearest the entrance of the hall. Music was played by a hired DJ as all awaited the arrival of the groom.

At 3.15, Ahmad and his convoy arrived at Samia's village and started blowing their car horns before coming to a halt in front of the *khalieh*. At the sound of the horns, the bride's mother along with a few female relatives formed a line next to Samia, while Samia's father, uncles and a few older men lined up at the entrance of the hall. The groom's party gathered in front of the *khalieh* and separated into two groups – males and females. The women, led by the groom's mother, made their way into the hall.[6] They greeted the men at a distance and walked to the line of women, shaking their hands and kissing occasionally. When they reached Samia they shook her hand before taking their place on seats that had been left empty for them. Ahmad, with his male companions, entered the *khalieh*, shook hands with the lined-up men and took their place on their appointed chairs. After about 15 minutes, three young males from Samia's family entered, each carrying a tray with *dyafeh*:[7] one had boxes of juice, the second sweets made from pistachio and coated with crunchy sugar, and the third decorated chocolates. They were followed by three young females carrying similar trays. The males went to the men's section of the hall and the females to the women's section, where they offered the *dyafeh* to all the guests – those invited by Samia's parents and those invited by Ahmad's parents. When all the guests had been offered the *dyafeh*, bridal music was played, followed by traditional *dabkeh*[8] music, whereupon Ahmad, surrounded by his male relatives and friends, walked up the middle of the hall to stand next to Samia. Then Ahmad's mother approached with his sister who was carrying a tray on which were displayed jewellery items including a gold set of necklace, bracelet, ring and earrings. Also displayed were the wedding bands, two more bracelets and two rings. Ahmad took each piece one by one and helped Samia put them on while all the people gathered around them watched and clapped as each item was put in place. When he was done, Samia took the wedding band and placed it on the middle finger of his left hand, and Ahmad did the same for her. That accomplished, many of those present, particularly uncles and aunts of both families, approached Samia, surrounded by onlookers, and presented her with a piece of jewellery, which they helped her to put on. All the while, and even before Ahmad had arrived at the *khalieh*, a professional photographer was taking pictures and a video was being made. When all the commotion surrounding the display of jewellery was over, the onlookers went back to their places and three young men and three young women from Ahmad's side carrying similar trays of *dyafeh* but loaded with different kinds of juice, sweets and chocolates went around all the guests. Greetings and congratulations were then exchanged and Ahmad and his family left, but not before Ahmad's mother had made sure that two trays of each kind of *dyafeh* remained behind to be offered to the guests who would, over a period of a month, visit Samia's parent's house to offer their congratulations. All would expect to receive Samia's *dyafeh* as well as her fiancé's.

The groom is expected to pay for the following at the engagement party: the dress worn by the bride, all the floral arrangements, the *dyafeh* offered by his family, the photographs and the making of the video, the music, and the jewellery presented on the tray. In Ahmad's case these amounted to:

- Bridal gown: $1,000
- Floral decorations: $600
- *Dyafeh*: $3,000
- DJ: $300
- Video and photos: $1,500
- Jewellery: $5,000.[9]

The bride's parents pay for the *dyafeh* they offer the guests.

After the engagement party, among very traditional Druze families, the groom becomes economically responsible for the bride. Samia's family did not request that Ahmad became financially responsible for Samia until after the wedding. Nevertheless, Samia made it explicitly clear to Ahmad that she expected him to send her a sum of money on a monthly basis that she would be able to use over the period of a year to prepare for the wedding.

Signing of the Marriage Contract

The signing of a marriage contract is yet another formal occasion in the series of events leading up to the actual marriage ceremony. Ahmad returned to Lebanon eight months after the engagement party and after his father had made an appointment with the Druze Personal Status Court for the signing of the marriage contract. On the assigned day, Ahmad with his father, mother, maternal grandmother (his grandfathers are dead), two paternal uncles with their wives, three paternal cousins, one maternal uncle, one maternal aunt, his brother and sister went to the court building. They were met there by Samia and her parents with a selection of relatives including her father, mother, brothers, sister, uncles and aunts. The total number present was 30.[10] The judge took his place in the courtroom and asked all those attending to sit on the benches with the bride and groom occupying the front bench next to their fathers. All the women, including Samia, covered their hair with the white veils they had brought with them for the occasion. Then the judge asked Samia and Ahmad if they consented to the marriage and they were asked to respond in a clear loud voice. The judge inquired about the specifications for the *mahr*, both in its paid and deferred form. He insisted that the amount of gold liras for the deferred amount be named, refusing to include the term 'agreed upon'. He wrote the amount down on the marriage contract and then asked Ahmad and his two witnesses to sign the contract, followed by Samia and her two witnesses. Finally the judge delivered a small prayer derived from the Islamic tradition and announced that the couple had become husband and wife. After that, a male from Ahmad's family went to the car and produced a tray of decorated chocolates that he offered to all those in the courtroom and to everyone in the court building. Ahmad's father then asked all those present to accompany them to a pre-arranged lunch at a restaurant to celebrate.[11]

Wedding Party

The date of the wedding day was agreed by the two families. Ahmad and Samia chose the wedding invitation card. Four hundred copies were printed and distributed to friends and distant family members on both sides. The brothers of the groom and bride issued verbal invitations to close relatives of both families. A paternal cousin of Ahmad's went to all the houses in his village to invite every person to the wedding.[12] Ahmad's invitees amounted to about 1,000 whereas Samia's invitees were around 400.

On the day of the wedding, events unfolded in much the same way as at the engagement party. People gathered at the groom's house and at the bride's *khalieh*. Ahmad went with about 200 guests to the hall where Samia, her family and some 350 guests were waiting. Samia, dressed in her white bridal gown, sat amidst an arrangement of flowers waiting for Ahmad's arrival. The entrance of the guests and the exchange of greetings were the same as at the engagement party. The only main difference was the presence of a traditional dance group – specially hired for the occasion – to dance and sing at specific moments of the celebration. Their first appearance was to dance and sing in front of Ahmad as he descended from his car and walked towards the *khalieh*, followed by all those who had accompanied him. The group also danced before the groom as he made his way towards Samia after the distribution of the *dyafeh* from the bride's side. When Ahmad and the group reached Samia, one of the dancers invited Samia to join in. Samia and Ahmad started to dance surrounded by relatives and the dance group, and Ahmad's sisters and immediate family relatives[13] then joined in the dancing with Ahmad and Samia. The band then retreated and Ahmad sat next to Samia as the couple received congratulatory greetings from guests while posing for pictures with relatives all the while. *Dyafeh* from Ahmad's family were distributed to all those present and then Ahmad was called by an older cousin to leave his bride's side and join the men. This was the cue to all those present that the groom's company was soon leaving with the bride. Females and some males who had accompanied Ahmad started leaving the hall amidst a hail of greetings, congratulations and thanks. Samia's father and older brother,[14] one on each side, walked with Samia to the entrance of the hall. They were followed by Samia's mother, sister, other brother and the rest of her close relatives. All the while, the hired group was dancing in front of Samia and singing emotional songs of a father bidding his daughter farewell and imploring the groom to take good care of his daughter. By the time they reached the entrance, Samia and most of the women were crying.[15] Then her father stopped and handed Samia over to Ahmad who was standing at the entrance between his father, brother and other male relatives – most of the women had either returned to the cars or were standing behind the men, all on one side.

Taking Samia's elbow, Ahmad guided her to the bridal car and helped her in. He then went back to join his father who had lined up with all the men from his family facing a line of men from Samia's family. Ahmad's father said in a loud voice, 'We thank you for your hospitality and your daughter has now become our daughter.' To which Samia's father replied, 'We do not consider that we have lost a daughter but have gained a son.' The men on both sides exchanged similar remarks, thanking each other and raising their hands to their chests in greetings, and then Ahmad was instructed[16] by his father to approach his father-in-law and *ysitaktir bi kheireh*, meaning to thank him for the good deed of giving him his daughter in marriage. He shook his father-in-law's hand and they exchanged kisses. Then, one by one, all the men from Ahmad's side went down the line shaking hands with all the men from Samia's side before climbing into their cars drawn up behind the bridal car. As the convoy left Samia's village, women and youngsters were lining the route and standing on balconies holding bowls filled with uncooked rice[17] to throw at the cars, especially the bridal car. One of the photographers videotaped the convoy from the back of a Range Rover driving slowly at the head of the procession. When the cars reached Ahmad's village, they all blew their horns to inform the people that the wedding convoy had arrived so they could come to his parents' house to offer their congratulations. The bridal car stopped some 250 metres before the house and the bride and groom walked the rest of the way preceded by the dancers and singers who had performed earlier. The dancing and singing continued for about half an hour in front of the house and then Ahmad and Samia were asked by his parents to enter. At the door, Ahmad's mother halted the bride and asked her to enter the house backwards as a sign that Samia would never divorce and leave the house.

Once inside, Ahmad and Samia sat on two armchairs surrounded by flowers. Ahmad's father, brother, uncles and some male relatives stood outside the house while his mother, sisters and aunts lined up inside the house near the entrance. They received guests for two hours. The guests shook hands with both the men and the women and then offered their congratulations to the bride and groom. As they had to rise to greet each guest, Samia and Ahmad found themselves unable to sit down for more than a few minutes during the whole of this two-hour period. More than a thousand guests came to the house and all were offered *dyafeh* including cups of ice cream, juice, Lebanese sweets called *baklaweh*, and wrapped decorated chocolates. After all the guests had left at 7.30, Ahmad's parents and immediate family members went to a restaurant to await 350 previously invited guests, who started arriving at 8.30. When all were seated, Ahmad and Samia made their entrance, preceded by the group of dancers who had changed into different outfits. Ahmad and Samia danced a little and then sat at their table while the group performed for about half an hour before leaving. A hired DJ provided the music as the dinner was served and dancing continued until 12.00 when a seven-tiered cake was cut and slices distributed to all the guests. The party ended at about 1.30 when all left. Ahmad and Samia stayed until the end, leaving after the last guest had gone.[18]

Both Ahmad's and Samia's parents continued to receive congratulations for more than a month. Those who visited Samia's parents received the same *dyafeh* offered at the wedding by both Samia's family and Ahmad's family. Those who visited Ahmad's family were offered Ahmad's family's *dyafeh* and did not expect to receive Samia's parents' *dyafeh*.

Cost of the wedding:[19]

- Invitation cards: $500
- Bridal dress: $2,000
- Groom's suit: $300
- Floral decorations at both groom's and bride's place: $2,000
- Floral decorations in the restaurant: $1,000
- *Dyafeh* of the groom: $4,000
- Car decoration: $200
- Car rental: $600
- DJ fees: $350
- Dancing group: $1,600
- Video and pictures: $1,500
- Dinner cost: $12,000
- Total cost of engagement and wedding paid for by Ahmad: $38,950

  On top of all this, the groom is expected to have a fully furnished home ready for his wife and to cover the cost of the honeymoon.

The above description of the process leading up to signing the contract and the actual marriage along with the accompanying costs associated with the whole process reveal the intricate nature of marriage among the Druze and the formalized steps that have to be followed by those wishing to get married. Before going on to the analysis of data pertaining to marriage contracts, a section covering the legal aspect is presented.

Legal Background

Marriage, among the Lebanese Druze, is regulated, legally speaking, by the Druze Personal Status Law of 1948, Articles 1 to 36. Marriage is considered to be a legally binding contract made by signature of two fully consenting parties, and since the Druze people do not regard marriage as a religious act, divorce is permitted. What is of the utmost importance is the principle of consent, which is considered the basic condition for the legitimacy of a wedding contract. This accords with the Druze's belief in freedom of action. An act that is not freely made is rejected and considered of no value by the Druze. The Druze had believed in *Tawheed* freely and without coercion, and they undertake everything in their life freely (or at least try to) – including marriage. If a judge does not hear the individuals consent freely to the marriage (or, in the case of a dumb person, see a given sign of assent), he will not allow the marriage contract to be signed. Agreement and consent are the two basic principles for the conclusion of a marriage contract, as clearly stipulated by Article 14 of the Druze Personal Status Law.

A second point worth noting is that only the judge (*Qadi*) of the court and the *Sheikh al-'Aql*[20] (Al-Awar, 1983: 22) can conclude a marriage contract, unlike other Islamic sects in Lebanon that allow a *Ma'zoun*[21] to do so. However, in recognition of the fact that the Druze are spread all over Lebanon but there are only six courts,[22] and that there are also many Druze immigrants in other parts of the world, Article 17 provides for some flexibility in this regard by allowing the *Qadi* and *Sheikh al-'Aql* to appoint, as necessary, a *Ma'zoun* to conduct marriage contracts in areas that are not close to the courts. However, the same article limits the freedom of this appointed *Ma'zoun* since he can write a contract only after acquiring written permission from the judge or the *Sheikh al-'Aql* to do so. Article 18 also restricts the freedom of the *Ma'zoun* since he is legally obliged to send the contracts upon their conclusion to the courthouse for ratification and official registration. The judge has acquired a number of rights in this regard resulting in the transition of a legal person into an active agent in the life of the Druze.

An important stipulation is that for any marriage contract to be considered legally binding, it has to be signed by the two individuals concerned, or their legal representatives if they are not able to appear in person, and by at least four witnesses. Article 14 states:

> A marriage contract is conducted upon the agreement and consent of both parties who should be present in person and in the presence of witnesses related to the betrothed parties, on condition that these witnesses are not less than four. The contract must be written and then signed by the marrying couple

> and their witnesses. If one party could not attend the session, a legal appointee may replace him/her as long as that person has obtained a written legal power-of-attorney that must be ratified by the local *mukhtar*.[23] The written document must include a specification of the *mahr* or a statement that the matter is to be left to the legal appointee to specify. This document should be then attached to the marriage contract.[24]

The emphasis placed by the Druze religious scriptures on freedom is reflected in that aspect of the Druze marriage laws that specifies the age at which a person can legally be married. For an individual to be able to show consent, and to do so freely and without coercion, as is required by Article 14, he or she must be mature enough to understand the commitment they are making. Unlike the Islamic laws that consider physical maturity a sufficient condition for marriage, the Druze law sets the marriage age at 17 for females and 18 for males. The first article of the Druze Personal Status Law states:

> The fiancé has the legal capacity for marriage when he completes the eighteenth year of age, whereas the fiancée has the legal capacity for marriage when she completes the seventeenth year of age.

However, in accordance with the principle of *taqiyya*[25] and under the influence of the surrounding Islamic society, the law makes allowance for earlier marriage. Articles 2 and 3 stipulate that a female can be married at 15 years and a male at 16 years upon the fulfilment of three conditions: the acquisition of a medical report proving puberty and physical ability, the permission of the individual's guardian,[26] and the agreement of the *Qadi* or *Sheikh al-'Aql*. If the guardian's permission is not granted, the marriage is not final since, according to Article 4, either party may request the annulment of the marriage contract within six months of reaching the age specified by Article 1. A female is required to acquire the permission of her legal guardian, normally the father, until she reaches the age of 21 (Article 6), after which she is free to marry as she wishes.

A particular difference between the Druze laws and other Islamic laws concerning marriage is that the former make no allowance for polygamy. If a man chooses to marry another woman while still married to the first, his second marriage is considered null. The first marriage continues to be considered legal and it is not considered resolved upon the husband's second marriage. It is only through a divorce – one concluded in and through the court – that a marriage is terminated. Article 10 states:

> Polygamy shall be prohibited and a man may not have two wives at the same time, and if he does the second marriage shall be invalid.

By Druze law, just as in other Islamic law systems, a man is obliged to pay his wife a *mahr.*[27] Every marriage contract therefore includes a specification of the *mahr*, which is paid in two forms – the immediately paid (*Mu'ajjal*) and the deferred (*Mu'ajjal*). The first part is normally paid before or upon the signature of the marriage contract, unless otherwise specified in the contract. In practice, especially among the Druze living in rural areas, the man becomes economically responsible for the female he is betrothed to, even before the actual marriage, which is defined as occurring after the cohabitation of the couple consummated through sexual intercourse. Some families even require that the groom takes care of the bride's every expense. The groom is also expected to give the bride money to spend on her *jihaz*, which includes clothes, linen and other necessities for her married life. The second part – the deferred – is usually paid to the wife either upon the death of the husband or upon divorce.[28] Article 21 states:

> The wife shall not be entitled to request the deferred portion of her *mahr* before the coming of one of the ends, either divorce or death.

This part of the *mahr* is viewed as a debt in the hands of the husband. After acquiring the first part of her *mahr* and after signing the contract, Article 22 affirms that a wife is legally required to join her husband in his residence – as long as it is considered suitable, meaning that the house should be similar in nature to those of people similar in background to the married couple. The house should also be the couple's private residence not to be shared with other family members such as a mother or a father.[29] The same article, furthermore, requires a wife to go with her husband to any country he chooses unless there is a reason to forbid it. A clarification of such reasons is not provided in the law but a lawyer explained that this might include variables such as war or a visible danger to the wife's well-being such as an epidemic area. Article 23 guarantees equality between the genders – a fundamental Druze belief – stipulating that:

> The husband should fairly treat his wife and consider her his equal, and the wife should also obey her husband in terms of the legitimate marital rights.

These are some of the laws that guide the Druze when it comes to marriage. It is clear from the above that the Druze legislators tried to accommodate Druze traditions and beliefs into the Personal Status Laws while at the same time trying to avoid any kind of confrontation such a process might cause with the predominant Islamic sects of which the Druze sect is considered a part.

Analysis of Marriage Practices

The research on marriage for this study covered all marriage contracts written at the Beirut Druze court between 1970 and 2003 inclusive. The number of marriages concluded over this 33-year period amounted to 2,986. Table 3.1 sets out the percentage distribution of these marriages by year.

The table reveals a marked increase in the number of marriage contracts signed each year over this period. More people were getting married each year, the explanation for which might be demographic in nature, such as an increase in the number of Druze in Lebanon or a decrease in the age of marriage among the Druze people. This will be fully analysed in relation to the variable 'elapse of time' and

Table 3.1 Distribution of Marriage Contracts per Year

Year	1970	1971	1972	1973	1974	1975	1976	1977	1978	1979
Number	8	21	21	14	11	8	0	6	9	4
Percentage	0.3%	0.7%	0.7%	0.5%	0.4%	0.3%	0.0%	0.2%	0.3%	0.1%
Year	1980	1981	1982	1983	1984	1985	1986	1987	1988	1989
Number	7	23	42	72	8	14	19	28	41	30
Percentage	0.2%	0.8%	1.4%	2.4%	0.3%	0.5%	0.6%	0.9%	1.4%	1.0%
Year	1990	1991	1992	1993	1994	1995	1996	1997	1998	1999
Number	195	134	216	269	300	192	238	210	154	169
Percentage	6.5%	4.5%	7.2%	9.0%	10.0%	6.4%	8.0%	7.0%	5.1%	5.3%
Year	2000	2001	2002	2003						
Number	145	119	129	139						
Percentage	4.9%	4.0%	4.3%	4.7%						

its influence on the marriage phenomena in the following section. However, one cannot help but notice that during certain years the number of marriages was remarkably low. For instance, in 1976 no marriages contracts were concluded or registered at the Beirut court. This can be explained in terms of the effect of the civil war that had broken out the year before. People may have been deterred from going to Beirut to get married, especially as under special circumstances – war being such – a Druze is allowed to register the marriage at another court. Similarly, the end of the civil war most probably lay at the root of the huge increase in the number of marriages concluded during the early 1990s.

The increase in the number of marriage contracts signed in Beirut peaked during 1993 and 1994. A reasonable explanation would be that three years after the end of the war the stability of Lebanon seemed assured and consequently large numbers of Druze immigrants returned there to find a wife and get married. It was, and still is, common for Druze men living temporarily or permanently abroad to make 'bride seeking' trips to Lebanon with the purpose of finding a suitable spouse from within the Druze community.[30] Another explanation for the increase of marriages between 1993 and 1994 might be related to the fact that after the war ended, all males became liable for military service at the age of 18, if not pursuing an education, or else immediately on finishing college. Many Druze males sought to escape military service by getting married, since according to the Lebanese law then in force, a man was excused from service on becoming the head of a household. According to one young man:

> I didn't want to get married at such an early age. I was only 21 years old when I got married but I had to do so. If I had not, I would have been forced to spend a whole year of my life in military service. My parents encouraged me to marry. I did. I do not regret it now. I am happy with my wife, but I was very young and took on the responsibility of a family at a very early age.

The aim was to study change in marriage practices through an analysis across time and controlling for urbanization. Four variables of marriage were investigated in particular. The first was the age of each spouse at the time of marriage. The second dealt with the age difference between the husband and the wife calculated by subtracting the wife's date of birth from that of her husband, the assumption being that husbands are generally older than their wives in the Arab world. The third was the presence or absence of any kind of relationship connecting the husband and wife before marriage, either by blood as revealed in their family names and those of their parents, both of which are included in the marriage contract, or by both spouses being from the same residential area. The last of the four was termed 'contractual variables' and referred to certain *mahr* specifications in each marriage contract.

All the four variables, which represent critical indicators of change, were analysed along two lines to study change. The first was that of the elapse of time and its effect on marriage practices among the Druze, and for this purpose the date of signing the marriage contracts was the determining factor. The second was the place of residence of each of the spouses, which would definitely influence individual marriage choices and practices. A person living in a village is very likely to behave in a different way to someone who lives in the city. The next section deals with the analysis of all four variables and the effect of both the elapse of time and residence on them is dealt with after that. The first variable to be analysed with regard to the effect of the elapse of time and residence upon them was the age at marriage of both husband and wife.

Age at Marriage

The age at which an individual – male or female – chooses to get married is largely a determinant of the economic variables and social values and norms at play in the society to which that individual belongs. Economic conditions have indeed undergone some changes over the past decades as, we may suppose, have the social values and norms of the Lebanese people. These changes can be expected to have left their mark on the Druze of Lebanon – particularly in matters relating to marriage age. An increase in the marriage age of women across the Arab world was notable during the early 1990s. A report published by ESCWA in 1999 revealed that the age at which women married rose from 22 years during the 1980s to 24 during the 1990s. The report itself related the age increase to economic factors, claiming that 'economic conditions in the Arab countries compel girls to work in order to earn an income allowing them to share equally in marriage costs and to help the husband in covering the high expenses associated with married life' (ESCWA, 1992: 51). The Lebanese Druze were expected to have experienced a similar increase in marriage age among both males and females.

a. Effect of Elapse of Time on Husband's Age at Marriage

The Lebanese Druze Personal Status Laws set the minimum age of marriage for males at 18, and with special permission, at 16. The marriage contracts concluded before the Beirut court reflected such age limitations. The youngest reported age at marriage for males, 16, was observed in only two instances of the whole sample of 2,986 marriages. The oldest man married before the Beirut court during 1970–2003 was 93 – a one-time occurrence. The highest concentration (57.7 per cent) was among males aged from 25 to 34, as Table 3.2 reveals.

Table 3.2 Frequency Distribution of Husband's Age at Marriage (1970–2003)

	Frequency	Percentage	Cumulative Percentage
Less than 19	34	1.1%	1.1%
20–24	449	15.0%	16.2%
25–29	914	30.6%	46.8%
30–34	810	27.1%	73.9%
35–39	396	13.3%	87.2%
More than 45	183	6.1%	93.3%
Missing	191	6.4%	99.7%
Total	2986	100%	100%

Out of the whole sample of marriage contracts under study, only 16.2 per cent of men chose to marry before the age of 24, and 32.1 per cent married after the age of 35. Such findings are reflective of the general situation in the Arab world, where the average marriage age for males was reported as 27 in the 1980s, rising to 29 in the 1990s (ESCWA, 1999: 29).

These percentages represent the general percentages for the whole sample; however, for change to be detected a specific form of data manipulation had to be carried out. The marriages that were concluded at the two extreme time intervals, 1970–75 and 1998–2003, were sampled out to study whether the age at marriage of males had undergone any change over time. The reader should be aware that these time intervals do not cover the whole sample, which is why the total number of cases in the table does not reflect the number of the whole sample. The general assumption is that with the increase in individualism and the socio-economic changes after the 1990s, an observable increase in the male age at marriage will be found.

The numbers reported in Table 3.3 are a cross-tabulation of the age of the husband at marriage, classified into intervals, against three time intervals indicating date of marriage. The first interval is the earliest one available, 1970–75, the second one represents the civil war period in Lebanon, 1980–90, and the third one is the latest, 1998–2003.

Table 3.3 Age of Husband vs. Selected Time Intervals

	< 24	25–34	>35	Total
1970–1975	19 23.1%	46 56.1%	17 20.8%	82 100%
1980–1990	108 22.5%	273 57.0%	98 20.4%	479 100%
1998–2003	86 10.3%	480 57.2%	273 32.5%	839 100%

The first and third time intervals offer a time-line for comparative purposes and the 1980–90 interval offers a glimpse into the situation of the family during the civil war.

Table 3.3 reveals an interesting finding. The overall general preference for marriage within the 25–34 age interval remained the same throughout, regardless of when the marriage was concluded. During the first time interval 1970–75, 56.1 per cent of husbands belonged to this age group, compared with 57.2 per cent in 1998–2003. Thus, there was no observable change in the overall trend. Such a general preference is understandable since a male in the Arab world, and no less so among the Druze, is the provider for the family and must possess the economic means to allow him to do so. Therefore he would be forced to wait until he had achieved at least a modicum of economic independence before getting married.

However, the direct assumption that no change has occurred defeats logic since this phenomenon could not have remained so immune to change among the Druze. Upon closer examination, change became relatively more apparent when the category (husband's age at marriage) was divided into five-year intervals, as shown in Table 3.4. The percentage of males marrying at the age of 25–29 during the 1970–75 time interval was 31.7 per cent, which decreased by 6 per cent in the 1998–2003 time interval. This decrease was reciprocated by the increase in males marrying at the age of 30–34: 24.4 per cent of males married in 1970–75 belonged to that age group, whereas 31.7 per cent did so in 1998–2003 – an increase of 7.1 per cent. Thus, the decrease

Table 3.4 Husband's Age Vs. Date of Marriage

	<19	20–24	25–29	30–34	35–39	40–44	>45	Missing	Total
1970–1975	1	18	26	20	8	5	4	0	82
	1.2%	22.0%	31.7%	24.4%	9.8%	6.1%	4.9%	0%	100%
1980–1990	5	103	170	103	49	28	21	0	479
	1.0%	21.5%	35.5%	21.5%	10.2%	5.8%	4.4%	0%	100%
1998–2003	8	78	216	264	153	66	53	1	839
	1.0%	9.3%	25.7%	31.5%	18.2%	7.9%	6.3%	0.1%	100%

in the first time interval was matched by an increase in the second. Therefore, it is safe to assume some change, which even if not a very pronounced one, remains significant especially when compared to the time interval 1980–90 covering the civil war period. The percentages in this time interval with regard to age categories closely resembled those for the 1970–75 period. In fact, there was a tendency during the war period for males to marry at an earlier age: 35.5 per cent at the age of 25–29 compared with 21.5 per cent at the age of 30–34. During the war, many Druze males married at an early age because they enjoyed the economical support of the militia to which they belonged – namely the Progressive Socialist Party. Parents also encouraged their children to marry at an early age. One man said, 'I encouraged him to marry at a young age. I thought that when he had a wife to worry about, he would become more careful and not jump into danger. His carefulness would increase once he got children.

It was further shown that the percentage of males who married at a very young age (20–24) remained the same during the 1970–75 and 1980–90 intervals, but decreased from 22.0 per cent during the 1970–75 interval to 9.3 per cent in the 1998–2003 interval. This change was balanced out in the higher age groups: 9.8 per cent of males who married during the 1970–75 time interval were aged 35–39, whereas this age group rose to 18.2 per cent during the 1998–2003 time interval – almost double the percentage. During the civil war interval the percentage for this group (10.2 per cent) remained comparable to the percentage (9.8 per cent) during the 1970–75 interval.

The explanation for such changes – small as they might appear to some – must lie with the socio-economic changes that occurred over time. In the early 1970s, most Druze were still centred in their villages, working in agriculture or in family businesses. In such societies, early marriages were favoured as they increased the pool of agricultural labour available to the family. Moreover, in such agriculturally based societies, a man did not have to wait until he had accumulated enough money to get married. He could constantly rely on his father for economic support. One 80-year-old man from a village in the upper Matn area clarified this by saying:

> Youngsters these days make a big deal out of nothing. What do you need to get married? Just find a *bint halal* (a good honourable girl to marry)[31] and that is it. In our days, this is how it was done. She'd live with you in your parents' house – eat the same food and live the same kind of life. Nowadays, young girls want a fully furnished house and a lot of appliances. It costs a lot to get married nowadays. In the past, things were much more natural (meaning easier).

This old man was clearly aware of the minimal economic cost of marriage before the 1980s and of the high increase in the cost of weddings and marriage in the 1990s.

During the civil war, when many Druze male youth joined the armed militia – namely the Progressive Socialist Party (PSP)[32] – the situation remained in socio-economic terms similar to the 1970s. They were paid wages and had enough money and economic support to allow them to marry. The family role as provider of the economic base for marriage was replaced by the political party, which paid enough money for a young man to be able to support a family, bearing in mind also that housing was not considered a major issue due to the Druze taking over the houses of the Christian population displaced by the fighting – a process that was in fact regulated by the PSP.

However, after the end of the war and the vast changes in the economic situation in Lebanon, all that altered. A Druze male could no longer rely on economic support from his family, thanks to the decline of the agricultural-based economy, and had lost the advantage of belonging to the PSP. He therefore found himself alone and could depend on no one but himself. In the process of acquiring enough economic independence to get married and take on the support of a household, he was forced to delay his marriage for a number of years, as the research reveals. Moreover, the cost of getting married and establishing a house increased remarkably in the 1990s. This factor is considered here, along with those of increased migration and increased education, both of which also impose a delay in the age of male marriage. If one looks simply at the price of domestic electrical equipment, one can appreciate the economic expense involved in setting up a married household, especially as a Druze male is required to pay for everything himself. But in addition to having responsibility for providing and furnishing a house, what has truly become a burden to the Druze male is the cost of the wedding itself. The groom has to pay for the bride's dress, hair and makeup, floral arrangements at both her house and his, the refreshments offered to the guests, pictures and video costs, and music. Recently a traditional dance group has become a necessity at any wedding, and many Druze families insist on holding a dinner after the wedding for which the groom is also expected to pay.[33] All this clearly calls for a delay in the male's marriage age until he is capable of securing the amount of money needed for all this.

One informant told the author that he could not marry, or even consider the prospect of a marriage, before he was 33 years old. In fact, he married at the age of 34. He said, 'I had to save enough money for the jewellery that is part of the *mahr*, the engagement party, and the largest sum was for the wedding party and the honeymoon. Even then, the money I had saved was not enough. I had to take a bank loan which was a burden as I had to pay it back after I married.'

b. Effect of the Elapse of Time on Wife's Age at Marriage

The traditional tendency for females throughout the Arab world to marry at an early age underwent a noticeable change in the early 1990s.[34] Such a change might be expected to be mirrored among the Druze.

The Lebanese Druze Personal Status Law sets the minimum age of marriage for females at 17, which may be brought down to 15 with special permission acquired from the court after securing a medical certificate testifying that the girl was medically mature and could marry.[35] The findings revealed that this lower age limit was breached in two cases only: a female aged 13 and another aged 14 whose marriages were registered at the Beirut court in the 1980s. In both cases, the judge had made a note beside the marriage contract stating that it was concluded under special circumstances – the nature of which were not clarified. In similar instances that have come to the author's attention in the Druze community, the situation has been either one of elopement or of rape. In cases of rape, the girl would be forced to marry her rapist so as to secure her honour and that of her family. In cases where a young girl has eloped with a male against her parents' wishes, the judge would be forced to marry the two, and both sets of parents compelled to agree to the marriage.

In one divorce case brought before the court in 1999, the wife's appeal clearly echoed such a situation, containing the following written statement:

> Four months ago, the marriage contract was signed after the husband had kidnapped the girl from her parents' home in Beirut. To preserve the honour of the family, her parents were forced to agree. He had threatened to kill her and then commit suicide if she refused, and thus she found herself forced to accompany him.

Another statement, in the same case, ran as follows:

> Your honour was the person who wrote the marriage contract and recall the circumstances under which it was carried out – the kidnapping and how he forced her parents to agree to the marriage and they had to after they knew that their daughter had become a woman...and to preserve honor and maintain traditions, they had to accept...The husband abuses the woman and her parents would not wish her to divorce under any other

situation because how will they be able to get someone else to marry her after she had become a woman.[36]

The oldest female to marry during the 33 years covered in the sample was 73, to a man aged 93. For the sake of statistical manipulation, the marriage age of females was grouped into five-year intervals and a number of findings were reported.

The study revealed that out of the 2,986 marriage contracts signed at the Beirut court in this period, 1,084 (36.3 per cent) were signed by females aged 20–24. This shows a general trend to marry at an early age. Such a trend becomes more pronounced if one looks at the cumulative percentages provided in Table 3.5, which show 59 per cent of all females marrying before the age of 24. A further 676 marriage contracts were signed by females aged 25–29. Table 3.5 reports the frequency distribution of females by age at the time of signing the marriage contract.
The table also reveals that only 18.2 per cent of females who married between 1970 and 2003 were aged 30 or over. Thus, the majority (81.6 per cent) were married before they celebrated their thirtieth birthday. The table supports the assumption that Arabs generally prefer women to marry early – the Druze being no different in this. However, to study more closely change in the marriage age of females, an analysis

Table 3.5 Frequency Distribution of Female's Age at Marriage

	Frequency	Percentage	Cumulative percentage
Less than 17	304	10.2%	10.2%
18–19	374	12.5%	22.7%
20–24	1084	36.3%	59.0%
25–29	676	22.6%	81.6%
30–34	274	9.2%	90.8%
35–39	148	5.0%	95.8%
More than 40	119	4.0%	99.8%
Missing	7	0.2%	100%
Total	1986	100%	

across time was carried out. Table 3.6 provides a cross-tabulation of female age groupings at marriage against selected time intervals.

The research revealed that the percentage of females who married at the age of 20–24 remained relatively stable over all selected time intervals: 36 per cent during the 1970–75 time interval compared with 33 per cent during the 1998–2003 time interval and 35.7 per cent during the 1980–90 (civil war) interval.[37] Thus the passage of time and the civil war seem to have had no effect on this trend, the percentage of female Druze who married at the age of 20–24 remaining reasonably stable. A decrease of 3 per cent is not so large as to consider the difference of great value – or an indicator of change.

However, one cannot and should not jump to the conclusion that the passage of time left no impact on the preferred marriage age for females. Table 3.6 reveals a very indicative change in relation to this phenomenon: it was observed that the percentage of females marrying under the age of 20 during the 1970–75 interval was a quite considerable 39 per cent. This percentage decreased almost by half to 14.9 per cent during 1998–2003, which is a huge reduction considering the Druze people's resistance to change as described by Betts. The same kind of change, but reversed, was observed with regard to females marrying after the age of 25: this percentage increased from 24.4 per cent during 1970–75 to 52.1 per cent during 1998–2003. Analysis of the percentages during the war period (1980–90) showed that they resembled those for the earliest time interval, 1970–75; however, some small observable percentage changes might be indicators for the change revealed in the latest time interval.

Table 3.6 Age of Female at Marriage vs. Date of Marriage

	Less than 20	20–24	More than 25
1970–1975	32 39.0%	30 36.0%	20 24.4%
1980–1990	159 33.2%	121 35.7%	149 31.1%
1998–2003	125 14.9%	277 33.0%	437 52.1%

It seems that with regard to females the trend in recent years has been to delay the age of marriage. This raised a number of further questions: What was the nature of the delay? Was the delay remarkable or not? Moreover, do more females marry before the age of 30 than after, and in what percentages? And has the age gap between husband and wife changed accordingly? All these will be covered in the next section.

Table 3.7 reveals a number of interesting findings relating to the marriage age of females across time. It was observed that during the 1970–75 time interval, a relatively high percentage (20.7 per cent) had married before reaching their eighteenth birthday. This percentage had dropped quite markedly to 5.5 per cent in the 1998–2003 time interval. A decrease by almost a half was also noticed for 18–19-year-old brides: 18.3 per cent in 1970–75, falling to 9.4 per cent in 1998–2003. This shows a trend towards delaying marriage that is quite remarkable. It can only be explained in the light of increased educational awareness among young women about the meaning of marriage and its ramifications. Increased education has also encouraged the idea of delaying marriage at least until after a young woman has completed her school education and, in some cases, her college education.

A similar rise was noted in the percentage of females marrying at the age of the 30–34, from 3.7 per cent during the 1970–75 time interval to 12.5 per cent during the 1998–2003 time interval. It seems that in recent years a female who has passed the age of 30 is no longer considered a spinster, as used to be the case. This becomes even clearer when we group the percentages of females marrying after the age of 30,

Table 3.7 Age of Female's Marriage vs. Date of Marriage

	<17	18–19	20–24	25–29	30–34	35–39	>40	Total
1970–1975	17 20.7%	15 18.3%	30 36.6%	15 18.3%	3 3.7%	0 0.0%	2 2.4%	82 100%
1998–2003	46 5.5%	79 9.4%	277 33.0%	232 27.7%	105 12.5%	59 7.0%	41 4.9%	839 100%

when we find that 6.1 per cent of females married during 1970–75 were over 30, compared with 24.4 per cent during 1998–2003; in other words, almost a quarter of recent brides belonged to an age group that was traditionally considered beyond marriage age. The explanation for this phenomenon once again must lie in the increased educational awareness and the greater economic participation of women.

Such changes in the marriage age of both males and females are simply reflections of wider changes in the socio-economic nature of Lebanese society. Men delay their marriage until they have the economic means to start a family. Women delay their marriage until after they have completed their education. Expressions like 'I want to realize my potential before I get stuck with a family and children' would never have been heard in traditional Druze society. They have become very common today. Of course, older people scornfully denounce such behaviour as 'the reason for the decline in family life'.

c. Effect of Place of Residence on Husband's Age at Marriage

The above analysis clearly revealed how the age of marriage had witnessed a change in relation to the time at which the marriage contract was concluded. Another factor that could be expected to be a determinant of, or at least to have an influence on, the age of marriage of both marriage partners was the place of residence of each. Someone residing in the city may be expected to behave in a way that is different from a village resident.

The marriage contracts concluded at the Beirut court and covered in the sample included individuals from different areas of Lebanon including Beirut, Aley, Chouiefat and a number of villages mainly in the Matn, Baabda and Chouf areas. For the sake of statistical manipulation, the variable place of residence was determined along the following lines: city residents were those who gave Beirut as their place of residence in the marriage contract. Town residents consisted of people residing in Aley and Chouiefat. Village residents were those who named any of the villages in the Matn, Baabda and the Chouf areas as their place of residence.

The husband's place of residence in the sample under study broke down into the following percentages: 77.8 per cent village residents,

6.6 per cent town residents, 10.3 per cent city residents. The husband's place of residence was expected to have a determining influence on the age at which he chooses to marry, the assumption being that males residing in villages would marry at a relatively earlier age than their counterparts in the city or towns. The reason for this assumption is that males in Druze villages are not economically independent but are supported by their parents. Lebanon is a patriarchal society and marriage is mostly patrilocal. It is not uncommon to find fathers saving money for the marriage of their sons. This allows a Druze male from a village to get married before he has actually collected the necessary amount of money – something that a city resident has to do for himself. Another determining factor is that the majority of Druze people in the villages own their own house and many own land too. A Druze father will frequently build an extra flat in his house with the idea that his son will live there too. This lessens the financial burden on a young man who is contemplating marriage and makes it possible for him to get married earlier than his urban counterpart.

When the husband's age at marriage was cross-tabulated against his recorded place of residence, the findings showed (Table 3.8) that 48.9 per cent of village males married before the age of 30, compared to 32.9 per cent of males in the city. This finding was reversed in the 30–39 age group: only 39.5 per cent of village males married in this group, compared to 47.6 per cent of city residents. It was notable that town residents behaved in a manner similar to the village. This might be explained by the fact that the towns are not very different, socially speaking,

Table 3.8 Age at Marriage vs. Husband's Residence

	Less than 29	30–39	More than 40	Total
Village	1138 48.9%	919 39.5%	267 11.5%	2324 100%
Town	84 42.4%	76 38.4%	38 19.2%	198 100%
City	102 32.9%	148 47.9%	59 19.1%	309 100%

from the villages surrounding them. The town of Aley, for example, is inhabited by a large number of religious men and women – *Ajaweed* – whose sight is quite common especially in the shopping area of the town. A large number of shops are owned and run by *Ajaweed*.[38] The Druze often say things like, 'Aley is not a town, it is simply a large village' when talking about social traditions and customs.

The finding that male city residents delay marriage is a strong reflection of the economic demands of married life in the city compared to the villages. Most villagers work in agriculture or in family businesses and even those who don't normally rely on parental support. As well as saving money for his son's marriage, a father will often sell a piece of land to make financial provision for him. A young man of 23 from a village in the upper Matn area fell in love with a girl from the same village and wanted to marry her. His father sold a piece of land a year before the wedding and built a house for his son next to his own. He also paid all the costs of the wedding. He commented:

> What else could I do? I could not leave the matter unattended to. What would have happened if they eloped? That would create many problems for our family and the girl's family. Sooner or later, my son would want to marry and the end result would be the same.

In villages, men still worry a lot about the marriages of their children and still consider the arrangements to be their own responsibility – not their sons. This is not common in the city where a man is expected to work for a number of years before getting married, not depending largely on what his parents might provide for him.[39]

d. Effect of Place of Residence on Wife's Age at Marriage

A wife's place of residence was also expected to influence the age at which she married. Some 81.6 per cent of women included in the sample lived in villages, 6.0 per cent in towns, and 7.7 per cent in the city of Beirut. The traditions and values upheld in the village community could be expected to lead to a younger marriage age for females in country areas. To study the influence of residence on the female's

Table 3.9 Wife's Residence vs. Age at Marriage

	Less than 24	25–34	More than 35	Total
Village	1471 60.4%	752 30.9%	214 9.7%	2437 100%
Town	99 55%	62 34.4%	19 10.6%	180 100%
City	111 48.3%	89 38.3%	30 13.1%	230 100%

age at marriage, her residence was cross-tabulated against her age at marriage at different time intervals.

The results reported in Table 3.9 supported the assumption of a difference in behaviour between women living in the city and those in the villages. Out of the total number of women living in villages, 60.4 per cent were married before the age of 24 compared to 48.3 per cent of city residents. More specifically, the research revealed (not reported in the table) that 23.2 per cent of village residents married before the age of 20 compared to 14.8 per cent of city residents. The findings also showed, like those for the husband's residence and age at marriage, that the behaviour of women in the towns was similar in nature to those in the villages, strengthening still further the idea that the towns are but huge villages with the same kind of value systems at play.

The preference of women in the villages for early marriage was evident from interviews carried out with girls living in these communities who welcome early marriage and for the most part expect to get married directly after finishing school or university. Work and self-realization are not considered prerequisites for marriage. This is not to say that Druze women do not work once they get married but most villagers do not consider work as crucial to their lives, whereas marriage definitely is. One 21-year-old university student from a village in Aley area told the researcher:

> Marriage is more important than work because work provides for an income whereas marriage provides a family and children.

> My husband has to provide for me so I do not need to work for money but I need to get married if I want a family and a meaningful future.

To this girl, marriage and future were synonymous, unlike work and future.

Spouses' Age Difference

An important aspect related to spouse selection is the age difference between husband and wife, which has decreased in the Arab world from about 14 years in the 1930s to eight years in the 1960s (Barakat, 1993: 11). This finding was further supported by ESCWA research that stated that the age difference in the 1980s and 1990s had decreased to five years (ESCWA, 1999: 30). As the marriage contracts studied in the research included the birth date of each spouse, it was easy to calculate the age difference between them. The results revealed that most Druze males choose to marry a female who is four to nine years younger than they are: 39.2 per cent of all married males displayed such a preference over the entire 33-year period covered in the sample. To be able to understand better the age difference, a number of age-difference intervals were selected so as to make the statistical manipulation of this variable easier and of more relevance to the question of social change. The intervals chosen were the following: (1) less than zero difference, in cases where a male married a female older than himself; (2) zero to six years difference, the normal age difference between people who may have met at work or college, admired each other, and fallen in love or come together for any other reason; (3) seven to ten years difference, taken to stand for the 'sought out' age difference among the Druze who intentionally seek a bride from within the community; (4) 11–15 years difference; (5) more than 15 years difference, chosen to cover any case that might fall outside the selected intervals.

The distribution of the age difference among spouses is reported in Table 3.10. It was found that the majority of Druze married couples (39.6 per cent) had an age difference of 0–6 years and 24.0 per cent had an age difference of seven to ten years. Those findings are an accurate

Table 3.10 Frequency Distribution of Husband–Wife Age Difference

	Frequency	Percentage	Cumulative percentage
Less than 0	276	9.2%	9.2%
0–6	1179	39.6%	48.8%
7–10	713	24.0%	72.8%
11–15	552	18.6%	91.4%
More than 15	266	8.6%	100%

reflection of the age difference between husband and wife in the Arab world at large.

a. Effect of Elapse of Time on Spouses' Age Difference

For the purpose of this research, the date of signing the contract was taken as a variable against which to compare the husband-wife age difference. The two five-year time intervals included for the purpose of this analysis were the oldest and most recent ones available in the sample: 1970–75 and 1998–2003.

Table 3.11 revealed a general trend in favour of a lower spouses' age difference over time. A 10 per cent increase in the zero to six years difference was observed across time, rising from 31.7 per cent of those married in 1970–75 to 41.6 per cent of those in 1998–2003. This increase over time was reversed for the group whose age difference was seven to ten years: the percentage of males choosing a wife within this category fell from 29.3 per cent in 1970–75 to 22.2 per cent in 1998–2003. Although the change is less than 10 per cent, it is indicative of a general trend that, intentionally or not, is bringing about a narrowing of the age difference between husband and wife. The only group that witnessed no change was among those whose age difference was 11–15 years: 19.5 per cent in the 1970–75 time interval and 18.1 per cent in the 1998–2003 time interval. Of course, one might find the explanation for this by identifying the age at marriage of those within this group, or studying the relationship between the spouses, but that goes beyond the limits of this research.

Table 3.11 Date of Marriage vs. Husband–Wife Age Difference

	<0	0–6	7–10	11–15	>15	Total
1970–1975	5	26	24	9	11	82
	6.1%	31.7%	29.3%	19.5%	13.4%	100%
1998–2003	85	349	186	152	67	839
	6.1%	41.6%	22.2%	18.1%	8.0%	100%

The trend towards a smaller age difference between marrying spouses is reflective of changes in Lebanon and the wider Arab world. A male, in these times, as many of my informants kept pointing out, seeks a marriage partner who is able to understand the ever-changing needs of modern-day society. If his wife was 10–15 years younger, she would not be able to cope with that, especially when one takes into account that the favoured age for marriage is 25–30 among males: thus a girl who is 10–15 years younger would still be a child. Young Druze men who are contemplating marriage will often say things like:

> I want a person to stand by me and not to give me trouble.
> I want a person to build a family and have kids with – not to marry a kid.

Still, there are many instances of Druze men marrying women more than 12 years younger. One man, reflecting on the age difference of 15 years between him and his wife, commented,

> It is true she's much younger but I am 42 and I want to marry to have children. The probability for a woman under 30 is higher. If I marry someone who is five years or less younger than me, we might end up with no offspring. If I were younger, I would have considered marrying a girl not much younger than me.

Many females commented on a large age difference as something favourable. One young girl of 18 said,

> A girl matures, mentally speaking, much faster than men. So when I am 22, have finished university, and want to marry,

> I will not even consider a man who is 24 or 25. Someone of 30 to 35 would be an acceptable marriage partner for me. He has to be capable of supporting me financially – so he must have a good income.[40]

What about love? Her response was that emotions were important but not everything is 'love', which will come later on in the relationship.

b. Effect of Residence on Spouses' Age Difference

The above clearly showed that the age difference between husbands and wives had decreased over time. Further analysis was carried out to see whether the place of residence of each partner influenced the choice of spouse in respect of age difference.

i. Husband's Residence and Age Difference

The place of residence of the husband was cross-tabulated with the age difference between husband and wife and the findings reported in Table 3.12. The resultant percentages indicate that with respect to those with an age difference of zero to six years, the husband's place of residence was not a determining factor since a stable 39.2 per cent of village residents, 37.4 per cent of town residents and 39.8 per cent of city residents married women in this category.

This stability was not maintained across the whole population under study, where noticeable differences emerged in other categories. For example, it was observed (Table 3.12) that 24.9 per cent of male

Table 3.12 Husband's Residence vs. Husband–Wife Age Difference

	<0	0–6	7–10	11–15	>16	Total
Village	215 9.3%	1161 39.2%	577 24.9%	407 17.5%	197 8.5%	2324 100%
Town	16 8.1%	74 37.4%	45 22.7%	40 20.2%	23 11.0%	198 100%
City	17 5.5%	123 39.8%	59 19.9%	77 24.9%	33 10.7%	309 100%

village residents were seven to ten years older than their wives, whereas the percentage for city residents with this age difference was lower – 19.9 per cent. When it came to the highest age difference (11–15 years), the opposite was observed: 17.5 per cent of village residents compared with a higher percentage of 24.9 per cent among city residents.

The higher age difference between husband and wife among city residents is explained by the fact that many urban men delay marriage for quite a long time until, say, the age of 45, when they are in an economic position to make the decision to marry. However, to be sure of having children and raising a family, they will choose a wife aged from 30 to 35. A purely economic consideration also operates: men above the age of 40 are economically well secure and young women will be tempted to choose a rich older husband over a poor younger one.

ii. Wife's Residence and Age Difference

The place of residence of the husband was shown to have a somewhat limited influence on the age difference between husband and wife. This part examines the influence, if any, of the wife's place of residence. Table 3.13 reports the findings of the cross-tabulation of the wife's place of residence vs. husband–wife age difference, which showed that although the overall preferred age difference was zero to six years, the percentage of women living in the city of Beirut who married men within this age difference was 46.5 per cent, higher than the 38.8 per cent reported for village residents. At 42.3 per cent, residents of

Table 3.13 Wife's Residence vs. Husband–Wife Age Difference

	<0	0–6	7–10	11–15	16>	Total
Village	216 8.9%	945 38.8%	592 23.3%	464 19.0%	220 9.0%	2437 100%
Town	22 12.2%	76 42.3%	32 17.8%	33 18.3%	17 9.4%	180 100%
City	22 9.6%	67 46.5%	47 20.5%	37 16.1%	17 7.4%	230 100%

the towns fell somewhere in the middle. When it came to marrying a male seven to ten years older, the percentages were not widely different: 23.3 per cent for village residents and 20.5 per cent for city residents. Percentage figures for residents of the two towns of Aley and Chouiefat were lower than those for city or village residents, with 17.8 per cent of marriages falling within the seven to ten years category. To summarize the findings of Table 3.13, we find that women in the villages married men who were more than six years older than themselves in 51.3 per cent of cases. Town residents did so in 45.5 per cent and city residents in 44.1 per cent of cases. Thus it seems that a wife's residence was not a determining variable in the age difference preference between spouses.

To conclude, the husband's place of residence was found to be a determining factor whereas that of the wife was not. More is demanded of males in Druze society than of females.[41] The financial demands a Druze male faces are huge, and if he does not have a family to rely on, he is often left with no option but to delay marrying until he is in a position to pay for all the expenses of the wedding. In the villages, where it is the practice for the groom's family to share in meeting the costs of the marriage and very often for the father to build his son a house, men can afford to marry earlier than those in the city.

Husband–Wife Kin Relationship

An important variable in any marriage is the person an individual chooses to marry. The Druze people are present in most areas of Lebanon, but the choice of marriage partner is often related to the individual's place of residence and the presence of transport infrastructure to facilitate wider contacts, allowing for marriage from outside the kin group. The study investigates whether marriage choices have changed across time in this respect.

a. In-Kin Marriages

The practice of kin marriage is highly favoured in the Arab world. One study carried out in Iraq found that marriage to non-relatives was as low as 17.7 per cent with similar findings reported in Syria (Barakat, 1993: 108). Alamuddine and Starr (1980) point out that Arabs generally encourage paternal cousin marriages as the first choice, followed by marriage within the kin group. The reason for this is that a female's kinship ties are not severed by marriage and kin loyalty is maintained.[42] At the same time divorce is avoided since it is assumed that cousin marriages and even in-kin marriages act as a strong deterrent to any open conflict (Alamuddine and Starr: 1980: 37–8). Sholkamy (2008) points out a similar practice in rural Egypt whereby women prefer to marry within the kin group, associating that with greater marital stability and family support. The practice of kin marriage continues to be dominant in rural areas. It remains to be seen whether the Druze covered in this study adopted such practices in their marriage choices.

The marriage contracts give the full name of each spouse as well as their mothers' name, thereby making it possible to identify whether the marrying couple belong to the same family in both its patriarchal and matriarchal branches. The relationship of the husband and wife was coded according to these categories: (1) same patriarchal family: spouses belonged to the same family; (2) maternally related: husband and wife were maternally related; (3) not related: the two were not related in the sense that their parents had different family names.

The frequencies reported in Table 3.14 show that the percentage of Druze from the sample marrying from within their own family was 17.6 per cent, while 9.4 per cent married individuals related to them through their mother. Thus, a total of 27 per cent of Druze were married to a relative – quite a high percentage, similar to that reported in Alamuddine's and Starr's study.

Table 3.14 Frequency Distribution of Husband–Wife Relationship

	Frequency	Percentages	Cumulative percentages
Same patriarchal family	525	17.6%	17.6%
Maternally related	281	9.4%	27.0%
Not related	2179	73%	100%
Total	2985	100%	

i. Effect of Elapse of Time on In-Kin Marriages

To discover whether the above factor was predominant at all times the variable 'date of marriage' had to be controlled. Table 3.15 shows the cross-tabulation of the husband and wife relationship against the date of marriage at intervals representing the earliest, the civil war period, and the most recent.

It is true that there is a general preference for marriage outside the family; however, there is detectable change in marriage preferences across time, according to Table 3.15. Out of the 82 marriages concluded from 1970–75, 28 per cent were among individuals of the same family. This percentage witnessed a sharp decline to 10.3 per cent in 1998–2003. This change is highly indicative of people's increased awareness of the negative health effects of marriage between relatives.

It was further observed that during the civil war, the percentages reported were similar to those reported in the early 1970s, with 21.7 per cent marrying within the same family. One explanation could be the fact that in times of war social relationships are limited, restricting the individual's marriage choices and increasing the likelihood of in-kin marriages. Another is that the huge changes in the socio-economic and cultural structure of Lebanese society did not begin to make themselves felt until after the war ended in 1990. The huge boom in information technologies brought about many changes in people's values and standards. It is interesting to note that in 42.1 per cent of the total sample, the husband's parents had belonged to the same

Table 3.15 Husband–Wife Relationship vs. Date of Marriage

	Same patriarchal family	Maternally related	Not related	Total
1970–1975	23	5	54	82
	28.0%	6.1%	65.9%	100%
1980–1990	104	51	324	479
	21.7%	10.7%	67.6%	100%
1998–2003	86	63	689	838
	10.3%	7.6%	82.2%	100%

family while the wife's parents had belonged to the same family in 39.2 per cent of cases. These figures show the extent to which kin marriages were practised before the 1970s. When the parents' relationship was also studied against the marriage date of their children (see Table 3.16) it emerged that the parents of women married in 1970–75 belonged to the same family in 53.7 per cent of cases, while in 1998–2003, the percentage was 34.8 per cent. The husband's parents belonged to the same family in 64.6 per cent of those married in 1970–75 and in 33.6 per cent of those married in 1998–2003.

The above finding clearly points to the strong tendency of the Lebanese Druze traditionally to marry within the kin group. This was very marked among the parents of the married couples covered in the study, became less so with those married during the 1970s, and declined further during the 1998–2003 period of the research. This diminution of the tendency to marry from within the same family is a particular reflection of changes in people's attitudes and perceptions, and even of their personal evaluation of the benefits of such marriages, although the practice remains in force.

ii. Effect of Residence on In-Kin Marriages

The above evidence tells us that the Druze community was distinguished by a relatively high degree of endogamous relationships, and particularly kin marriages, although this practice is diminishing. The place of residence is expected to have an influence on the occurrence of blood-related marriages since city residents will have a wider choice of marriage partners from among non-family members.

Table 3.16 Parent's Relationship vs. Husband–Wife Marriage Date

	Husband's parents of same family	Wife's parents of same family
1970–1975	53 64.6%	44 53.7%
1998–2003	282 33.6%	291 34.8%

(a) Husband's Residence. The research revealed that the place of residence played a part in influencing the husband's choice of a blood relative as spouse. For this part of the research, the relationship between the husband and wife was described in one of two ways: (1) related: when the spouses were related in any way, whether patriarchal or matriarchal; (2) non-related. Table 3.17 reveals that males living in the villages married a blood relative in 29.3 per cent of the whole sample, whereas city residents reported a lesser figure of 16.2 per cent, and town residents a not dissimilar 18.7 per cent. The high percentage of almost 30 per cent among males in villages is evidently a particularity of where they lived.

b) Wife's Residence. The place of residence of a wife was also found to have an influence on the choice of a blood relative as spouse. Table 3.18 reveals that village women married a blood relative in 28.8 per cent of cases, whereas city residents did so in 15.5 per cent of cases. Town residents fell

Table 3.17 Husband's Residence vs. Husband–Wife as Relatives

	Related	Not related	Total
Village	682 29.3%	1641 70.6%	2323 100%
Town	37 16.7%	161 81.3%	198 100%
City	50 16.2%	259 83.8%	309 100%

Table 3.18 Wife's Residence vs. Husband–Wife as Related

	Related	Not related	Total
Village	701 28.8%	1735 71.2%	2336 100%
Town	33 18.3%	147 81.7%	180 100%
City	35 15.2%	195 84.8%	230 100%

in between with 18.3 per cent. Therefore, women in the villages were twice as likely to marry a relative than those in the city.

In general, city residents, whether controlling for the husband's or wife's place of residence, showed a preference for non-related marriages. The reasons for this are manifold. First of all, city residents are more exposed to the effect of the mass media, education and medical information that all point up the health risks accompanying kin marriages. Secondly, city residents have a wide range of choice in terms of numbers of people and are more likely to meet individuals from outside the family, whether at work, social gatherings or elsewhere. Village residents, on the other hand, don't enjoy such privileges, simply because of the demographic structure of Druze villages: one or two families dominate the whole village and marriages are normally among members of restricted groups that, in one way or another, promote related marriages. Thirdly, city residents delay their marriages, thereby increasing the possibility of meeting a range of people from other families. All these factors taken together promote non-related marriages among city residents while playing an opposite role among those in the villages.

b. Spouses of the Same Place of Residence

The choice to marry from within the village or to venture outside the limits of one's immediate contacts was also expected to have witnessed a change across time. Areas that seemed beyond reach during the 1970s became a car-ride away during the 1990s and 2000s. This transformation can be expected to show itself in wider marriage choices since the Druze social network extended to distant mountainous areas that were very hard to reach decades before.

Effect of Elapse of Time on Same Residence Marriages

Table 3.19 represents a cross-tabulation of the date of marriage and the proximity of residence between husband and wife. The proximity of residence was grouped as follows: (1) same residence: the husband and wife come from the same village, town or city; (2) adjacent residence: husband and wife come from adjacent villages or towns (the city was excluded since the closest Druze town or village was considered too far);

Table 3.19 Date of Marriage vs. Husband–Wife Residence

	Same residence	Adjacent residence	Same vicinity	Others	Total
1970–1975	31	6	6	39	82
	37.8%	7.3%	7.3%	47.6%	100%
1980–1990	152	53	61	213	479
	31.7%	11.1%	12.8%	44.5%	100%
1998–2003	159	38	92	550	839
	19.0%	4.5%	10.9%	65.6%	100%

(3) same vicinity: husband and wife come from villages in the same vicinity – separated by one or more village; (4) others: all other variations, including marriage to Druze in Palestine or Syria.

The research revealed a decrease in the percentage of spouses coming from the same and adjacent villages across time. It was observed (Table 3.19) that 37.8 per cent of couples married during the 1970–75 interval belonged to the same village and 7.3 per cent to adjacent villages. These percentages fell in 1998–2003 to 19.0 per cent and 4.5 per cent respectively. This shows that after the passage of about 30 years the Druze were opting for marriage from outside their villages. This was supported by the increase in the number of people marrying from areas that are not in close proximity. The percentage rose from 47.6 per cent in 1970–75 to 65.6 per cent in 1998–2003. As with other factors, the civil war period resembled the early 1970s in all aspects.

Evidently, the increased availability of cars, increased movement to urban areas for work, and increased exposure to higher education contributed to the growing tendency among the Druze to marry from outside their villages, town or residential area. When a person is able to commute to distant areas, new social connections are formed and social relationships with residents from other villages are maintained. This encourages the formation of connections with other families that may in itself bring about extensive marriage choices including that of a spouse from beyond the village's geographical boundaries.

One 70-year-old man married to his maternal cousin who is also from the same village and the same family commented:

> I married at a very young age. I was 20 and my wife was 15. We knew each other all our lives. It was normal then to marry someone from your same family. Where would I meet someone from another family? Girls at that time were not like today – they would not leave their houses and be seen on the street. At least with my cousin, I knew what she looked like. With another girl, I would have to rely on what my mother said. As for marrying someone from outside the village, that was very rare. There were only a few cars in our village and one bus. If we needed to go outside the village, we had to wait for days until one of the car owners decided to go and then we would try to get a place in the car. Or we would have to save enough money to pay the bus fare and also wait for a long time for the bus on the side of the road. Mostly, we walked so, even if we could meet a girl from another village, it would be a great trouble to go visit her. A girl from the village is much less trouble.[43]

Contractual Variables

The variables included in this section are related to the nature of the marriage contract itself.[44] The marriage contract utilized at the Druze court includes a specific section allocated to the specification of the *mahr* in both its prompt and deferred form. Article 24 of the law specifies that the *mahr* is the amount of money that must be specified in the marriage contract and constitutes the money the husband is obliged to pay the wife as soon as the marriage contract is signed. The article clarifies further that when the amount is left unspecified, the judge is to assume that the sum equals that to be paid to one of a similar social position. This article, as such, leaves it to the judge to assign the *mahr.* The dowries mentioned in the contracts under study included items ranging from money and gold coins to regular household items such as sewing machines, carpets, bedrooms,[45] and even kitchen utensils. A notable aspect of the *mahr* among the Druze was the mention of a sewing machine and/or a bedroom. When informants were asked the reason for including these two items in the *mahr*, most answered that it was the traditional way of doing things. One woman aged 65 said:

> No marriage contract is considered 'right' without these. That is the way things have been done for a long time and there is no need to change things now.

A more logical explanation in sociological terms may be found in the Druze's traditional base in agriculture and the predominant extended family structure. A male would marry and bring his wife into his father's household. The whole family lived and worked together. Under such a system, the only thing a wife needs is a bedroom. As for the sewing machine, the explanation is of a more economic nature. A female in traditional Druze society was expected to know how to tailor clothes – both for herself and her family. The sewing and embroidery were even taught to girls in school up until the 1970s and remain the practice in a few schools of a religious affiliation, taught under the subject of arts and crafts. A sewing machine, looked at from this angle, would be considered of great value. Moreover, a sewing machine would also act as an economic (income) asset to a Druze woman if widowed or divorced. As one old lady put it, 'If destiny leaves her without support, a woman can always use her sewing machine.' Old people of the community told stories of how they and their children wore clothes that were tailored at home by their mothers' sewing machines. One man recalls how the old women in his village used to cut out wheat sacks made from soft cloth and tailor them into clothes for the children. A sewing machine was essential in these times as it was largely used in most households.[46]

The mention of both the bedroom and the sewing machine was quite understandable in past times under the above mentioned condition. However, it would be quite exceptional if the mention of these elements continued into recent times, especially during the latest time interval covered in the sample (1998–2003).[47] The following sections will deal with the presence of these two items in marriage contracts.

a. Sewing Machines

The study revealed that out of the 2,986 marriage contracts covered in the sample, 1,669 (55.9 per cent) included a mention of a sewing machine. Its inclusion in the *mahr* was expected to be influenced by a number of factors such as the passage of time and the place of residence of the spouses.

i. Effect of Elapse of Time on the Mention of Sewing Machines

The presence of a sewing machine was analysed across time. The results are reported in Table 3.20.

The findings are quite remarkable since they show no change over a period of 33 years. The contracts that included a mention of a sewing machine in 1970–75 amounted to 40.2 per cent of the whole sample and remarkably enough the percentage remained almost constant – 40.4 per cent in the 1998–2003 time interval. It seems that the Druze conform to tradition in this regard. They evidently do not question the norms and as the old woman said 'the right way of doing things'. The fact that the percentages have remained the same shows a resilience to change, or if taken at a lighter level, simply a lack of concern on the part of more recent spouses to confront and change the traditional custom. Many young individuals are unconcerned about the whole business and respond to questioning with 'I don't care. Such details are of no importance. The judge may write whatever he wishes, I don't care.' This may be the cause, but the fact still remains that most

Table 3.20 Marriage Date vs. Sewing Machine's Presence

	Sewing machine mentioned	No sewing machine	Total
1970–1975	33 40.2%	49 59.8%	82 100%
1980–1990	278 58.0%	201 42.0%	479 100%
1998–2003	339 40.4%	500 59.6%	839 100%

Druze continue to abide by a practice that seems to be very traditional and outmoded.[48]

Noteworthy in this regard was the fact that the mention of a sewing machine as part of the *mahr* increased to 58 per cent during the war interval. The reason for this might lie in the fact that the possibility of a wife being widowed increases in wartime and thus it makes sense for the sewing machine to be included, since it will provide a means of income in case of bereavement. How this phenomenon relates to urban and rural residents is covered next.

ii. Effect of Residence on the Mention of Sewing Machines

The research revealed that the mention of a sewing machine as part of the *mahr* was more likely to occur when the husband was from a village than from either the city or town. A reference to a sewing machine was recorded in 60.2 per cent of dowries where the husband was a village resident compared with 33.8 per cent of town residents and 41.7 per cent of city residents.

With respect to the influence of a wife's residence on the mention of a sewing machine, the percentages revealed little difference. It was included as part of the *mahr* of 58.8 per cent of female village residents and 47.0 per cent of female city residents though the percentage fell to 33.9 per cent with respect to town residents. All these percentages are fairly high, indicating that the Druze generally include the mention of the sewing machine independent of their place of residence.

b. Bedroom Furniture

The bedroom, as mentioned previously, was a notable part of the wedding contracts among the Druze. It was observed that a bedroom[49] was included in the female's *mahr* more frequently than a sewing machine. The bedroom was mentioned in 2,117 (70.9 per cent) of marriage contracts out of the total of 2,986.

i. Effect of Elapse of Time on the Mention of Bedroom Furniture

This section will analyse whether there is any difference between marriage contracts signed during the early 1970s, the 1990s and early 2000s.

Table 3.21 Date of Marriage vs. Bedroom Mentioned in *Mahr*

	Bedroom mentioned	No bedroom	Total
1970–1975	45 54.9%	37 45.1%	82 100%
1980–1990	343 71.6%	136 28.4%	479 100%
1998–2003	502 59.8%	337 40.2%	839 100%

The trend revealed in Table 3.21, which analysed the mention of a bedroom in the *mahr* during different time intervals, echoed that reported for a sewing machine. Out of the 82 marriage contracts signed in 1970–75, 54.9 per cent included a bedroom, compared with 59.8 per cent in 1998–2003 (839 contracts). Thus the consistency noted in the Druze *mahr* specifications with regard to sewing machines held good for bedrooms too. The percentage during the civil war interval was even higher – 71.6 per cent. One can only speculate about the reason for this. It may be that in a time of war people are not particular or picky, and many couples may have told the judge simply to write down the traditional *mahr* items. If anything, the findings related to both sewing machines and bedrooms run counter to the argument that a change in such behaviour would be expected.

Clearly, the above does not mean, nor is intended to mean, that all the Druze have abided by this behaviour, but simply that the percentage of people who chose to include either or both items showed no perceptible change over time, remaining at roughly 70 per cent for bedrooms and 50 per cent for sewing machines. Indeed, clauses reflecting recent social changes have been included in the *mahr* specifications of some marriage contracts. For instance, out of the 532 marriage contracts signed after 2000, ten provided as part of the deferred *mahr* the following: 'half of whatever is brought into the marital house after the marriage is the right of the wife' – meaning, of course, in the case of divorce or the death of the husband. Moreover, 15 contracts included mention of the 'latest computer' as part of the *mahr*, another indication of how the ideas of a younger generation of Druze are changing. However, the traditional patriarchal nature of Druze society continues to limit change – even within the legal system, where the head of the court is usually a Druze male sheikh.[50] A Druze couple who were married in 2007 reported what took place while they were signing the marriage contract:

> The judge asked them what to write in the deferred *mahr*. The man answered that he wanted the judge to write half of all his property at the time of his death or upon divorce. The judge simply refused, threatening not to continue with the session, and consequently the husband was forced to give in after much debate and upon the interference of both his family and the bride's. The judge told him that it was against the traditional way of doing things and if the husband really wanted to do that he could write it in his will or sign some agreement with his wife but not include it in *mahr*.

This shows that despite some changes in attitudes, younger Druze people continue to adhere to traditional custom – or are forced to do so, as in the above case. It is true that the judge was offering a compromise or a solution for the young man's predicament through suggesting a will; however, his suggestion does not stand in contradiction to Druze customs. Freedom of testation is part of the Druze tradition and is guaranteed by law. A male giving his wife half of his property through a will is accepted and does not contradict the religious teachings, but including such a stipulation in the *mahr* is not accepted.

Another explanation for the continuity of this traditional behaviour is the reaction of the young marrying couple who feel the burden of the formality of the situation. The signing of the marriage contract is a very important aspect of one's life because it transforms the person's status establishing a connection with others – not just the spouses but all of the spouses' families. 'On making such a contract a person's legal status undergoes a radical transformation; the person is viewed as qualitatively changed' (Stewart, 2007: 135). The marrying couple find themselves under the influence of this transformation brought forth by the status contract[51] and, subsequently, consider the whole question of the *mahr* not worth fighting about, taking the line of 'Let's get the matter over and done with'. In the words of one young Druze man, 'It's all just a formality.' And so the practice carries on.

During the signing of one marriage contract I attended at the Aley court in 2010, the judge did not even bother to ask the couple if they wished to have a sewing machine and a bedroom included in the delayed *mahr* specification. He only asked how many gold liras (coins) to include. When he read out what he had written down as the *mahr* specification, one of those present burst out laughing on hearing the mention of a sewing machine, saying that the machine's make and model should be specified, and suggesting 'Singer'. He added that it should be replaced with a computer since everyone knew that the wife did not even know how to use a needle and thread, let alone a sewing machine. With a stern face, the judge remarked: 'This is our Druze tradition and we will abide by it!' I was left with the impression that this was one method by which the religious court is struggling to maintain its control over young Druze people.

ii. Effect of Residence on the Mention of Bedroom Furniture

When the mention of a bedroom in the *mahr* was analysed against the place of residence of both spouses, the data revealed that the husband's residence was not a determining element in this particular: 74.1 per cent of male village residents mentioned a bedroom, compared with 62.5 per cent of city residents. Although the gap of 11.6 per cent points to some difference between city and village residents, the mere fact that over 50 per cent in both categories opted to mention it indicates a general preference for the inclusion of a bedroom in the *mahr*.

A similar result occurred when the residence of the wife was analysed against the mention of the bedroom. It was included in 61.7 per cent of contracts in which the wife was a village resident and 73.4 per cent of those from the city. Here, too, it is safe to assume that with respect to women, residence was not a determining factor in the inclusion of a bedroom in the *mahr*.

To conclude, it does not appear that the place of residence of either spouse had any influence on the inclusion of a sewing machine or a bedroom in the *mahr*. This shows an acceptance of traditional customs whose purpose was understandable in earlier times but is not so today – especially with regard to the sewing machine. The explanation may have its roots in the religious upbringing of young Druze people, for as one young Druze male explained:

> We know nothing of our religion. We just know that we have to respect the religious men and that they know more. We do not go to religious *Khalweh* (Druze prayer place) and do not read the religious books. When we are confronted by a religious sheikh, we are taught not to question his words. We just accept what he says, even if we do not agree. We are not brought up to question religious authority since our parents don't know and don't teach us the religion but they teach us to respect and show reverence to the religious sheikhs – who apparently know the secrets of the religion. So, when I went to the courthouse to sign the marriage contract, I simply signed and agreed to whatever the judge said was the normal thing – as did my wife. Now, we both agree that including a sewing machine was silly since she doesn't even know how to operate one, but we found ourselves agreeing to the traditions – blindly so.

A change in values across generations is evidently present and there is the lurking tension between the older generation represented by religious-legal authority and the younger generation represented by the marrying couple. However, this tension is kept under check as most Druze, young and old alike, emphasize their Druze identity above all else.

c. Nature of the Paid Mahr

As was made clear at the beginning of the chapter, each contract includes a specification of a paid *mahr* or a *Mu'ajjal*. The paid *mahr* is whatever the husband gives to his wife before or directly upon signature of the marriage contract. Study of the marriage contracts revealed variations in assigning the paid *mahr*. Some contracts included mention of household items such as a cupboard, carpet, set of pots, set of sofas, a couple of gold bracelets and in some rare cases a computer. Others named a particular sum of money in the form of jewellery bought for the wife or mentioned gold coins. Some contracts even referred to the paid *mahr* given to the wife as 'agreed upon' meaning that the husband and wife had agreed the amount of the *mahr* between themselves and preferred to leave it unspecified. In my conversation with the judge, he indicated that the court requires the couple to clarify and specify what they had agreed to as judges are facing problems in divorce proceedings when the matter is left ambiguous. The paid *mahr* – not the deferred – is the wife's automatic right upon divorce and when this is not clearly outlined in the marriage contract, it increases the amount of conflict as the judge finds himself forced to deal with conflicting claims from the contending parties as to what was actually agreed to. Some contracts also mentioned, as part of the paid *mahr*, the whole or parts of the Druze religious books, *Kutub Al-Hikma*. This provision is found only among the religious strata of *Ajaweed*. The *Kutub Al-Hikma* was mentioned in 53 contracts, representing 1.8 per cent of the whole sample.

i. Effect of Elapse of Time on Paid Mahr

The *mahr* specifications may be expected to have witnessed changes over time if only by reason of the economic changes that took place in Lebanon over the period from 1970 to 2003. Table 3.22 offers an overview of how details of the paid *mahr* have altered. It should be noted that for the sake of statistical manipulation the paid *mahr* has been classified in the following groups: (1) money: refers to mention of a specific sum; (2) gold coins: refers to instances where a particular number of coins was specified; (3) agreed upon: refers to instances

Table 3.22 Paid *Mahr* vs. Date of Marriage

	Money	Coins	Agreed upon	Other	Total
1970–1975	65 78.3%	0 0%	17 20.5%	1 1.2%	83 100%
1998–2003	474 56.3%	21 2.5%	336 39.9%	11 1.3%	842 100%

where the couple declared the matter to have been settled between themselves without specifying the details in the contract although in recent years judges are insisting that the amount be explicitly specified as they are facing problems in its evaluation when faced with a divorce case; (4) other: refers to anything else that was mentioned including household furniture (other than a bedroom), gold jewellery (a ring, necklace or other), a carpet, etc.

The nature of the paid *mahr* was cross-tabulated against two five-year intervals, the earliest and the most recent covered in the study. The findings revealed a notable change over time. In 1970–75 78.3 per cent of contracts specified a sum of money in the paid *mahr*. This dropped to 56.3 per cent in 1998–2003. Over the same period the percentages of those who preferred to leave the matter unspecified – agreed upon – increased from 20.5 per cent to 39.9 per cent, nearly double.

These obvious changes may reflect a change in people's understandings of the marriage contract. Young people marrying today generally refuse to admit the economic factor as integral to the marriage, preferring to emphasize the emotional aspect. That is why they prefer not to specify the *mahr*. One young girl said that she particularly hated that aspect of the marriage contract because it made her feel as if the husband was exchanging money for his wife, which she thought was degrading. It seemed more romantic to her not to specify the *mahr* since whatever the husband gave his bride before the marriage would be viewed as an outright gift and not as payment in exchange. Yet, in a large percentage of all marriage contracts signed at the Beirut court in the period under study, a specified sum was included, which leaves one wondering to what extent these young Druze really are rejecting the traditions.

Signing the marriage contract is not a private matter restricted to the couple getting married. Parents, grandparents, uncles, aunts and cousins are present transforming the incident into a public event. The couple find themselves under the scrutinizing eyes of all those present which as one couple said, 'it was very awkward. There was the judge asking about the amount to write and we were silent. We did not know what he expected us to say.' In another incident, the judge took up a more active role. The husband told the judge to write 'agreed upon' but the judge insisted that an amount be specified. He then asked the husband to tell him how much gold he got for his bride (for the engagement). The man answered $5,000 upon which the judge commented, 'That is not an amount to be ashamed of. Why were you hesitating to mention it?' and he wrote the amount as paid *mahr* ignoring the request of the groom not to specify anything. Here, again the judge took up an active role in defining what is normative.

ii. Effect of Residence on Paid Mahr

The place of residence of both the husband and the wife was studied to assess their influence on the nature of the paid *mahr.* The findings revealed that the place of residence did not play a significant role. Out of the whole sample, the percentage of male city residents who chose to specify a sum of money as paid *mahr* was 42.7 per cent, while among village residents it was 50.0 per cent. Urbanization, with all the differences it makes to an individual's way of life, had no impact among the Druze in this regard. It is important to clarify that the Druze who are from Beirut are not migrants to urban areas but are descendents of Druze families who resided and owned land in Beirut even before the establishment of Lebanon as an independent country.[52]

The analysis of a wife's place of residence similarly pointed to little difference in behaviour between village and city residents regarding the *mahr* specification. The percentage of female village residents whose paid *mahr* specification included a sum of money was 49.0 per cent compared with 44.8 per cent among city residents.

It seems that Druze people remain constant in their behaviour no matter where they live. Social customs are strong, independent of residence. One lawyer explained it to me like this:

> The Druze in the cities become more attached to their religion and their sect's practices and particularities. In this way, they attempt to prove that city life has not taken hold of them and that they are still as Druze as the Druze people in the mountains. They actually became stricter in certain aspects.

Therefore, upholding certain customs and traditions may act as a way of asserting identity – of 'being a Druze',[53] members of a sectarian minority group whose home is normally in the mountains which they consider their territorial sanctuary. When some Druze families settled in Beirut, they found themselves a minority within a huge majority. Since they could not integrate with the majority because of their different religious traditions and teachings, they further secluded themselves by trying to remain as traditional and conforming as their village counterparts.

d. Nature of Delayed Mahr

The delayed *mahr* – *mu'ajjal* – is considered an integral part of a marriage contract and it is rare to find a contract (three only out of all 2,986 marriage contracts studied) that does not include a *mahr* specification. The amount specified in the delayed *mahr* ranged from a sum of money or number of gold coins to a plot of land or a house. Most Druze people who married at the Beirut court during the 33 years of the study assigned the delayed *mahr* in terms of gold coins (71.5 per cent), the reason no doubt being that a gold lira will not lose much of its value over time. Currency, on the other hand, is subject to socio-economic factors and may devalue over time, as actually happened in Lebanon. This might explain why a mere 21 per cent of the whole sample specified a sum of money. Furthermore, 171 contracts (5.7 per cent) limited the *mahr* to one gold coin only.

The influence of parents and other family members cannot be denied. Even when young couples feel that the assigning of a *mahr* is uncalled for since rarely does a person marry thinking of divorce, the signing of the marriage contract is a public event in which family members of both sides are present. What gets written in marriage contracts become the public 'news' (the gossip) to be exchanged in the community and evaluated as reflecting the bride's worth and the groom's generosity. Among the Druze, bride's who insist on a very large sum are criticized as greedy and those who settle for a very small sum are subject of gossip as unworthy of more. It is a predicament that many youngsters find themselves in. One woman, reflecting on news she heard regarding a high *mahr* allocated to a bride said, 'Can you believe it? The bride's father told the judge to write one hundred golden liras. It is true that she is more educated than the groom but that is too much.'

The Druze will use the *mahr* as a bargaining tool in certain cases where an individual marries without the agreement of the parents or where the couples come from different social backgrounds. A father may require a large sum of money as a deferred *mahr* if he feels that his daughter is marrying someone who is either less educated than she is or is of a lower class. The purpose of a large deferred *mahr* is to be able to force the husband to agree to a divorce quickly if the wife is not happy. The *mahr* acts as a lever that allows the wife and her family a larger control over the marriage. On another level, a husband who knows he would have to pay such a large sum of money would not create conflict that might lead to divorce, since the delayed *mahr* is the wife's right upon divorce. Some parents further insist on a large delayed *mahr* because they are not happy with the marriage in the first place.

In one divorce case brought before the court in 1999, this reason was clearly emphasized. The man was born in 1973 and the woman in 1981. The case revealed that he had actually abducted her from her parents' home in Beirut and the family was forced to agree to the marriage as the girl had supposedly lost her virginity: 'to preserve the reputation of the family, the wife's family had to agree to the marriage'. The *mahr* detailed in the marriage contract was as follows:

- Paid *mahr*: 10,000 US dollars to be paid upon demand, and the complete furniture of a house.
- Deferred *mahr*: 300 gold liras.

The wife's family was able to use these terms to force the husband to agree to a divorce only eight months after the marriage although he had tried without success to persuade his wife not to leave him. The wife waived her right to the *mahr* in return for a divorce in agreement.[54]

i. Effect of Elapse of Time on Delayed Mahr

The kind of delayed *mahr* included in a marriage contract was analysed across time and the findings were largely related to changes in the economic climate. Table 3.23 clearly shows that during the early period of 1970–75 the percentage of contracts specifying a sum of money as delayed

Table 3.23 Date of Marriage vs. Kind of Delayed *Mahr*

	Money	Coins	1 Lira	Other	Total
1970–1975	83 100%	0 0%	0 0%	0 0%	83 100%
1998–2003	94 11.2%	650 77.2%	86 10.2%	12 1.4%	842 100%

mahr was 100 per cent, decreasing steeply to 11.2 per cent in the 1998–2003 time interval. As explained above, the reason for this lies in the staggering decline in the value of the Lebanese lira (pound) and the fluctuations of the monetary market. For instance, the amount of money specified during the early 1970s ranged from 500 LBP up to a maximum of 50,000 LBP, the value of which is negligible today,[55] and this motivated most people to change the specification of the delayed *mahr* from a sum of money to gold coins.

Another important finding revealed in this section was that concerning the specification of the amount of *mahr* as one gold lira. Out of the 842 marriage contracts signed in 1998–2003, 86 (10.2 per cent) had a delayed *mahr* of one gold lira. This might reflect the fact that working women are rejecting the idea of demanding money upon the divorce or death of the husband. One informant said:

> If we reach a stage of divorce, I'm not going to ask for money. That would be silly. I'd earn the money that would be registered in my *mahr* in a period of a couple of months through my work. I won't humiliate myself by asking for money.

Of course, not all females are working and definitely do not share this opinion. However, 10.2 per cent, even if not large, is nonetheless indicative of some change that might be 'fermenting' within Druze society.

ii. Effect of Residence on Delayed Mahr

The place of residence of both husband and wife seem to play no role in the allocation of a delayed *mahr*. Of those allocating a sum of money,

22.7 per cent husbands lived in the city, 27.3 per cent in towns, and 20.4 per cent in the villages. Relatively similar percentages were found with regard to the allocation of coins: 68 per cent were city residents, 66.2 town residents, and 72.3 per cent village residents.

The wife's place of residence also seemed to have no impact on the kind of *mahr* specified. A sum of money was specified for 23.9 per cent of female city residents, 28.9 per cent of female town residents, and 19.7 per cent of female village residents. Nor was there any observable difference between city and village in the allocation of gold coins: 67.4 per cent and 73.2 per cent respectively. Therefore, the place where people lived seemed to have no influence on the kind of *mahr* mentioned.[56]

Concluding Remarks

Marriage practices among the Lebanese Druze as revealed through the study of the marriage contracts at the Beirut Druze court were a strong reflection of the intricate nature of the Druze community. Some aspects of marriage practice remained resilient to change over the 33 years covered in the research. The inclusion in the *mahr* of certain traditional elements, such as the sewing machine and the bedroom, remained stable over time, as did the practice of specifying a *mahr*. It is true that the nature of the delayed *mahr* changed from allocating a sum of money to allocating a certain number of gold coins, but these changes were a reflection of economic factors in Lebanon – basically the devaluing of the Lebanese pound. The essence and the purpose of the *mahr* had not changed.

On the other hand, there were a number of detectable changes within the general framework of continuities. Changes were reported in the increased preference over the 33 years for delaying marriage, for both males and females. Among the most notable changes related to marriage preferences was the decrease in the percentage of in-kin marriages, accompanied by a preference for marriage from outside one's own village. Evidently in-kin marriage and marriage from the same village have not died out completely. Many still opt for these marriage practices but their occurrence is decreasing significantly across generations.

Socio-economic changes that have significantly influenced the Lebanese society after the 1990s have left their impact on the Druze family life. After the war ended in 1990, Lebanon underwent a process of reconstruction of the infrastructure, revival of educational institutions and emergence of effective communication networks all of which left their impact on the society. Values of youngsters changed and were reflected in marriage practices. However, these changes interacted with an already existing habitus that regulated the behaviour of the group and hence the continuities that were persistent. The Druze individual does not make choices and take actions that only reflect the socio-economic changes. These choices and actions are incorporated within a history that interacts with the changes formulating the outcome – the changes and continuities. The habitus 'captures how we carry within us our history, how we bring this history into our present circumstances, and how we then make choices to act in certain ways and not others. This is an ongoing and active process – we are engaged in a continuous process of making history, but not under conditions entirely of our own making' (Maton, 2008: 52) Thus, the practices of marriage are not outside of what constitutes the Druze identity – which is a reflection of the experiences of a community that constantly seeks to maintain its inner solidarity and continuity as a minority, a fact which the Druze youngest are aware of.

To further understand the marriage practices, these must be situated within the framework of what happens in the court during the signing of the marriage contracts – particularly the role that the judge, a sheikh, plays. The judge becomes an agent concerned with the continuity of traditions. The continuity in the specification of the *mahr* does not occur outside of the court setting. It is a process that is situated and settled within the court, particularly by the judge who refuses to endorse non-traditional behaviour insisting on the continuity of traditions as part of the Druze identity and demanding submission to collective rhythms that represent the group (Bourdieu, 1977: 163). The courtroom itself with the judge and the people present become a minute representation of the Druze community with all the tension between continuity and change. This is manifested in the tension that the young experience. They want to change but find themselves unable to either because they are confronted by an unrelenting judge or because they feel the power of the social structure which they cannot question – the legal setting itself. Some are even not consciously aware of the power that this structure has over them and thus fail to react but succumb to the normative order that is imposed by the legal field that limits their behaviour because 'what can be done is also shaped by the conditions of the field' (Thomson, 2008: 69).

In summary, certain aspects of Druze behaviour remained the same over a period of three decades, but changes were witnessed in other areas, especially when socio-economic factors rendered them necessary. Behavioural changes were observable but were confined within a general framework that remained somewhat traditional in character.

CHAPTER FOUR

DIVORCE AMONG THE DRUZE

The court is located on the first floor of an otherwise residential building.[1] When I arrived at the court, the bailiff as always asked me if I had my *mandeel* with me.[2] I pulled my *mandeel* from my handbag and asked him if the judge was in the courtroom. He informed me that the judge was seeing some people in his office. I entered the courtroom and sat on the last bench next to a man who had some papers with him. There was also an old woman sitting on a side bench. A young woman with two young men sitting next to her was seated a little further from the old woman. The young woman was crying silently and the two men with solemn looks on their faces kept looking at their shoes avoiding my eyes whenever I looked in their direction. The man sitting next to me told me that he was in the court to submit a few documents that the judge had required from him. He was in the middle of a divorce. The man had told the judge in a previous session that his wife had intentionally sabotaged his minibus from which he made his living by transporting students to the university. His wife was not attending the court sessions and the judge could not question her so he needed the man to get him proof which he got from the police department since he had filed a complaint against his wife and he had taken some photos of his smashed minibus. He was at court to submit these as evidence.[3] After about 15 minutes, he was called to the judge's office and left soon afterwards. A few other people had entered the court by the time the judge made his appearance. All those present stood up as the judge wearing the Druze religious attire entered the courtroom. He casually greeted all those present and took his place at the bench, as did the secretary, also a religious *sheikh*. Case after case was called upon, ending with the last case, the *Jamal* v. *Souad*. The young woman and the young man sitting next to her stood up. The judge looked at the file and read:

> We the undersigned, Jamal and Souad, declare without pressure by anyone that we want to divorce and have come before the court to ask that our divorce be validated.

The judge finished reading and looked up at the two. He asked, 'Do you two still want to divorce?' The man looking at the floor said, 'Yes.' The woman, who had not stopped crying, said nothing. The judge asked her, 'Why are you crying? Do you want to divorce your husband or not? If someone is forcing you to come to court just say so.' The woman continued crying and said nothing. The judge then announced that the case would be moved to the conference room. He rose from his bench and asked the couple to follow him. The other man told the judge that he was the man's brother and asked if he could accompany them. The judge asked the couple if they wanted him present and they both said yes, so he gave him permission to go with them. The judge then looked at me and said, 'Come with us. Maybe she (meaning the woman) will talk to you and then you can help me understand what's going on.' We all sat around an oval table and the judge told the man and his wife that he would not sign the divorce agreement until after the wife stopped crying and announced that it was her wish as well. The wife continued to cry and in between sobs said that she wanted to divorce her husband. The judge told her that he was not convinced it was what she really wanted. He then asked me to try to understand what the problem was and left the room to go to his office. I asked the woman to calm down so we could talk. All the time, her husband was offering her tissues to dry her tears and trying to comfort her with comments like, 'Please, stop crying', 'Everything will be fine' and 'Don't worry.' It was his brother who talked and told me the story. He said that his brother cared about his wife as did he but the problem was with her uncle. Souad was an orphan and she was orphaned at a young age. Her uncle had custody over her and had placed her at the Druze orphanage. He then made her marry at a young age. Her first husband died leaving her with two children. When her first husband died, she went back to the orphanage. She then married Jamal who was also a widow with two children. Her uncle was against the marriage and would not let them be and had been making their life miserable. Her uncle would show up at their house and beat Souad, terrorizing the children. Her husband had tried his best to stand up to her uncle but he was afraid for his children since her uncle had threatened him that he would harm the children. I asked the wife if the story was correct and she nodded adding, 'He is ruining my life.' After that, her husband said, 'I do not want to divorce her but I have my own children to think of.' She then explained to me that she wanted to go back to the Druze orphanage where she and her children would be cared for and protected as her uncle would not dare approach her there. Her brother-in-law then explained that because of her uncle's constant threat she developed a severe nervous breakdown and was being medicated. She had even left the four children all alone at home and was gone for the whole day. When she returned she said that her uncle would not harm her if he did not find her.

After that, I explained the whole situation to the judge. He spent a few minutes thinking and then said that if there were no children involved he would not sign the agreement but he had to consider the children's welfare. He could not keep them with a disturbed mother who was not even capable of taking care of herself and could rely on no relative for support. Her own children would go back to the orphanage and receive proper care and the husband's children would be protected. Then the judge told the couple that he would sign the divorce but that he was giving them a two month period to finalize the divorce, in case they wanted to go back on the decision.

Jamal and Souad had signed an agreement and brought the agreement to the court to simply be endorsed by the judge. The judge did not immediately agree to their agreement as he had enough reasons to doubt that the agreement was not really by consent. He took certain measures to help him reach his decision which was mostly based on his evaluations and judgement – a thing that was reflected in several cases though my research in the court. Before providing an analysis of the divorce court records, a legal overview of articles related to divorce is provided.

Legal Background

The Druze laws governing divorce, as with all other legal matters, are basically derived from the Islamic *Hanafi* and *Maliki* schools of law and the Islamic *Shari'a* (Al-Awar, 1983: 18). However, a number of modifications were introduced, specifically related to Druze customs and inherent beliefs. Freedom and equality, as previously mentioned (in Chapter 2), are fundamental to the Druze people and find resonance in their legal system. Guided by these beliefs, the Druze legislators treated both genders equally in the laws governing divorce, its causes and practice. The mainstream Islamic jurisdictions restrict divorce rights to the husband. The Druze law, on the other hand, allocates an equal right to husband and wife to file for divorce, which is described by former Judge Al-Awar as without precedent in other systems[4] in Lebanon (Al-Awar, 1983: 12).

Divorce, according to Druze law, is the termination of a marriage contract binding two Druze individuals. Once it is ended, the wife leads a life totally separate from her husband's: he is not allowed to meet his divorced wife nor to go back on the divorce and remarry her (Al-Awar, 1983: 40). It is even considered *haram* – meaning religiously sinful – to see one's spouse after divorce. Should former spouses happen to attend the same social function, they will avoid each other and try not to look in each other's direction.[5]

If a Druze couple get a divorce and later, for whatever reason, wish to remarry they cannot do so under Druze law but will be forced to obtain a civil marriage or change their religion altogether. Civil marriage is not available for anyone in Lebanon and people must travel abroad to arrange one – usually to Cyprus or Turkey. The stipulation concerning the relationship between divorcees is contained in Article 11, which lays down that once a divorce is announced, it is forbidden for any divorced husband to remarry his ex-wife. This is further confirmed in Article 38, which stipulates the following:

> A man has no right to remarry his divorced wife after the judge renders the separation judgment.

Although both husband and wife can seek a divorce, the actual annulment or end of the marriage – the declaration of the divorce – is in the hands of neither. That right is legally restricted to the court in the person of the judge.

Article 37 of the Druze law particularly stipulates that no marriage contract can be dissolved except by a sentence issued by the judge. This freed women from the Islamic practice of instant repudiation through the mere uttering of the word *taliq* (you are divorced) by the husband.[6] This Druze practice is in line with the *Muwahhiddeen* belief in the 'supremacy of reason' – the *'Aql*. According to Druze beliefs, it runs against reason to allocate the right to divorce to either the husband or the wife since both are capable of utilizing this right illogically or in a moment of anger. So, to prevent such a probability, the right to divorce was given to the judge who is required to use all measures to prevent a divorce. For this purpose, a judge is further required by law to appoint an adjudicator from both contesting parties. Article 47 stipulates:

> In the event of a dispute or discord between husband and wife, and either of them refers the case to the judge, the latter shall appoint an adjudicator from the husband's family and another one from the wife's family. If none of their relatives has the legal capacity to be an adjudicator, the judge shall appoint a non-relative adjudicator.

The role of this adjudicator[7] is to try to find out the causes of the disagreement and to do his utmost to reconcile the parties. If the fault was with the husband, the judge must issue a sentence allocating the wronged wife part of or all her *mahr*. He should also decide upon any form of harm or injury compensation that is the right of the innocent party. The law even sets apart an article dealing with the matter. Article 49 stipulates:

> In the event where the judge considers that divorce is not legally grounded, he may decide to have the husband pay damage and harm to the wife in addition to the deferred *mahr* provided that the moral and physical damage are taken into consideration.

The Druze law enumerates a number of conditions upon which the wife is entitled to ask for divorce without renouncing her rights to a *mahr* and harm or injury compensation. Articles 39, 40, 41, 43, 44 and 45 provide that a wife may ask for a divorce if her husband suffers from an incurable, contagious disease that precludes a safe married life, or if her husband is mad, has committed adultery, was imprisoned for more than five years, was absent for three years without sending maintenance or for five years with maintenance. In all these cases, her economic rights are upheld. The same rights of divorce are afforded to the husband,[8] with the further addition of *noshouz*, referring to a wife who refuses to have any sexual relationship with her husband or leaves the house without due cause and does not return.

A Druze couple may divorce by agreement as stipulated under Article 42. They do not have to explain the causes to the judge as long as they had agreed to the divorce before coming to court. Close consideration of the articles governing divorce among the Druze leads one to conclude that in many ways the law is quite progressive. However, what is of interest to this research is whether the Druze practices of divorce changed over the 33 years under study.

Analysis of Divorce Practice

The research covered all divorce cases brought before the Druze Beirut court from the beginning of 1970 to the end of 2003. All the cases were hand-copied; these amounted to a total of 1,066, but after some analysis it was decided that not all could be considered as actual divorces.[9] In 237 of the 1,066 cases, the divorce had occurred before the actual marriage was consummated – in other words, they represented a sort of engagement breaking and not an actual divorce. These cases will be analysed in the section below entitled 'Pseudo-divorce' since the behavioural phenomenon that led these couples to marry 'officially' and then 'separate' calls for special attention. The cases of actual divorce during the 33-year period amounted to 829.

The distribution of cases over the 33-year period varied from year to year. Of course, taking the numbers on their own, without comparing them to marriage rates, reveals no specific finding except that the number of divorces per year has increased over time. The war had a definite bearing on family life among the Druze and to account fully for its effects, the war years had to be taken as a variable to compare against other variables. However, before embarking on an analysis of the different variables to disclose any change in divorce practice, it is essential to provide an overview of custody laws that directly reflect and influence divorce practices among the Druze.[10]

Articles 54 to 66 are concerned with child custody. According to Druze law, the mother has the right of custody to a son if he is under the age of seven and to a daughter if she is under the age of nine (Article 64). The mother's right to custody of her children cannot be questioned except when she is not considered fit to carry out that duty (Article 54). Moreover, Article 60 states that any custodian of a child has the right to maintenance to be paid by the father. If that person happens to be the mother, then according to Article 61, the father is to pay her the child maintenance, in addition to providing a suitable place of residence, if she does not have one, and a servant to look after the child if the father is rich enough to afford one. As the analysis revealed, these custody laws have a direct bearing on the nature of the divorce in cases where children are involved.

Type of Divorce

Before analysing the data, it is important to point out certain facts. To start with, the Druze consist of an enclosed community that has witnessed only a very limited degree of internal conflict. It is worth noting that, even during the civil war, the Druze people remained for the most part internally cohesive. Although historically the Druze have been, and to a large extent still are, divided between the prominent Yazbaki and Junblatti families, this division has rarely manifested itself to the outside world in the form of observable internal fights or disagreements. The Druze people constantly emphasize their internal cohesion and solidarity and dislike any form of internal strife or disharmony. This is apparent in the way the family manages its own affairs and particularly in the type of divorce brought before the court.

Conflict within the family is always kept within bounds and Druze people are commonly heard saying things like 'We solve our problems internally', 'It is a shame to wash your dirty linen in public', or 'Family issues are solved inside the family.' This rejection of conflict and emphasis on 'peaceful' solutions without involving an outside arbiter in the form of the court reveals itself in the type of divorce cases brought before it.

The first variable to be analysed is that related to the type of divorce cases brought before the court. They were sorted into three groups: (1) divorce in agreement: the couple had agreed to a divorce before coming to court and had settled all matters outside the court setting; (2) contested but ending in agreement in court: the couples brought their divorce before the court and reached agreement after court intervention; (3) contested divorce: one or both parties brought the divorce before the court but they did not reach agreement. Consequently, the judge issued a ruling that was imposed upon both individuals. Figure A reveals the nature of divorce cases brought before the court.

It is evident that out of the 829 cases brought before the court, 537 (64.8 per cent) were divorce by agreement. This means that the majority of couples had agreed beforehand to the divorce and its ramifications; they had settled all their disagreements outside the court and signed an agreement before coming to court without any legal intervention from outside the family. This agreement becomes a legal document outside of and parallel to the court system – revealing a plurality in legal procedures through the practice of divorce by mutual consent *(talaq bi al-taradi)*.[11] Evidently, conflict does occur and divorcing couples make their conflicts known within the family or the community. However, most rely on family intervention to put an end

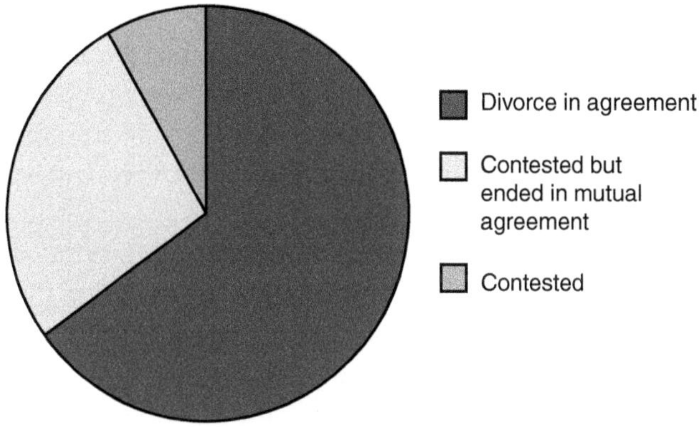

Figure A Type of Divorce

to the conflict or, if that fails, allow just enough escalation to settle upon a divorce without taking the issues before the court. This is in line with the Druze practice of solving all conflicts internally without allowing any form of outward conflict manifestation.

Another explanation for the predominance of consent cases among the Druze is that mediation can result in a better outcome for all. Mnookin and Kornhauser point out that 'the range of negotiated outcome would be limited to those that leave both parents as well off as they would be in the absence of the bargain' (Mnookin and Kornhauser, 1995: 112). Thus resolving conflict through family members and out of court may actually serve the contesting parties better than not doing so.

The rest of the cases were contested in front of the court. However, all did not end with the court imposing its judgment on the contesting parties. As Mr Fuad Hamdan, a trainee judge at the Beirut court at the time I was conducting my research, explained, the court, in the person of the judge (and also in some instances the lawyers), always favours a non-contested resolution of conflicts, working to persuade the couple to reach an amicable agreement with the aim of bringing about a more positive result for the contesting parties, emotionally speaking. When an agreement is reached, the couples depart with at least a 'workable' relationship in place, which reflects positively on the relationship between the families – extended and kin group – especially when children are involved. The significance of this becomes greater when we note that 50 per cent of the divorcing couples in the sample had children.

Some 222 of the total number of divorce cases (26.8 per cent) brought before the court over the 33-year period ended in agreement in court (shown in the lightest middle shade on the pie chart). One of the contesting parties brings the case before the court and it is during the legal procedure that a workable agreement is thrashed out. What normally happens is that the judge will urge the couple to reach an agreement, calling upon their family members as well as their lawyers to intervene.

Evlanger, Chamblis and Melli (1995) point out that in most cases pressure for informal divorce settlement came from lawyers and judges to end the dispute because these most often have better end results on all family members who are not left feeling bitter about the end result since these most often include compromises that take into account the desires of each party. On another level, informal in court agreements

> allow parties to participate in decision making. This is related to the benefits of flexibility, in that participation is the method by which flexibility is achieved. But participation is also considered meaningful in its own right for when the parties have more control over decisions, they are more likely to take responsibility for them. Furthermore, they will be more satisfied with a 'self' imposed result than with one that is court imposed. (Evlanger, Chamblis and Melli, 1995: 120)

The following case reveals how a self-imposed agreement may be better for both parties. The wife was born in 1959 and the husband in 1949. They married in 1981 and have two children, one born in 1985 and the second in 1988. The case was brought before the court in 1991 by the wife who claimed that the husband did not economically support the family. They had a house which they had co-bought but which he had sold and later spent the money. He was living in Switzerland alone, leaving his wife and children in Lebanon at her parent's house. She demanded divorce, maintenance, child custody and custodian fees. The husband responded that the money from the sale of the house was put in the bank account at the bank where his wife worked and that she had withdrawn all the money and spent it herself. He claimed that his wife could not keep the children as she worked at the bank and then had to attend to her shop, that her parent's house was not large enough to house all of them hand that he lived alone with his mother and his mother was more suited to care for the children.

They reached an agreement which ran as follows: (1) announcement of divorce; (2) the wife forgoes all her deferred *mahr*; (3) the wife keeps her jewellery; (4) the girls stay with their mother until the youngest reaches eight years old. The wife takes care of all the economical needs of the girls as long as they are staying with her and the husband has the right to see the girls for 48 hours every 15 days. After the youngest girl is eight, the girls join their father and he takes over economic responsibility. The wife has the right to take the children for 48 hours every week as well as alternating whole weeks during the summer.

This agreement gives each some benefit which would not have been possible if they had not reached the agreement alone. The wife benefited from the out of court agreement by keeping both her children with her for a period of five years. Although the youngest would end up staying with her mother one year less than the legally specified end of custody age of nine, the older one would stay with her mother for two more years. Another benefit is that the girls would not get separated. In return, the wife gave up some of her economic rights and took on the economic burden of bringing up the two daughters. This is the husband's benefit from the agreement. Each party asked for what he/she considered beneficial and came out of the agreement with their needs partially met. The following case is another example of such an outcome.

The case was brought before the court in 1995. The husband was born in 1957 and the wife in 1965. They married in 1988. The husband petitioned for divorce claiming that his wife had left him in Saudi Arabia and returned to Lebanon with their daughter. She then refused to return. The husband said that he was patient with her behaviour until he received a letter from her uncle accusing him of abandoning his family and asking him to take responsibility of his daughter or otherwise to divorce his wife. He was asking through the court that his wife return to her marital house. The wife answered with a counter petition six months later in which she detailed the nature of her relationship with her husband claiming that he was not committed to her and was psychologically abusive. He had previously forced her to have an abortion and had at that time informed her of his intentions for divorce. After exchanging a number of accusations, the couple reached an agreement – a year after the husband's first petition. The agreement specified the following: the daughter remains with her mother until she reaches the age of 11. The custody period is subject to extension upon the agreement of both parties. The wife's custody rights would be annulled if she remarried. The husband would pay the wife a sum of $500 as maintenance. The husband would also pay the tuition fees of a good school. He would also provide for all the medical needs of the daughter. The wife acknowledges that she had received all her legal rights. The husband retains his right to see the daughter once a week and in case he was absent all year from Lebanon, he has the right to take his daughter for 15 days during the summer. The daughter's parental grandfather has the right to see his grand-daughter once a week. If the mother's custody rights are annulled, she would have the same rights awarded to the husband under the agreement

This agreement is also beneficial for both parties. The husband wanted to stay uncommitted and taking his daughter would tie him down, especially since his mother was dead. He would not be able to rely on anyone's help. The wife got a lot more than what the law would guarantee her.

If one or both of the parties fail to reach agreement in any other way, the court will legally appoint an adjudicator or adjudicators to mediate in the case. The adjudicators are suggested by the spouse but appointed by the court and hence the judge's acceptance of these suggested names is essential. The research showed that adjudicators were appointed in 35 of the cases under review. The fact is that lawyers and even court employees consider the appointment of these mediators to be controversial. One court employee pointed out that the adjudicators are required to submit a written report of their attempts to resolve the conflict, but in most cases these are subjective and cannot be used as legal documents upon which to base a judgment. The data showed that in most cases the adjudicator's report favoured the party on whose behalf he was appointed,[12] as the following case, brought before the court in 1992, clearly indicates.

The husband and wife had been married in 1978 and had three children. The wife claimed that her husband abused her physically and refused to support her economically. He had also threatened her with guns and accused her of extra-marital affairs.

The husband claimed that his wife had been dishonest from the beginning of the marriage since she was a divorced woman and not single as she had claimed at the time. He also claimed that she hated his family, was an over-spender and had psychological problems. The husband refused to appoint an adjudicator on his behalf, as he did not see room for reconciliation. The wife's adjudicator wrote the following:

> The husband is blinded by jealousy and he constantly thinks badly of his wife. He hits her and threatens her and doubts her every move. Trust is missing between the two and there is no basis for an understanding. My only solution is, as required by the wife, divorce.

In another case brought before the court in 1974, the couple had married in 1963. The husband was born in 1937 and the wife in 1946. The wife claimed that he constantly beat her but she put up with his abuse for the sake of her children until the conditions became too unbearable. The husband denied his abuse claiming that they occasionally disagreed as was normal in all marriages. Adjudicators were appointed to try to reconcile the couple. The husband's adjudicator submitted the report while the wife's did not. The report was as follows:

> Upon becoming familiar with the case and because I know about the nature of the problems between the two, I can say that the wife was happily living with her husband and children in one house. Then in September 1974, she left the house and

> went to an unknown destination with a person. After making the necessary connections and searching for her with the help of Mr. XX, she returned after she promised to raise her children and live with her husband. A few months later, she left the house and until the time of writing this report, her whereabouts are unknown. Please take this information into consideration, especially since the husband has no one to help him.

In this case the adjudicator had already decided who the guilty party was and had passed his sentence without attempting to resolve the conflict.

In another case brought before the court in 2001, the husband (born 1972) and the wife (born 1970) had been married in 1999 and had one daughter. The wife was a teacher and had shared the costs of building and furnishing the husband's house. She wanted to divorce her husband because she claimed that he had married her simply to take control of her income. He also listened to his parents complaints about her and, in the end, had even begun to hit her.

The husband claimed that she did not respect him. He wanted her to stop working and take care of their daughter, especially as she gave her mother money instead of spending it on her own household. The judge appointed adjudicators on behalf of each party.

The wife's adjudicator wrote the following report:

> The husband wants his wife to leave her work, stop visiting her mother and stop driving a car. I asked the husband to meet with his wife in the presence of her brother but the husband has refused. All of the husband's conditions are impossible to abide by especially since his income is not enough to support the family. As for the wife, she's ready to return to the marital house if he promised to respect her and stand by her against his mother.

The husband's adjudicator's report said.

> I tried to reach an agreement but the wife refused to meet with the husband except in the presence of her adjudicator, which was

> impossible as he was away from Lebanon. She refused to return and the husband claimed that she often challenged him by telling him that she would have extra-marital affairs right in front of his eyes just to spite him. She left the house leaving behind a written note with the words 'Don't ask about me until you've changed your mental attitude'. She does not want to return.

As these cases show, the appointed adjudicators actually come to the case with preconceived ideas that the other party is at fault. Furthermore, most adjudicators are not aware of the role they are supposed to play and instead of trying to resolve the matter they end up taking sides and even becoming part of the conflict. Since these adjudicators are appointed upon the suggestions of the litigants themselves, they are most likely to feel some kind of loyalty towards the party that named them, even when they are not related by any kinship ties to the parties. The following case, brought before the court in 1983, shows this clearly.

The husband and wife were married in 1957 and had children. The wife claimed that her husband was mean and uncaring, gambled a lot, and took no interest in his children. The husband accused the wife of stealing their shared bank account and being in a relationship with her work partner (she owned a shop).

The wife's adjudicator wrote:

> The husband's adjudicator must be changed because he has deviated from his job and showed no cooperation and he is not trying to reconcile the couple which could have been done if he had taken his role more seriously.

The husband's adjudicator wrote:

> I request that some other adjudicator on behalf of the wife be appointed since he has refused to meet with me and her brother threatened me with a gun.

This totally negates the role and function an adjudicator[13] is supposed to play.

In recent cases, after the 1990s, it was observed that in a number of cases the assistance of a psychiatrist and a social worker was utilized. This psychiatrist and the social worker were both females. They were asked by the judge to try to resolve the matter between the contesting parties. After that, she was asked to submit a written report detailing the particulars of her meetings with both parties and her suggestions as to whether the divorce is unavoidable.[14] The following cases reveal the kind of work and the report that the psychiatrist carried out and submitted.

The case was presented before the court in 1997 and the marriage took place in 1995. The husband was born in 1975 and the wife in 1980. Although the age difference between the two was just five years, which is not considered a huge age difference, the reader should note that the wife was barely 15 at the time of marriage. At the time the case was brought to court, they had a daughter who was one and a half. The psychologist's report included the following:

1. The marriage took place four years ago which means that the wife was actually 13 and not 15. She bore the treatment of the husband and his family . . . and the husband kept repeating that he was not economically capable saying 'do you want me to steal to meet her demands?'
2. Her parents in law forced her to wear the outfit of the religious group but her husband beat her when she did . . . but he was too weak to stand up to his parents. Once his father beat her because she told her husband that she had seen his father, who was a religious *sheikh*, smoking cigarettes.[15] Her husband did not protect her.
3. It became clear that his father was dominating and controlled his son's behaviour.
4. The husband did not ask, for three days, about his wife after she gave birth.
5. I explained to the husband's father that it was easy to buy furniture for the house and settle the matter in payments. He refused, saying that he would not help because he did not want his son's wife to return, so the problem was not economic.

6. The wife was accused by the husband's parents, brother and cousins of having an affair and she did not deny it before them so they hit her. The wife said that she did not deny it because her husband did not try to defend her allowing his relatives to accuse her. The husband said that it was not an accusation but that they had asked her a question.
7. When the wife approached the court for divorce, the father promised to buy a bedroom but then went back on the agreement.
8. The wife refused to go to the house that the husband rented because she did not trust him.
9. The husband promised me to send his wife clothes and money for the little daughter but then did not which forced her to buy the things the daughter needed.
10. My Analysis: The husband is immature, does not work and suffers from epilepsy which he does not acknowledge and as such refuses to get the needed medication. The wife married while she was still a child but she has a good nature and personality. Divorce is the solution as the husband did not take responsibility of the family and the wife is young with her life before her.

The judge acted upon the recommendation of the psychiatrist and declared a divorce.

In another case also brought before the court in 1997, the psychiatrist's help was also required. The man was born in 1975 and the wife in 1977. They had married in 1995 after he had kidnapped her. She wanted to divorce him because he refused to support her economically and did not provide a suitable residence. The psychologist presented the following report:

> We met but the wife's father refused to stay in the same room with the husband and took his daughter and left. I explained to her father, after the husband left, that his attitude was not helping and that the husband had to be present. The husband promised to finish building his house. After a year of separation, we re-met and the wife demanded the house be furnished.

> We agreed that I would accompany them to choose the furniture. On the agreed upon day, the husband did not meet us outside his parent's house, although I saw him looking at us from behind the curtains. Then he pressed charges against his father in law claiming that the father in law had threatened him.
>
> My Analysis: The husband does not assume responsibility of his wife and will not. The wife is a victim. They should divorce because if the husband really wanted his wife he would have finished building and furnishing the house in the past year.

The judge pronounced a divorce but held them both responsible for paying the legal costs of the divorce and the psychiatrist.

Although these cases are in fact small in number, yet they show that even in contemporary times the tradition of trying to contain and limit the conflict is maintained. The process may also point to the applied use of an up-to-date mechanism for conflict resolution, showing that many are willing to adopt modern procedures when they help to attain their particular goals. Thus, change is accepted – even welcomed – if it serves to preserve the sect's unity and solidarity. In 2007, a female lawyer was appointed at the Beirut court tasked with aiding the judge and the couples to reach an agreement, if not achieve full reconciliation.[16]

Returning to the analysis of types of divorce, the pie chart shows that only in 69 cases out of the total of 829, a mere 8.3 per cent, did the court actually impose a legal ruling of divorce. This low percentage further supports the idea that the Druze people disdain disagreement and favour a peaceful resolution to their internal conflicts. The pie chart reveals that the Druze prefer agreement in cases of marital conflict to a contested divorce. But how does this finding relate to other variables such as gender, time and residence? In other words, who favours agreement and who favours contested resolutions of conflicts, and how has the passage of time affected people's choices?

a. Type of Divorce across Time

The first point to be established was whether the decision to resolve marital conflicts by agreement has been influenced by the passage of time and whether there has been any change during the 33 years under examination. The change might show itself by comparing the earliest years with the most recent. In Table 4.1 the type of divorce cases were cross-tabulated against three selected time periods within the overall timeframe: 1970–75, accounting for the earliest cases in the study; 1998–2003, for the most recent; and 1980–90, when the influence of the civil wars in Lebanon was at its most intense. It should be noted that this cross-tabulation does not account for all the cases collected in the sample since the five years from 1975–80 and eight years from 1990–98 fall outside its chosen scope. The reader should not confuse the total number shown in the table in this part with the total number of cases in the whole sample. Table 4.1 indicateds that the passage of time had a limited influence on the Druze preference for resolving their internal family conflicts discreetly. The practice or tradition of resolving conflict without court interference seemed to be resilient to change. It is true that rulings in mutual consent cases are given very quickly is the ultimate object of the contesting parties. The fact is that this trend has somewhat remained stable over a period of 33 years with a percentage of change of only about 4.6. The percentage of consent cases was 70.6 of the total in 1970–75, compared with 66.0 per cent in 1998–2003. Whether this will remain constant or change over time remains to be seen in future research and as more time elapses. What Table 4.1 shows is that the Druze preferred to solve their intra-family disputes outside the court in the 1970s and, after the passage of 33 years, continued to show this preference. Such behaviour aims at strengthening the internal solidarity and unity of the group. Placing all kinds of conflict under control limits and diminishes the opportunities for internal friction. The preference for 'peaceful' resolution of conflicts is further reflected in the

Table 4.1 Type of Divorce vs. Time Intervals

	Consent	End in agreement	Contested	Total
1970–75	72 70.6%	21 20.6%	9 8.8%	102 100%
1980–90	104 65.4%	40 25.2%	15 9.4%	159 100%
1998–2003	167 66.0%	55 21.7%	31 12.3%	253 100%

findings relating to court-imposed resolutions in contested cases. The percentage of these was 8.8 per cent in the early 1970s and remained comparatively low, 12.3 per cent, in 1998–2003, thus reinforcing the preference for a 'peaceful' divorce.

The research also revealed that in most contested cases, frequent reference was made in the court records to attempts by family members to resolve the conflict. The fact is that parents and individuals from the kin group, normally referred to as the reconcilers, generally intervene to try to resolve the conflict.

For example, in one case the husband and wife had married in 1967 and brought the divorce before the court in 1973. The mention of reconcilers was specifically noted by the wife who wrote:

> He (the husband) had mistreated me from the beginning of our marriage and I would leave the house but then return after intermediaries mediate and work at resolving our conflict – a thing that happened again and again during the years of our marriage.

In another case, dated 1980, the wife's claim included the following:

> I have lived with my husband in continuous strife and insults which made me leave the house more than eight times but each time the reconcilers intervened to make me return.

In another case, the husband and wife were married in 1980. They brought the divorce before the court in 1998. The wife wrote:

> Life with him was a case of continuous suffering because of his physical violence which had made me miscarry. But I used to return to him upon the intervention of his family members.

In a more recent case (2002), the couple were married in 1980 and the wife wrote:

> He had beaten me and I had to be taken to the hospital but I returned to his house after his uncle intervened and convinced

> me to do so promising me that my husband would stop beating me.

Yet another case brought before the court, also in 2000, further revealed similar reference to the intervention of others. The couple had married in 1973 and in her claim submitted through a lawyer the wife's petition said,

> It is worth mentioning that his method of dealing with his wife was physical and psychological violence accompanied by insults. She put up with his behaviour for the sake of her parents and because of her parents intervention until she has reached a stage where she's losing her sanity and health which was the reason behind petitioning for divorce.

These and other cases point to the fact that the Druze prefer to resolve their interior conflicts within the family circle. This is done basically through the intervention of family members who try to reconcile the couple or at least reach a workable agreement – a divorce by consent.

It is worth mentioning that the civil war does not seem to have had an influence on this issue since the percentage of those who chose to settle their divorce by agreement without court intervention was 65.4 per cent of the total number of divorces in 1980–90, comparable to that for the other time interval. It seems obvious that fewer people would opt for an in-court divorce during the war since they would understandably want to avoid the risks of travelling to and fro to attend court sessions, and consequently it was only to be expected that more people would divorce by consent. However, the fact that the percentage remained more or less stable across the whole study shows that the practice, in itself, was not affected by the time variable. The Druze favour divorce by consent simply because they have always solved their problems within the institution of the family. To account for this, it should be noted that their court was only established in the late 1940s. Prior to that date, the Druze used to solve their matters on their own and to marry and divorce without going to court.[17] Moreover, people of the older generation upheld beliefs that ran contrary to the laws then in force and most often applied their own. For example, some people still hold that it is against family honour for a wife to return to her husband once he has uttered the word *taliq*. In one case, the wife actually asked for a divorce because the husband had announced that he had divorced her. She wrote in her appeal, 'He threw me out a week ago and said "you are *taliq*"', adding that she considered this was ample enough reason to file for divorce – accepting the rule of an on-the-spot oral decision. Clearly, such an action is no longer common, but people of the older generation still respect the traditions.

b. Type of Divorce and Residence

Another factor that might influence the decision to seek a court divorce is the place of residence of the contesting parties. It may reasonably be assumed that city people are less under the influence of their family and therefore more liable to resolve their conflicts through the court. They lack the protective presence of the extended family, which normally interferes to prevent the escalation of any problem or to solve the conflict before it reaches court.

i. Husband's Place of Residence

When the place of residence of the husband was cross-tabulated against the type of divorce (Table 4.2), the findings reflected these assumptions to a remarkable degree. However, the reader should be aware that the total number of cases considered in this analysis differs from the total number of cases in the whole sample simply because not all cases were considered in the variables. For instance, people whose place of residence was documented as being in Syria were excluded since it was found that these were mostly Syrians residing in Lebanon. Other cases were excluded because the information was not provided in the case's documents. If the statistic arrived at in Table 4.2 is taken at its face value, it shows that only 4.3 per cent of divorces sought by city residents are contested, compared to 7.2 per cent of those residing in villages – a higher percentage that seems flatly to contradict the above assumption. However, on closer examination, the statistics reveal an opposite result. It is true that a smaller percentage of husbands residing in Beirut file for a contested divorce, yet a very significant percentage – 46.7 per cent –

Table 4.2 Type of Divorce vs. Husband's Residence

	Consent	In court agreement	Contested	Total
Village	354 70.4%	113 22.5%	36 7.2%	503 100%
City	46 50.0%	43 46.7%	3 4.3%	92 100%
Town	39 67.2%	14 24.1%	5 8.6%	58 100%
Emigrants	76 55.9%	44 32.4%	16 11.8%	136 100%

approach the court but later divorce by agreement compared to only 22.5 per cent of village residents. Thus, the court for city residents fulfils the role of the family in the villages, since the reality is that a much higher percentage of city couples come to the court with an unresolved conflict than do those in the villages. The percentage of male city residents who approach the court with a resolved conflict (shown in the table as 'consent') is 50 per cent compared to 46.7 per cent who come to the court to resolve their conflict ('in court agreement') and only 4.3 per cent who are actually seeking a contested divorce. So it seems that residents of Beirut view the court as an integral part of their conflict resolution mechanism, unlike village residents, who generally view the legal system as foreign and prefer to settle their conflicts within the boundaries of the family. It appears that city residents have adapted the legal system so that it has come to play the role of the extended family in the villages.

This finding was echoed by those for husbands who gave their place of residence as outside Lebanon. Table 4.2 reveals that 55.9 per cent of emigrants approached the court for a divorce by consent. Some 32.4 per cent of cases ended in agreement inside the court. Therefore, for male emigrants, the court seemed to play the same role that the husband's family plays in the villages and towns. What is also notable is the fact that the highest percentage of contested divorces ending in a court-imposed sentence is found among male emigrants: 11.8 per cent compared to 7.2 per cent among those from the villages, 8.6 per cent from the towns and 4.3 per cent from the city. One possible explanation for this may be that, although these male emigrants approached the court to resolve their marital conflicts, the mere fact that they were living outside Lebanon was in itself an obstacle. Basically, they were not always present to solve their conflict before it escalated, and they may even have found it less costly in money terms to have a court-imposed decision. The fact is that the *mahr* included in the marriage contract, which is normally paid to the wife upon divorce, rarely exceeds the travelling costs from a distant country.[18]

Table 4.2 reveals, as well, an important finding along a different line. It was evident that males living in the villages and those in the towns made similar or at least comparable choices with regard to the type of divorce they preferred. Some 70.4 per cent of those divorcing in agreement came from the villages and 67.2 per cent from the town – a negligible difference, which also holds for the other variables in the table. As was noted in Chapter 3 in regard to dowry choices, the Druze towns of Chouiefat and Aley have retained a way of life very similar to that of the villages. The people are closely connected and their families live in close proximity to the world of the villages.

ii. Wife's Place of Residence

This section deals with the analysis of the wife's place of residence and its influence, if any, on the type of divorce brought before the court. Here, too, the total number of cases does not equal the total number of cases in the study (1,066) since Table 4.3 accounts for only four variables related to residence: residents of villages, towns and cities, and emigrants. Missing cases were excluded. When the wife's place of residence was cross-tabulated against the type of divorce brought before the court, the findings revealed that, as a general rule, women preferred divorce by agreement to court intervention – 65.3 per cent in the case of village residents, 53.7 per cent of city residents, 61.5 per cent of town residents and 69.8 per cent of those living outside Lebanon. Once again, as in the findings related to the husband's place of residence, it was remarkable that 41.1 per cent of city residents who approached the court to divorce reached an agreement inside the court.

Table 4.3 Residence of Wife vs. Type of Divorce

	Consent	End in agreement	Contested	Total
Village	333 65.3%	138 27.1%	39 7.6%	510 100%
City	51 53.7%	39 41.1%	5 5.3%	95 100%
Town	48 61.5%	19 24.4%	11 14.1%	78 100%
Emigrants	74 69.8%	20 18.9%	12 11.3%	106 100%

Therefore, the findings revealed two general trends among the Druze. The first is that, independent of gender, the Druze people prefer agreement to conflict. Second, the majority of city residents, male or female, who approach the court to divorce, reach an agreement inside the court through the intervention of the judge, lawyers and adjudicators.

The basic difference regarding the gender of petitioners concerned the divorce procedures of emigrants. When the wife lived outside Lebanon, the result showed gender-related discrepancies, with more females in this group divorcing by consent. Although the difference between the two is only 13.9 per cent (55.9 per cent of husbands and 69.8 per cent of wives), yet it remains significant especially if compared to the difference between those living outside Lebanon whose divorce ends in agreement in the court: 32.4 per cent of husbands and 18.9 per cent of wives. This time the difference of 13.5 per cent was tipped towards the husband, with more reaching an agreement inside the court. The reason for the preference of females living outside Lebanon for an uncontested divorce may lie in the nature of the relationship of Druze women to their families. Among the Druze, a divorced wife or widow is considered the responsibility of her kin group – her father and brothers. The term used to refer to unmarried, divorced or widowed Druze females is *Qati'a* – a cut-off. Once a female is categorized as a *Qati'a*, she becomes the responsibility of her male kin[19] and thus a female facing a divorce usually seeks the help of her kin group even when living abroad.

For example, in one case brought before the court in 1987, the woman wrote the following in her statement to the court:

> I felt I was a burden to my mother-in-law (because her husband had left her with her son and moved from the United States to Germany and) so I travelled to Venezuela. My parents and brother reside there and they will take care of me and help me.

Another woman (married in 1964, divorced in 1977) wrote that after she quarrelled with her husband she 'returned to Lebanon to my parents and they gave me money to care for myself and my children'.

A woman's male kin generally act as intermediaries and try to resolve the conflict before the matter reaches the court. Female Druze living abroad continue to remain connected to their kin group and so do not tend to use the court as a mechanism for conflict resolution. As indicated above, the statistics show that men living outside Lebanon adopt the opposite attitude, preferring to allow the conflict to end through a court-imposed decision. It may be that the husband refuses to come before the court because of the costs he is likely to incur, or for any other reason. A female living abroad, on the other hand, will often prefer to settle the conflicts outside the court through her family's intervention.

An important observation made while attending the court sessions related to the Druze way of approaching the court and sheds further light on how the court may be used as a conflict-resolution mechanism – a place to reach an agreement. During the three-month period I attended divorce sessions I observed that people tend to approach the court in a relatively informal manner. Some females, especially those belonging to the older generation and who appeared before the court without a lawyer, addressed the judge quite familiarly:

> You are like my father. The court is my only resort. I have no one to aid me – only you. I address you like a son, a brother or a father.

The judge himself often appeared to be moved by such people, who seemed unaware of the nature of the legal process. For instance, in one case an old woman was seeking divorce because her husband refused to support her – of course, she asked for maintenance and not a divorce but later told the judge that she actually wanted a divorce because her brother would then support her. The judge realized that she was ignorant in legal matters. Her husband had submitted a written statement in which he made a number of legal claims and these needed to be addressed by the wife in a legal manner which the old woman seemed not to be aware of. The judge tried in more than one way to explain the law to her. When she seemed not to understand, he called a court employee and instructed him to help her, adding: 'Better help her so that she doesn't say that the court was unfair'. Dupret (2002) describes this moral predicament a judge might find himself/herself in. Judges often find themselves in a position whereby they feel the need to justify themselves before an audience while staying within the objective boundaries of morality and integrity (Dupret, 2002: 47–8). The judge in this instance found himself in a predicament.[20] On the one hand, he was confined by the law which forced him to judge based upon the legal allegation he had in the file. On the other hand, he wanted to help the old woman and felt a moral obligation towards her.

The research also led to the realization that the judge was often 'partial' to the woman – especially in cases where the husband seemed to be totally at fault and she appeared to be very pious and only had the interest of her children at heart. In one such case, the husband and wife were married in 1983 and the divorce was brought before the court in 1997. The wife petitioned that her husband had forced her and her children to leave the house and refused to pay maintenance. The husband remained stubborn throughout, even after the intervention of adjudicators who declared that it was difficult to reason with him. His parents declared before the court that they were not ready to bring up the children (two boys born in 1984 and 1990 and a girl born in 1986). He insisted on divorce and even announced at court that he was planning to marry another woman. The judge's sentence was the following:

> Since the husband's only aim is to remarry and since the wife did nothing to make him hate her, the following was decided: 1) *Nafaqa* (maintenance): The husband is to pay the wife the

> sum of seven million LBP,[21] and a sum of 20 million LBP to his children; 2) Since it was proved that the husband continuously threatened to kill his wife and had actually beaten his wife and children, and since a normal husband's role is to offer protection and support which he does not do, then the wife gets custody of the children until they all reach adulthood – especially since his family members declared that they did not want to care for the children. The husband is further requested to pay, at court, 250,000 LBP per month for the children's support. He is also forced to pay a sum of 3,000,000 LPB as *mahr*, 10 gold liras as delayed dowry, a lump sum of 30,000,000 LBP as 'harm and injury' {compensation} to the wife, in addition to court expenses.

In another case, the husband brought the divorce before the court in 2000 after five years of marriage. He claimed that his wife did not care about her household and ignored her duties towards him and their child. The wife answered that the husband spent most of his time abroad and when he came to Lebanon, it was only to cause trouble. He had even tried to kill her a week before by trying to sabotage her car brakes. She wanted to divorce him because she was scared of him. She added that she did not have any money and did not work and so could not keep her son. The judge saw that the wife was not at fault and understood that she could not care for the child and so he issued the following ruling:

> Since the husband insisted on the divorce, he should give his wife all her rights which include $2000 *mahr*, 3,000,000 LBP to cover a bedroom cost (part of the *mahr*), 30 gold liras and another 3,000,000 LBP as harm and injury.

Another case brought before the court in 2000 concerned a husband and wife who had married in 1987. The husband wanted to divorce his wife, claiming that she was disobedient and constantly doubted his word. The wife stated that he wanted to marry another woman, which he later did, and had actually left his two children at the Druze orphanage before travelling to the United Arab Emirates. That proved that he did not care about his children. The judged issued the following sentence:

1. With regard to divorce: since the husband insisted on the divorce and he did not submit any proof of his wife's disobedience and his negligence towards his children was proven and since the wife had not specified any amount for the *mahr* or harm and damage but has left the matter for the court, the judge decides that the husband should pay the wife a sum total of 20 million LBP.
2. Maintenance of children: the husband must pay the wife enough money to cover caring for the children including education and medical care.
3. The husband must provide a suitable residence for the children. As such the wife is to remain with them in the marital house and the husband is denied access to the house.
4. The wife has sole custody over the children until they are 18 years old.
5. The husband has to pay all legal expenses of the case.

This case illustrates the extent to which the judge may take the rights of the children into consideration, as well as women who have been wronged by their husbands. In one case brought before the court in 2001, the wife and husband went through a series of court appeals and questioning sessions, before reaching an agreement that their son would spend two days with his mother and two days with his father. The judge, however, considered this agreement inappropriate and refused to abide by it. Rather, he issued a ruling whereby the son would remain in his mother's custody until he was seven years old, after which the father would take over custody. The father was given the right to see his son for 48 hours every week, to start on Friday evening and end on Sunday evening.

c. Who Files for What Type of Divorce?

A further question relating to the nature of the divorce cases brought before the Beirut court asked which party filed for a contested divorce.

Table 4.4 Type of Divorce vs. Who Filed for Divorce

	Consent	Contested + in court agreement
Husband	13	100
Wife	8	190
Both	518	0

In order to study this variable, the total number of divorce cases was divided in two by grouping divorces by court agreement and contested divorces together. It was found that nearly twice as many women filed for contested divorces as men, proof that Druze women do actually practise their rights to divorce – an observation worthy of note, since the situation was the opposite for Druze living abroad. The reason for this may lie in the fact that Druze women seem to possess a high level of awareness when it comes to their legal rights and are prepared to claim them before the court. As one female put it:

> He drove me crazy! He tried everything to make me leave the house and forego my rights. He only wished to throw me out on the street but I refused to go. I know the court will get me my rights. If he won't listen to me, he will be forced to listen to the court.

This reveals the fact that the wives have approached the court as a last resort, after all other attempts to reason with their husband have failed, and not because they are more accepting or in favour of contested divorce than men. As one woman put it, the court became 'my final resort after no one was able to influence my husband. I had to think of my life and my children.'

The above analysis clearly indicates that the Druze place great importance on their internal solidarity and consistently try to avoid conflict. When it comes to the breakdown of marriage, the Druze, in old times and new, village and city resident, those who have emigrated and those living in Lebanon alike, will try to obtain a divorce by agreement and avoid conflict. This process is further upheld by the legal system, which instructs the judge to utilize all possible means to resolve the conflict before he takes the step of pronouncing a couple's divorce. This practice has remained constant and stable across time. However, it could not be expected that all matters relating to divorce would remain unchanged over the 33 years of the study. The next section studies the influence the passage of time might have had on some aspects of divorce.

Passage of Time and Divorce

As already stated, a total of 829 divorces were brought before the Beirut court between 1970 and 2003. The first thing to strike one is the fact – already pointed out – that over this time the number of divorces have steadily increased, with certain interruptions such as during the war in Lebanon. As Table 4.5 shows, the average number of cases during the 1970s was 17.5 per year. This fell to 12.9 during the 1980s, then increased to an average of 34.5 in the 1990s, and rose still further to 42.25 cases per year in the early 2000s. However, this overall increase in the average yearly number of divorces does not necessarily indicate that divorce rates have actually increased – this will only become clear by comparing divorce rates against marriage rates, which will be the focus of Chapter 5.

The frequency distribution in Table 4.5 reveals one outstanding figure: only two recorded cases of divorce in 1976. This was the lowest

Table 4.5 Number of Cases per Year

1970	1971	1972	1973	1974	1975	1976	1977	1978	1979	**Av.**
6	26	18	16	18	19	2	29	28	12	17.5
1980	1981	1982	1983	1984	1985	1986	1987	1988	1989	
18	6	12	19	18	6	12	12	22	16	12.9
1990	1991	1992	1993	1994	1995	1996	1997	1998	1999	
18	31	27	31	38	44	44	28	43	41	34.5
2000	2001	2002	2003							
42	45	32	50							42.25

number over the entire 33 years of the study, and may be related to the outbreak of the civil war the year before. As already noted, the overall decline in cases during the 1980s is also explained within the context of the civil war, then at its peak. In times of war, when basic physical survival is at stake, people are less concerned with resolving inter-familial conflicts and less prone to endanger their lives by attending court sessions. Not unnaturally, familial conflicts tend to take a back-seat in comparison to fighting a civil war, and can be addressed later once things return more or less to normal.

The highest number of divorces – 50 – was recorded in 2003, the last year of the study. This relatively large number occurred after a relatively stable increase over the preceding decade and suggests that this trend is most likely set to continue. Indeed, while I was doing my research the *Ra'is al-Qalam* (head of the registry office in the court) informed me that the number had in fact risen to about 60–65 in 2006. The trend can be better appreciated if plotted along a graph.

Graph 1 clearly illustrates the decline in the number of divorces during the civil war as well as the sharp increase after the end of the fighting. The reader should note that in the last bar in the graph the number of years covered are only three, which accounts for it being lower than the one preceding it.

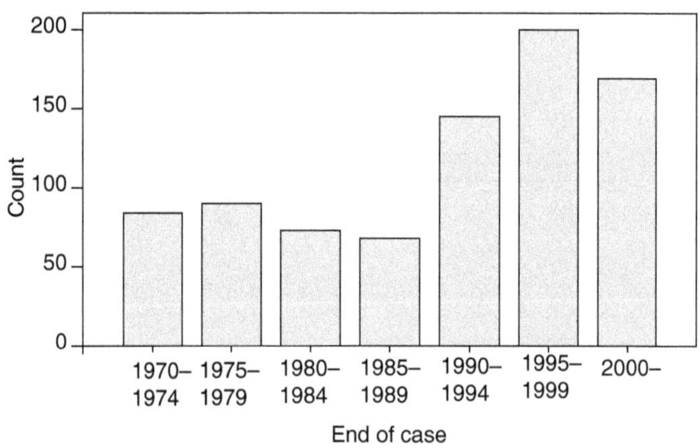

Graph 1 Number of Cases per Five-Year Time Interval

To study change, three time intervals were sampled out: 1970–75, 1980–90 and 1998–2003 to account for any war-time change. Comparison of the time intervals at the beginning and end of the sample should account for any changes over time.

a. Gender and Time

The first topic to be analysed is that of gender and change. Over the last 50 years or so, Druze women have increasingly been entering the workplace, increasingly exposed to Western ideas of freedom and equality, and increasingly enjoying better education. Consequently they could be expected to express their individualism and to assert their rights more forcefully than before. One gender question to be raised in relation to this research is whether wives are more likely, over time, to approach the court for a divorce in an attempt to assert their right to divorce. The data revealed quite the opposite. Amazingly enough, over a period of more than three decades, the behaviour of Druze females exhibited a remarkable stability. It appears that Betts's claim about the nature of the Druze's resilience to change was more correct than my assumption, prior to the research, that change is likely to be depicted in both women's and men's decisions. Table 4.6, which shows whether the husband or wife brought the case before the court (divorces by mutual consent have been excluded) for both the earliest and latest time intervals, reveals quite remarkably the stable, static nature of women's behaviour in this respect. During the early 1970s, 69 per cent of contested divorces were brought before the court by the wife. Two decades later, in 1998–2003, the figure was 68.2 per cent.

Table 4.6 Person Who Brought Contested Divorce Before Court vs. Time Intervals

	Husband	Wife	Total
1970–1975	13 31.0%	29 69.0%	42 100%
1998–2003	28 31.8%	60 68.2%	88 100%

This negligible difference of only 0.8 per cent (quite evidently the figures for males remained unchanged as well, at 31 per cent) demonstrates that for both women and men this aspect of divorce remained resilient to change and to the pressures of modernization. However, the same cannot be expected of other aspects relating to the divorce process. While it is necessary to keep in mind the Druze mentality, described earlier, that predisposes them to avoid internal conflict and strive to resolve their conflicts with as little tension as possible, yet it seems certain that change will be expressed elsewhere.

This research indeed depicted certain changes in the nature of the decision issued by the court at the end of the divorce. What is being referred to here is the final ruling of the judge, which is basically a summing up of the court's proceedings – the claims and demands of each contesting party and, in agreement cases, the settlement reached between them. The court decisions were grouped under five headings: (1) *ibra' zima*: each party frees the other of any legal claim; (2) money/benefits: the wife gets her *mahr*, money or other benefits; (3) custody: the wife gets custody of her children; (4) visitation rights: the wife gets visitation rights of her children; (5) forgoes all: the wife forgoes all her rights. Table 4.7 cross-tabulates the different elements of the court's decision against three time intervals. The resultant percentages show that a change has actually occurred between the oldest and most recent time intervals. Basically, it is only to be expected that over three decades and with increased equality between husband and wife arising from women's greater participation in the workplace, increased education and increased self-awareness, the wife will be more likely to assert her rights. The results shown in Table 4.7 reflect such a trend. It was observed that the only variable that remained unchanged over time was the court decision related to *Ibra' Zima*. This is the decision that is usually registered when the parties come before the court in agreement having, in most cases, settled matters outside of court. In the first time interval the percentage was 52, remaining at a stable 51 per cent in the most recent time interval.

Parties whose divorce cases were resolved in court attempted to assert their rights and to express their problems more willingly and openly in front of the judge. It was observed that women increasingly did so in recent years, especially with respect to their rights to visit

Table 4.7 Elements of Court Decision vs. Time Interval

	Ibra zima	Money/ benefits	Custody	Visitation rights	Forgoes all	Total
1970–75	53	20	6	2	21	102
	52.0%	19.6%	5.9%	2.0%	20.6%	100%
1980–90	92	18	7	17	25	159
	57.9%	11.3%	4.4%	10.7%	15.7%	100%
1998–2003	129	25	16	64	19	253
	51.0%	9.9%	6.3%	25.3%	7.5%	100%

their children, as specified by the laws. Only 2 per cent of females who divorced in 1970–75 were awarded children's visitation rights, compared to 25.3 per cent in 1998–2003, representing an increase of 23.3 per cent. This may be considered a high percentage when set against the changeless nature of Druze society that Betts claims. It is in line with a second finding relating to the court decision requiring women to forgo their rights. In 1970–75, 20.6 per cent of females were asked to forgo their rights. This fell to 7.5 per cent in 1998–2003. These two variables most definitely reflect the effect of the passage of time on women's behaviour. They were asserting their rights in a more forceful manner, and this was reflected in the court decisions. Maybe the court's perception of women had also undergone some change.

The point worth noting here is that while females are obtaining some of their rights, this is not the case across the board. Table 4.7 shows quite clearly that the rights they are getting are related to their children, but once it comes to their material rights, the statistics paint a different picture. The fact is that the wife's claim to money or benefits has witnessed a decrease from 19.6 per cent to 9.9 per cent. It is safe to claim that economic factors no longer play the important role in divorce settlements they did in the 1970s. This might be for a number of reasons. First of all, more women are working and are no longer dependent on their husband's money for economic survival; hence the decrease in their claims to the *mahr* or money benefits. They can, therefore, assert their rights regarding their children: they can afford to visit them, and take them into their homes at weekends. This has not been a sudden trend but occurred steadily over time since it was observed that in the time interval from 1980–90 a similar, though slighter, increase was observed in the court's decision to grant women the right to visit their children. Another finding of Table 4.7 is that 10.7 per cent of females were given visitation rights to their children during the period of the civil war, and this was accompanied by a decrease in court decisions asking them to forgo their rights, which fell to 15.7 per cent. In some cases, when they had room to manoeuvre, women did not choose to forgo their economic rights.

In one such case the woman had two children aged above 24 and thus did not have to deal with visitation rights. She had been born in 1950 and her husband in 1943. They were married in 1971 and the case was brought before the court in 1998. The wife was working and earned enough income to support herself, but she insisted on all her rights. The case was brought before the court by the husband and started with an appeal by him to force his wife to return to the marital home. He claimed that she had left the house for no legitimate reason and refused to live with him, preferring to live with her parents in Beirut. She responded that her husband was abusive, constantly threatened her, and was stingy, making it impossible to live with him. She worked and he took her money and forced her to pay the tuition fees of their younger son who was at university. He owned plots of land but refused to sell them to meet the financial demands of running the house; she submitted a list of things that she had bought for the house and that he refused to pay for. She was forced to use her own money. The husband responded that he was not stingy but simply calculated the expenses that they needed as a family and that she had forced him to send the children to expensive schools and universities and he could not afford everything she demanded. He added that her father constantly interfered in their life and wanted them to separate. She answered that all his allegations were false and that he refused to spend his money on his family.

The judge issued the following sentence:

> Since the husband did not question his wife's allegations that she had bought things for the house and since he did not deny that his wife spent her salary in the house then the husband is to pay

> the wife the total amount of 40 million LBP as a compensation for what she had spent in the house, 820,500 LBP as *mahr*, hand over all the wife's personal belongings that the husband still has in his house, and pay for all the legal costs.

Although more women are demanding their rights regarding visitation of their children, this has occurred at the expense of their material benefits. Today, women are sufficiently self-supporting to be able to use their economic rights as a bargaining tool. They are prepared to forgo them in exchange for their children, a thing they could not afford to do in years gone by.

The following case reflects this reality. The husband, born in 1949, and the wife, born in 1961, were married in 1976. The wife brought the case before the court in 1984 and in her petition she said:

> We were married and now have a daughter who is six years old. Our relationship worsened and life together became impossible due to his bad temper. He beats me in front of our neighbours and insults and threatens me constantly. This had caused me to have a nervous breakdown which required hospitalization . . . forcing me to leave my house. I ask for a divorce and waive all my economic rights and my right to the custody of my daughter, just to be able to live in peace.

An agreement was reached between the husband and wife whereby the wife got custody of her daughter, with the husband providing maintenance and support. In this case the wife was prepared to bargain. In the end, she got more than what she was expecting because she appeared willing to let go of her economic rights.

In one case brought before the court in 1997 (the couple were married in 1979), the wife had a well-paid job and was able to support her children. She and her husband reached the following agreement:

> The wife exonerates her husband of all her material rights. The husband waives his right to the custody of his children until they

> reach adulthood and he pays them nothing. The wife is expected to cover all their educational, medical and personal expenses and she is not to remarry. The husband has the right to see his children for 15 days every year but at his own expense.

In this case, even during the 1970s, the wife was sufficiently well off to be able to force her husband to agree to waive his right to custody. However, one might wonder about the economic burden that visiting children may impose on female divorcees. What are the costs of looking after children for a day or two per week? Why is the factor of economic independence so important, especially as most wives are not asking for full custody of their children but for visitation rights only? Yet, on thinking over the question more deeply, the economic reality becomes apparent. As one divorcee said,

> When my children come I prepare special food. I always make sure to cook meat and chicken and to bake a cake or make a special kind of dessert they like. I also take them to the shop so they can buy some treats. Whenever I can, I buy them some clothing items. I try to compensate in any way I can.

This woman has two children; a boy aged eight and a girl aged 12. Her husband had left her when she was pregnant with her son. Her family, mainly her mother and brother, was supportive and she kept her children until the boy was seven, when her divorced husband took them away. She worked selling goods to people in her village and the surrounding area. This clearly shows that indeed some economic factors are involved in the question of visitation rights, which, no matter how restricted, are a burden to mothers on limited income or with no income whatsoever.

The experience of this woman is a common one in Druze villages, but family members are not always as supportive. One female I talked to stopped visiting her three-year-old daughter simply because she could not afford the cost of a taxi from her village to that of her ex-husband as the judge had given her the right to see her daughter once a week at the house of a *sheikh* from his family. Her parents wanted to marry her off to a relative and refused to pay her transportation expenses. She had married at the age of 17 after leaving school, did not have any kind of education or vocational training, and consequently could not find a job to support herself. She said:

> I had to surrender to my lot. I can do nothing to fight for my daughter and I have no means of supporting her.

She has since remarried and has not seen her daughter in more than ten years.

Women's economic independence has increased lately due to their increased participation in the workplace, and this means they can now afford to demand visitation rights. This has to be taken into account in relation to another factor – the fact that out of the 829 divorce cases brought before the court during the period of the study, only 155 couples (19.8 per cent) had children under the age of custody. This will be dealt with in greater detail in the part dealing with children and divorce but is mentioned here to give a fuller appreciation of the idea that women will generally fight for their rights to visit their children when they have the economic means and enough family support to do so.

b. Causes for Divorce over Time

The effect of time was evident not only through consideration of the court's decision at different periods but also by examining the causes upon which husband and wife based their claim to divorce. When dealing with causes mentioned in files, one has to be cautious of an important reality. Litigants in court try to instrumentalize the law dealing with the whole process as a means to an end and proposing a cause for divorce which might not be the aim actually intended (Dupret, 2002; Osanloo, 2009). For example, a wife may file for support but in fact want divorce. Evidently, this became clear once the case become labelled under divorce and was hence controlled for in this study. Although, normally, each party mentions a number of causes, for the sake of manageable statistical data, the first cause named in each of the contesting claims was taken as the primary cause for divorce. The first section will analyse the change that has occurred over time regarding the wife's primary cause for divorce.

i. Wife's Causes for Divorce over Time

More than half of the divorce cases brought before the Druze Beirut Court from 1970 to 2003 were 'divorces in agreement'. Since these cases do not name the actual cause or causes of the divorce they were excluded from the following analysis.

After an overview of all the data, the causes most frequently mentioned by the wife in contested divorces were grouped into the following categories: (1) violence: the husband physically beat his wife; (2) husband's infidelity: the husband cheated on his wife and had a relationship outside the marriage; (3) non-supportive: the husband was not supporting his wife; (4) other: all other reasons such as parental interference, psychological problems, etc.

There were a number of changes over time. Table 4.8 clearly shows that during the early 1970s the major causes for divorce named by wives were their husband's refusal to give support (23.5 per cent), in equal place with violence (also 23.5 per cent), followed by their husband's infidelity (17.7 per cent). Infidelity and the withholding of support both witnessed a sharp decline during the 1998–2003 time interval, balanced by a huge increase in the mention of violence, which almost doubled from 23.5 per cent in 1970–75 to 47.4 per cent. This increase was observed even from the beginning of the 1980s, when the percentage of wives claiming violence as the main cause

Table 4.8 Wife's Causes for Divorce vs. Time Interval

	Violence	Husband's infidelity	Non-supportive	Other	Total
1970–1975	8	6	8	12	34
	23.5%	17.7%	23.5%	35.3%	100%
1980–1990	29	4	3	21	57
	50.9%	7.0%	5.3%	36.8%	100%
1998–2003	37	5	11	25	78
	47.4%	6.4%	14.1%	32.1%	100%

for divorce was a high 50.9 per cent – a stark reminder of how the civil war in Lebanon adversely affected families and family relationships. It was observed that in a large number of cases brought before the court during the war, reference was made to various war-related incidents, ranging from displacement, loss of income or a house, to the use of guns to threaten the spouse, this last being named as a cause for divorce by a number of wives. Several cases give striking evidence of this.

In one case, brought before the court in 1986, the wife filed a claim for divorce against her husband whom she had married in 1981 on the grounds that he had threatened her with a gun. They had two children and the husband was a militia man. Her lawyer wrote:

> she moved to her husband's house after her 18th birthday and she was still young. After five months and due to a misunderstanding with his parents for which she was not responsible, as he himself acknowledged, the relationship started turning violent. The husband used to curse her all the time and would leave her alone for long periods of time and even force her to sleep outside the house. She remained patient until they had a daughter and she was hopeful that the daughter would change her husband, making him kinder. However, he did not change. He was always tense and anxious. His anger escalated and once he threatened her with his gun in front of many neighbours. He used to stay away for months leaving her while pregnant and her daughter alone in the village (Matn area). He only returned to beat her, curse her and treat her like a servant. Things remained this way until the end of the Tripartite Accord[22] and the outbreak of military skirmishing in the Matn area. The armed militia in the village ordered all the people to evacuate the village, especially women and children. Instead of doing that, he left them and promised to return a couple of days later, which he did not. She got very scared, hired a taxi, left the village with her children, and went to her parents in Aley. He came to Aley, but only to curse her for leaving the village, and then he later returned with three fully armed men to force her to return. When her father

> stood up to him, the men fired their guns inside the house and did not leave until some of the neighbours came to her father's aid. They left after they had spread terror in the hearts of the children and her family. This resulted in her suffering from a nervous breakdown that required medication. Life with him is impossible due to fear, and thus the wife asks for a divorce and demands her rights to custody of her children as the girl is six and the boy is one year old.

The husband's lawyer answered that the appeal had no basis since the husband had never hit his wife but treated her like a loving father. As for the husband's absence, it was largely because the husband:

> Belonged to the Progressive Socialist Party[23] and is a brave fighter. He was among the first to take up the role of a fighter defending the Druze honour, land, religion and dignity so it was normal to be away from home fighting and not for any other reason. In fact, the people of the village were actually ordered by the PSP party to stay in the village to offer moral support to the fighters and we have a certificate from the commander of the area that testifies to the truth of that. She had left her husband, the hero, at the frontier and gone to her parents without any due cause. When he had gone to get her from Aley, her father used his gun against him in an attempt to prevent him from taking his wife back home. Her mother had even thrown the little boy, his son, on the ground as the report from Dr. XX proves and I have filed a legal suit against the family for that. Due to her parents' misconduct people started trying to mediate but all attempts ended in failure. The husband wants his wife to return to the house and does not want divorce. He wants his wife to return as staying away from her husband runs contrary to all Druze teachings.

The couple agreed to a divorce a month later. The wife gave up custody of the children.

Guns were also mentioned in a case brought before the court in 1981. The couple had married in 1980. According to the wife's claim she had asked him to provide a separate residence, which he refused. He then threatened her saying that he belonged to a militia, and would ask his friends to help him kill her and her parents. The divorce took place a month later.

In yet a third case involving guns, brought before the court in 1988, the wife's lawyer wrote in his petition:

> Towards the end of 1982, the husband, accompanied by a number of armed men (two men were named) forcefully entered the School XYZ and, threatening her with a gun, kidnapped the wife, who was 16 years old. They beat her brother and fired their weapons in the school campus. They threatened the students which prevented any of the teachers present from interfering. Then the girl was transported and accompanied by armed men, according to a well outlined plan, to the man's paternal uncle. She was afterwards kept at the house of the village's *mukhtar* where she was coerced after 20 days to marry her husband. She refused to marry someone she did not know. The *mukhtar* and a number of his relatives tried to convince him to return the girl to her parents but he refused. Later on, he threatened her that he would kill her parents and she was forced to agree to the marriage in the absence of her parents.[24] The husband forced her to live with his parents in a house that was occupied and used to beat her all the time. After seven months she could bear it no longer and tried to kill herself. To punish her for her attempt, he took her to a deserted house, threatened to shoot her, and kept her locked up. After some time, she escaped and hid at the house of a paternal uncle who was a colonel in the Lebanese army which was why the husband had not been able to re-kidnap her.

The husband stopped attending the court sessions and she obtained a divorce sentence after six months.

The civil war aside, the rise of violence, as the main cause for divorce, and the fall in claims of infidelity and withholding of support, reflected changes that had taken place across the whole of society in the 1990s. As women acquired greater economic independence, claims for material support naturally decreased in number since hardship could no longer be argued as a legitimate cause for divorce if the wife was evidently a wage-earner. Along the same lines, as women became more assertive of their rights, they refused to accept domestic violence as a normal occurrence in the family. The physical beating of wives was previously widely practised and was generally accepted by an older generation of women as right and natural and not a thing to be fought against. As Azzam points out in *Gender and Religion*:

> There is a prevalent belief, especially among the older generation, that battered women usually call their fate upon themselves by being disobedient, inconsiderate, or confrontational with their husbands. Expressions like 'a good wife does not give her husband a cause to beat her,' or 'an obedient wife does not give her husband a reason to beat her' are common among older women who continue to reinforce patriarchal attitudes. (Azzam, 2007: 176)

The *Ajaweed* strata accepted the right of a husband to beat his wife if it was done to guide her to 'correct' behaviour, as laid down in the teachings of Sayyid Abdullah.[25] Echoes of this idea were evident in a number of cases brought before the court in the three decades covered in the research. For example, an elderly religious woman brought a case before the court in 1980. She had married in 1958 and she had stayed with her husband even though he used constantly to beat her. She had even sold her jewellery to pay for him to have an operation. She remained at his side and took care of him after his leg was amputated but could finally bear no more when he fired a gun at her. It was this attempt to kill her and the intervention of her 19-year-old son that persuaded her to leave him and ask for a divorce. Furthermore, she informed the judge that she had done so only because some relatives told her that he intended to 'smear' her reputation by saying she used to cheat on him.

Thus a religious woman was willing to accept physical violence and to put up with any kind of abuse from her husband.[26] It was only when he threatened to tarnish her reputation – her honour – that she decided to file for divorce. Her case, however, does not stand as a general rule for all Druze women. Indeed, especially in more recent times, the opposite trend was observed, with more and more women citing domestic violence as their reason for seeking a divorce. As soon as they found out about their husband's violent nature, they refused to put up with it, as the previous generation had done, but immediately sought to end the marriage.

The following case reflects this change in attitude. The couple married in 1988. The husband was born in 1966 and the wife in 1967. The case was brought to court a mere five months after the marriage. The wife's petition for divorce, put through a lawyer, claimed that:

> Since the first day of marriage, the husband insulted and offended his wife for no reason whatsoever until his abusive behaviour escalated to hitting her. He was also very stingy, which was the reason behind asking for divorce.

The husband's petition stated:

> He was a religious man and would not behave in any manner contrary to his religion. His sister was in fact married to his wife's brother and they are related. The wife left the house for no apparent reason and refused to return.

The wife responded with a detailed description of his violent behaviour:

> As soon as they married the husband's violent nature, as an abusive person, emerged. He did not spare her any kind of abuse. He would throw garbage at her face calling her a maid. He would not let her sleep on the bed but made her sleep on the floor. He forced her to drink dirty water and threatened to run her over with his car. When she got sick, he refused to take her to the hospital. Instead, her neighbours took her. He even denied her food forcing her to eat from the same plate for three consecutive days.

Both were questioned by the court and it became evident that the wife's brother was abusing the husband's sister. The husband had married his wife to avenge his sister. The judge ordered a divorce and gave the wife all her rights, which amounted to 3 million LBP and 20 gold liras.

A case brought before the court in 2001 is a further illustration of this trend. The couple had officially married in 1999, but the actual marriage ceremony was delayed until 2000. Only five months later, the wife brought a case for divorce before the court. She claimed that her husband had beaten her and caused her to miscarry. She refused to put up with his behaviour and so she had left his house. This is an extreme example but it is revealing of how women's attitudes to traditional norms of behaviour have changed. As they became more aware of their rights and on a more equal footing with men – and, also, may be less economically dependent on their husbands – they began to reject violence as a normal occurrence in the home. What these women are, in fact, depicting is a change in their self-perception. They are taking on a 'rights defined self'. They perceive themselves as humans with rights who have become victims actively taking action against their husbands which requires a 'substantial identity change' (Engle Merry, 2003: 244–5).

ii. Husband's Causes for Divorce over Time

We now turn to the possible changes over time in respect to the causes of divorce most frequently cited by husbands. Naturally, these are different from those mentioned by wives. The husbands mostly named the following reasons: (1) wife's infidelity: the wife had cheated on her husband; (2) *noshouz*: the wife had deserted the marriage; (3) no children: the wife had failed to conceive; (4) parental interference: the wife's parents interfered between husband and wife; (5) other: all other causes named by the husbands such as slovenliness, failure to keep house properly, overspending, etc.[27]

It was found that the husbands mentioned *noshouz* – meaning the wife's refusal to have sexual relations and her desertion of the marital home – as the primary cause in all the time intervals. This word used to hold a very negative, pejorative meaning for Druze people. One informant told me:

> It was not enough that I had stood by him at all times. I put up with his love affair with his secretary and I put up with his constant absence. I had to bear everything because of my two

daughters. I could not leave them and where would I go? My parents cannot support me. I had to bear everything. But what I really cannot understand was how he could threaten me with a divorce because of *noshouz*. I – to be called a *nashez*[28] – after all I had put up with. No! I preferred to reach an out of court agreement and leave. The judge explained that through a lawyer I could make him pay a lot of money. I refused. I did not want to be called by him a *nashez* and I will not stand before the father of my children at court and accuse him of relationships with women.[29]

Even nowadays people belonging to the older generation react strongly to this word. However, people belonging to the younger generation consider it less offensive and do not view the matter in such a negative light as their parents. Yet it remains the most frequently named cause for divorce by husbands. The reason for this may be the fact that the law stipulates *noshouz* as a legitimate reason for a divorce to be granted without giving the wife the *mahr*.

Table 4.9 shows that the naming of *nahouz* as the reason for divorce by husbands witnessed an increase over time, rising from 29.4 per cent in 1970–1975 to 44.9 per cent in the most recent time interval. Husbands are actually making more use of this cause today than they did in the past. This may be due to several reasons, most evident of which is an increased realization among husbands that such a reason would result in the least economic costly divorce since they would not be forced to

Table 4.9 Husband's Causes for Divorce vs. Time Intervals

	Wife's Infidelity	Noshouz	No children	Parental interference	Other	Total
1970–1975	3	10	2	4	15	34
	8.8%	29.4%	5.9%	11.8%	44.1%	100%
1980–1990	6	23	1	3	18	41
	11.8%	45.1%	1.9%	5.9%	35.3%	100%
1998–2003	7	31	3	2	26	69
	10.1%	44.9%	4.3%	2.9%	37.7%	100%

pay the delayed *mahr.* Adopting a literal interpretation of the data, it could be assumed that women are actually practicing *noshouz* more in recent times. In other words, women are increasingly choosing to leave their husbands, although in many cases women claim that they were asked by their husbands to leave. When this is the case, the judge questions the husband and wife and when the husband does not deny the wife's allegations, the judge would not consider the wife as *nashez.*

Another variable that has also seen a change over time is the mention of interference from the wife's parents as a cause for divorce, which decreased from 11.8 per cent to 5.9 per cent. This decline was already evident during the 1980–90 time interval, which indicates that the change did not occur suddenly but has been a gradual process. The reasons have to do with the changing condition of women whereby they are no longer perceived as a burden on the male members of the family but are better educated, have greater economic freedom, and are viewed as productive members of their families. They are better able to cope with their own problems and can fend for themselves without involving their parents in decisions regarding their own life and family. So there is generally less reason for parental interference in the marriages of today.

Place of Residence and Causes for Divorce

Another factor that might definitely be expected to influence the causes of divorce is the place of residence of the contesting parties. Villagers are likely to divorce in a manner quite different from people in the cities or towns. The named causes will naturally be influenced by whether the whole extended family, and even the whole village, knows why the marriage has broken down and the nature of the conflict between the couple. Moreover, the place of residence is also likely to influence which of the two parties brings the case before the court. For instance, it is easier for a woman who lives in Beirut to bring her case to the court, which happens to be located in Beirut, than it would be for one living in a village, simply on grounds of distance and practicalities of travel.

a. Wive's Place of Residence and Causes for Divorce

The first part of this section analyzes the effect of wife's place of residence on a number of different factors in the divorce. The statistics in this part include only the cases where the wife was resident in Lebanon. People living outside Lebanon and those whose documents were missing were excluded from the analysis. This left a total of 603 cases (out of 829 in the complete sample). Of these, 61.7 per cent concerned wives who lived in a village, 9.4 per cent in a town (basically Aley and Chouiefat) and 11.5 per cent in the city of Beirut.

The place of residence was cross-tabulated against a number of variables to discover what, if any, effect it might have. The first variables to be checked against the place of residence were the causes of divorce mentioned by the wife. The analysis also included divorces by agreement.

Although Table 4.10 reveals broadly comparable percentages across each variable, there are nonetheless some significant differences to be accounted for. The first relates to the number of divorces in agreement obtained by village and city residents. The difference between them is about 15 per cent, which, to a community as enclosed as the Druze, is nonetheless substantial enough. Women (and men) living in the villages are under greater pressure from their kin

Table 4.10 Wife's Place of Residence vs. Causes of Divorce According to Wife

	Violence	Husband's infidelity	Parental interference	Non-supportive	Divorce in agreement	Other	total
Village	75 14.7%	12 2.4%	3 0.6%	25 4.9%	350 68.6%	45 8.8%	510
Town	15 19.3%	0 0%	1 1.3%	8 10.3%	47 60.3%	7 9.0%	78
City	16 16.8%	6 6.3%	1 1.1%	8 8.4%	51 53.7%	11 13.7%	95

group to end things in agreement rather than face the bitter claims and counter-claims of a court divorces. As one villager put it:

> The divorce is going to happen and the damage take place so why add to the catastrophe and incur further harm?

The mention of violence was also clearly influenced by the wife's place of residence. Being the most 'socially' legitimate causes for divorce, it is generally the excuse most utilized by women. After all, a female is not likely to incur social blame if she names marital violence as her reason for asking for a divorce.

Once the in-agreement cases are factored out as in Table 4.11, we find that the percentage of women mentioning violence is 46.9 per cent for village residents, 36.9 per cent for city residents and 48.4 per cent for town residents. Villagers chose to mention violence as a cause since it is considered an acceptable reason to file for divorce and wives using this pretext would not have to face social criticism. However, they are reluctant to cite violence as a cause when bringing a case to court since the wife would be compelled to reveal intimate details of her husband's violent behaviour to the judge – a male and, still more shame-inducing, a *sheikh* – and to the general public as the court sessions are open to all unless otherwise stipulated. This would add to the 'shame' felt by a woman who was reticent about revealing intimate details and humiliating incidents. One particular story that came to my knowledge concerned a

Table 4.11 Wife's Place of Residence vs. Causes for Divorce

	Violence	Husband's infidelity	Parental interference	Non-supportive	Other	Total
Village	75 46.9%	12 7.5%	3 1.9%	25 15.6%	45 28.1%	160 100%
Town	15 48.4%	0 0.0%	1 3.2%	8 25.8%	7 9.0%	31 100%
City	16 36.9%	6 13.6%	1 2.3%	8 18.9%	11 25.0%	44 100%

woman in her mid-30s. Her husband was very violent, and she was beaten again and again and even burned on different parts of her body. She did not tell any member of her family about these experiences until after the couple were divorced; in her petitioned to the court she had claimed 'irreconcilable differences'. She later said that the way her husband had treated her had been humiliating enough and she refused to add to that public humiliation by recounting her experiences in front of the court. She added, 'I felt miserable enough without the whole world knowing my story!' For this woman, divorce itself was stigma enough and she did not want to add to that the stigma of admitting in public to being physically abused. The reason she refused to tell her family about her husband's abuse from the beginning was because she knew her parents and brothers would not allow it and would force her to divorce her husband. She was hoping he would change and she would be spared a divorce. In the end she realized he never would, and so she had to go through with it.

The wife's place of residence also seemed to influence her decision to seek a divorce from the court. When contested cases were analyzed against the wife's place of residence, the findings, reported in Table 4.12, revealed that the wife was more likely to have instigated the action, with 10 per cent more village residents doing so than those living in the city. Villagers have the support of their male kin who are very likely to intervene on the side of the wife, forcing her husband to concede as

Table 4.12 Who Brings the Case Before Court vs. Wife's Place of Residence

	Husband	Wife	Total
Village	54 29.2%	131 70.8%	185 100%
Town	6 18.2%	27 81.8%	33 100%
city	18 39.1%	28 60.9%	46 100%

many of her 'rights' as possible. Even in the city, women continue to be the responsibility of their kin group and can, in most cases, count on the support of their family members in times of trouble – but evidently not to the same extent as in the villages.

b. Husband's Place of Residence and Causes for Divorce

The place of residence of the husband was also analyzed to ascertain what influence it might have on the decision to bring the case before the court, the assumption being that city residents would ask for divorce for different reasons than those living in the villages or towns. To verify the influence of this factor the husband's place of residence was cross-tabulated against the reasons for divorce cited in his claim for divorce. As before, this analysis excluded husbands living outside Lebanon and cases lacking the relevant data.

The table shows that, regardless of the husband's place of residence, the cause for divorce cited most frequently by all males was *noshouz*: 52.6 per cent of village residents, 56.3 per cent of town residents, and 48.6 per cent of city residents, a generally high percentage. Here Goode's comments that people tend to base their claim for divorce on what is likely to get them the quickest and most favourable decision is highly relevant since, as already noted, the Druze personal status law allows a husband to divorce his wife upon allegations of *noshouz* without giving her any of the legally stipulated rights – essentially her *mahr*. Therefore, it is not surprising that males use this excuse as their main cause for divorce.

Table 4.13 Husband's Place of Residence vs. Husband's Causes for Divorce

	Wife's infidelity	Noshouz	No children	Wife's work	Other	Total
Village	15	70	6	5	57	133
	11.3%	52.6%	4.5%	3.8%	27.8%	100%
Town	0	9	0	3	4	16
	0%	56.3%	0%	18.7%	25.0%	100%
City	5	17	1	4	8	35
	8.6%	48.6%	2.9%	11.4%	22.9%	100%

The percentages for other causes of divorce showed no sizeable differences between village, town, and city. The only factor that stood out and may be related to the husband's place of residence was the wife's going to work, which was mentioned as a cause for divorce by 11.4 per cent of city residents, and 18.5 per cent of town residents, almost triple the percentage of village residents (3.8 per cent) that named it as a factor. This is not surprising since locality definitely influences the opportunities for a woman to obtain work outside the home. A wife living in the cities or town is more likely to find a job, and, if she does so without her husband's agreement, it could be a potential cause for marital conflict. The possibility of a wife working in the village without her husband's total acceptance of the situation is much less plausible.

The following case, brought in 1991, shows how a husband might use his wife's employment as a cause for disagreement, and even as a reason to deny her custody of the children. The couple had married in 1981 and resided in Beirut. The husband's claim included the following:

> It is true that custody is a women's right, however, not in her case. She is an employee and her work takes up all her time. So she has no time for her children especially since she is not just a bank employee but had recently opened her own shop in which she stays after bank hours. Therefore, she had no time for her children and her parent's house is not large enough to house all of them whereas my mother is alone and can better take care of the children.

Following another line, the research investigated whether the husband's place of residence had any influence on his decision to bring his case for divorce before the court. Generally speaking, it was the wife who brought the divorce before the court in contested cases, and this remained so even when controlling for the husband's place of residence. However, a slight divergence was revealed in the findings for husbands from the city. Table 4.14 shows that only among city residents was the percentages of husbands and wives bringing the divorce comparable – in fact, they were almost the same. This was a significant finding.

Table 4.14 Husband's Place of Residence vs. Who Brought Case Before the Court

	Husband	Wife	Total
Village	58 36.5%	101 63.5%	159 100%
Town	6 30.0%	14 70.0%	20 100%
City	20 41.7%	28 58.3%	48 100%

In cities, males and females can be expected to exhibit similar behaviour, because differences based on gender become minimized.

Immigration and Divorce

What influence might immigration be expected to have on the nature of the divorce process among the Druze? We have seen in chapter two that Druze immigrants display the classic behaviour that anthropologists identify among immigrant groups in general – that is, they react to the larger migrant community by turning in on themselves and clinging more closely to their own culture. Druze individuals immigrate to a foreign country tend to live among people they recognize as their own – relatives or people belonging to the same village. They form their own group within the larger community and continue to practice their own customs and traditions. They take their village and Druze ethos with them and build their own society within the larger society.[30] Thus, they may be expected to solve their conflicts in the same way as they settled such matters in their country of origin.

One particular case clearly reveals the intense social pressures felt by the Druze, even when they live outside Lebanon. The couple was married in 1971 in Lebanon after the wife had met her husband on one of her family's visits. They set up home in the United States. After four years, they brought a case for divorce before the Beirut court because she had asked for divorce in the United States. The reason for the divorce was that the husband had a psychological problem and could not approach her in bed. The wife had not told her parents what was going until she could bear things no longer. She had kept the fact that she had not enjoyed sexual relations with him at any time in their marriage a secret although he used to beat her and was extremely jealous.

This case reveals that even among long-time Druze immigrants – the wife had been born in the United States and had lived there most of her life – traditional values remain strong. She found it hard to talk about her husband's sexual problems or even to tell her parents that he was physically violent. She waited for four years before she brought the matter before the court.

In the next parts we shall examine the influence of immigration on divorce with respect to both husbands and wives.

a. Immigrant Husbands and Divorce

The statistical analysis revealed that immigration did not appear to change how husbands behaved in respect of the cause for divorce, who brought the divorce before the court, and other similar matters. This was an important discovery, quantitatively supporting the hypothesis outlined above that no large difference exists between immigrants (Druze living abroad) and non-immigrants (those living in Lebanon).

The only factor in which immigrants differed from non-immigrants husbands was in the number of years the couple were married before the divorce took place. Table 4.15 shows the relationship between the length of the marriage and the status of the husband. It reveals that the likelihood of an immigrant husband seeking an early divorce was statistically lower than a non-immigrant husband. In the case of the

Table 4.15 Immigrant Status of Husband vs. Years of Marriage

	Less than 5	6 to 10	More than 10
Immigrant	45 25.7%	43 24.6%	87 49.7%
Non-immigrant	243 40.1%	127 21.2%	228 38.1%

former, it was found that 49.7 per cent of marriages had lasted for more than ten years before the divorce. When the husband was not an immigrant, it was found that 40.1 per cent of the marriages had lasted for less than five years. The explanation for this behaviour is related to the experience of the immigrant. When an individual, male or female, leaves their country to live in a foreign country, they are more willing to remain in a troubled marriage than to leave it and face a strange society. In their home country, divorcing individuals have the support of their family members and this is often lacking in their new country, especially when there is no existing Druze community to identify with. With regard to men with children, family support is of the utmost important since among the Druze it is normal when a husband divorces for him to get custody of the children and for his mother to take care of them. This arrangement is not possible outside Lebanon. The question of who cares for the children consequently becomes of primary importance to male immigrants and may motivate them to delay divorce.

Another explanation might have to do with the laws of the country in which they are residing. For example, individuals residing in the United States are required by law to pay maintenance to a divorced wife and give her an equitable share of the marital property. This they are not forced to do under Druze law and it may be another powerful motivating factor in putting off divorce for as long as possible.

b. Immigrant Wives and Divorce

The same findings were observed in cases where immigrant wives had sought the divorce. Table 4.16 reveals that 54.5 per cent of immigrant wives did not leave an unhappy marriage before ten years. By

Table 4.16 Immigrant Status of Wife vs. Years of Marriage

	Less than 5	6–10	More than 10
Immigrant	42 27.2%	28 18.2%	84 54.5%
Non-immigrant	250 41.1%	136 22.4%	222 36.6%

comparison, it was observed that 41.1 per cent of non-immigrant wives divorced before five years of marriage and only 36.6 per cent after ten years.

A case brought before the court in 2001 describes one such immigrant wife's experiences. She was born in 1963 and was married in 1979 to a man 12 years her senior. The wife's petition before the court said:

> I was 16 years old when my parents forced me to marry and I did not know what to do. Ever since I gave birth to my first son, my misery and torture began. My husband did not care about my son and me. He was authoritative and had no respect for me. I remained patient because I was afraid, all alone in a foreign land and I feared my son would be thrown on the streets.

After seven years and another child, he sent her back to Lebanon and did not follow. She kept her suffering a secret until she ran out of money after she had sold all her jewellery. After that, she filed for divorce but later went back on the divorce because as she wrote:

> My parents intervened, especially my brother who said it was better not to break up my family. So I returned to him.

To prevent the same thing happening again, she found a job and worked. After five years, her husband told her he intended to buy a house in Lebanon and asked her to give him all the money she had saved. She agreed as she was hoping this would improve the relationship between them. However, he spent all the money and asked for more without buying the house and he lied about the reasons. She knew he was cheating on her especially after the children found some letters from his lover but she ignored them. His behaviour worsened and he started beating her until the children asked her to call the police. She refused because she wanted to protect the honour of the family:

> However, his behaviour did not change and became threatening to the kids and now I seek to divorce him.

Her son was by then 16 years old and no longer under his father's authority. The divorce took place ten months after it was brought before the court and the sentence was issued by a judge after the couple had failed to reach an agreement. The judge's ruling allowed the children the right to live with whichever parent they chose and gave the wife the right to her *mahr* but not to maintenance as she was still living in the house rented by the husband at the time of divorce, nor to compensation for harm and damage as eyewitness proof had not been forthcoming.

> In another case, the couple, who belonged to the same family, had migrated to the African state of Gabon immediately after the marriage in 1962. They brought the divorce before the court in 1972, ten years later. The conflict between them started a year after the birth of a son in 1964. She became pregnant for second time and he forced her to have an abortion and began to mistreat her, shouting, beating her and even telling her to return to her parents. She did just that but three years later she returned to him, to discover that he was living with a Frenchwoman who was pregnant with his child. He threw her out of the house and told her to return to Lebanon, which she did only to find out that he had banned her from leaving the country again.[31]

In his cross-petition before the court, the husband claimed that she was the one cheating on him and that she had wanted to leave him to marry her boyfriend. This was proved to be a lie and thus the court disregarded his statement. The divorcing couple failed to reach a settlement and remained in disagreement until her parents found out what he had done and insisted that she sought a divorce sentence from the court, which she finally did in 1978.

Some wives put up with their abusive husbands for even longer. One couple married in 1959. They were related – the wife's mother was the husband's first cousin – and the wife was born in 1946 (information regarding the husband's date of birth was missing from the documents). He was living in Australia, and the marriage was arranged. The marriage contract was concluded in the absence of the husband, and his 13-year-old wife travelled out to join him. Her petition for divorce submitted to the Beirut court included detailed descriptions of his violence. He used to get drunk and beat her so that many times she was forced to flee to his brother's house or to the house of a neighbour to escape his violence. After one such assault, the wife took her children and went to live with one of her cousins. People intervened and asked her to return to her husband. She did so but he carried on with his beatings, until she could bear it no longer and filed for a divorce in Australia. This was in 1980, after suffering 21 years of abuse.

These cases are examples of how Druze wives living outside Lebanon 'put up' with their husband's misbehaviour and do not leave the marriage, thereby breaking up the household, until all forms of reconciliation have failed. These women's actions were condoned and even encouraged by members of their own family who evidently upheld the traditional view that a woman is meant to suffer while a man's misdeeds are considered mistakes that are capable of remedy. To family members, divorce was a measure only to be contemplated when all other methods failed to work – even at the cost of the wife's, or even the children's, welfare and happiness. The claim that a wife should bear up for the sake of her family and not break up the household carries strong echoes of traditional patriarchal attitudes.

The above findings provide clear evidence of how a particular 'traditional' religious sect witnessed a number of changes in certain aspects of divorce. These changes, nevertheless, had to take place within the limitations imposed by the sect's most basic survival strategies – namely the preservation of their internal solidarity. All forms of conflict – political or social – have to be kept under control and are never allowed to be fully expressed. In other words, divorce, which is a 'natural' phenomenon of family life in most modern societies, occurs among the Druze but most divorces are made by mutual consent. Even when contested cases were brought before the court, numerous attempts were made to end the conflict by agreement.

Change: Case Studies

To clearly understand the complex nature of change that has occurred in perceptions of divorce and the purpose of marriage, it should be enough to study the following cases. The petitions, both brought by the wife, display a difference in approach and language. The first offers an insight into what might be considered a traditional viewpoint as to the role of a wife offered by a woman who is of the *Ajaweed* strata – a religious woman.[32] The other cases offer the opposite perspective.

The first case was brought before the court in 2002. The marriage had taken place in 1971 and the couple had four children. The divorce was granted in 2003, nine months after the wife's petition was presented. It was handwritten by the woman herself and not by a lawyer on her behalf, and included the following:

This woman was indeed granted a divorce and her husband was made to pay all her rights in addition to sum of money to compensate for the harm and injury she had suffered.

> I poor XX, praise be to God who ruled that my lot be with YYY and I became his wife and we had four children. My parents loved him and helped him at all times although he was uncaring and did not reciprocate their good behaviour. He was brutal towards me, treated me disrespectfully and beat me although I am a religious woman. He used to make me work with him and he would collect my pay and leave me nothing. At that time, I used to work with him at the school XYZ… I remained patient because I wanted to take care of my children and he always used to threaten me with divorce. I did not tell a person so that the matter will not reach my parents and the 'infavourable end reached' (literally meaning divorce). When he was building the house, I helped with the work. I mixed the concrete and carrying the blocks. He would not have pity on me when I would complain that I was tired and could not work, he would threaten me by saying, 'I will send you back to your parent's house.' I put up with his ruthless behaviour. My brother

got married and he did not allow me to attend his wedding and I did not disobey him. Despite everything, I obeyed him and did as he wished until lately he left us and took a separate residence. He stopped giving me money. When I would ask him for anything, he would say, 'Go to the Court and ask for your rights.' I believe in God and his judgment and that it was my lot and destiny and that God knew better ... I used to go to his house and clean and cook for him ... One day his neighbour told me that he had said that he'd divorce me and that he wanted to marry another woman... I rushed to him and implored him not to do that because it was illegal and ran against the *Tawheed Shari'a* and that would reflect badly upon our reputation and our children especially our married daughter. I went to him and lived with him for a few months but was cautious as I heard that he was planning to marry someone else. However, he refused to listen to me and even threatened me and beat me. I actually heard recently that he had asked a woman's hand in marriage and that, she had accepted. The neighbours told me he had actually gotten engaged to another woman. I remained silent and visited him every now and then. I would clean his house, wash his clothes, and prepare his food. One day a strange man came to the house and my husband asked me to leave the room. I refused and he hit me on the shoulder. I left and went to the kitchen but could hear what was being said. When the man left, I asked my husband about the stranger's visit and he hit me and kicked me out of the house. I went back home and cried. His brother heard me and when I told him what happed, his brother informed me that that man was a 'match maker' and that he had taken $50 from my husband to find him a wife. He told me that his brother had actually asked him to accompany him on the *tolbeh* visit but his brother refused. Should this be done to a Druze woman? I beg your help and the help of your court and I request the legal and religious procedure, in God's name, to help correct the wrong that is about to happen and only to prevent a bigger wrong that I ask for divorce and for my rights.

That case shows a very traditional approach to divorce and to the court especially by comparison with the one that follows, which was brought before the court in 1992. The marriage had taken place in 1987. The wife's petition ran as follows:

> Because of a difference in our ways of thinking and because we are not able to continue our married life, I ask for divorce.

The husband agreed and they divorced one month later.

The next case also illustrates the contrast between current and past outlooks to divorce and to family life. It was brought before the court in 1996, the year the couple had married, and the divorce took place four months after the petition was entered, in 1997. In her petition for divorce the wife wrote:

> ... After some time, he began to hit me and so I left and asked for a divorce.

The psychologist who was appointed to the case said in her report:

> The husband doesn't assume any responsibility towards his wife and there is no agreement between the two. It is better to allow them to divorce especially as there are no children yet.

Taken together, these three cases show how women's perceptions of the role of the wife and the mechanisms of divorce have changed, revealing the difference in mentality between the old generation and the new one. The elderly woman in the first case remained, to use her terms, a patient and a good Druze wife until her husband decided to remarry. Only then, did she feel that she should divorce him. The beatings, continuous humiliation, and even separation were not reason enough to ask for a divorce. It was not until he did something totally unacceptable – attempt to take a new wife – that she sought to end the marriage. In the second case, the wife felt that a difference with her husband's ways of thinking was ample reason for divorce. Similarly, the woman in the last case refused to be beaten, petitioned for divorce, and got it after only four months of marriage.

Modern Technologies

The recent past has witnessed huge technological advances in the field of communications and these found their way into divorce and family life. Over the last few years, records of telephone conversations have been mentioned in a number of divorce cases. Some people taped their spouse's phone calls to prove disloyalty or love relationships and used the recordings to petition for divorce on grounds of infidelity.

For example, in one case, the couple had married in 1988, and the husband brought the divorce before the court in 2000. He claimed that he had recently spotted some changes in his wife's behaviour towards him and their children. He noticed that she had begun to receive longer than normal phone calls, and after noting down a number of such incidents, he began to doubt her. Once she left the house without preparing food for the children and was absent for a long time. She had told him that she was going to get her glasses fixed. After waiting for her return, he asked her parents, who lived in the same building, where she was and, according to his statement:

> They told me that she was visiting one of her friends and named her friend. I called my wife on her cell phone and asked her where she was. She told me at her friend's but gave me a different name. That was when I installed a recording machine connected to the phone and was surprised when I found out that she was having an affair with a man who used to come to my house and so I left my house and took the children with me and filed for divorce.

He sent a copy of the recording to the wife's parents. The wife's lawyer kept insisting that the recording was not admissible because it was made without her consent and the recording could have been technically tampered with. They divorced in agreement reached in court but the wife did not get custody of her children.

In another case brought before the court in 1998, the husband asked for divorce after one year of marriage. His petition said:

> Since my married life is stained by distrust and I have certain proofs, witnesses and a recording that prove that this woman is immorally involved with other people and thus I ask for divorce.

Another case involving the use of tape recordings was brought before the court in 2001. The husband, born in 1943, and the wife, born in 1960, were maternal cousins. The case was brought by the wife who claimed that her husband neglected her and their three children. He had a weak personality and was largely influenced by his brothers. He had asked her to leave his house based on unfounded and imaginary accusations and allegations. She demanded all her rights and custody over the children as he rarely took care of them.

In his response the husband said that he had not kicked his wife out but that she had left of her own accord after he had discovered her outrageous behaviour which constituted a criminal act. Nevertheless he had asked her not to leave but to reach a divorce agreement by consent. He requested a secret hearing to tell the judge the actual cause for divorce, adding that he refused to allow his children to spend another night with their mother. She could see her children but might not spend any time alone with them because she was trying to poison their thoughts against their father.

The judge called the husband and wife to a private session in which the husband presented a recording as evidence. The wife refused to listen to it. The tape revealed unethical behaviour and adultery. On being questioned, the husband admitted that he knew of his wife's adulterous behaviour. When he questioned her about it, she confessed to having an affair with Mr. XX who would spend the night with her, and admitted she also used to give him money. The wife denied her husband's allegations, claiming that everything was fabricated. The judge admitted the recording as evidence and his judgment was as follows:

1) Since the husband insisted on the divorce after he was sure of his wife's misbehaviour and since it became clear to the court that it was impossible for the marriage to continue and upon hearing the recording of the wife talking to a non-Lebanese stranger which proved that his wife had ill intentions that the wife could not deny ... the wife was responsible for the breakdown of the marriage.
2) Since neither required a sum of money as harm or injury, none is allocated.

3) Maintenance is not to be allocated to the wife as she left the house.
4) The wife is to see the children once every two weeks for a period of four hours only.
5) The wife shall pay all legal costs.

On this occasion, the judge considered the tape recordings to be admissible evidence[33] and pronounced his judgment accordingly. However, this is not always the case. For example, a Druze immigrant male living in the USA brought a case before the Beirut court in which the judge rejected the use of recorded evidence.

The husband claimed that his wife, who was still in the USA, had removed everything from the house, kidnapped their daughter and left. The wife answered that her husband had changed after a trip to Lebanon and upon returning had moved to a different state. He then threatened her and tried to take away her daughter as a result of which she had had to apply to the courts in the United States for custody. The husband replied that his wife hated his parents and always created problems with them, which made life miserable for him, especially as his parents used to visit them once a year. To prove his allegations, he quoted from a secret tape he had made of his wife talking on the phone to her mother and presented the recording as evidence to the court. The quotes included,

> His father is good but his mother is a dog. I [the wife] have spent the last five months doing nothing but receiving guests and am so joyous that they have left and now I can rest since they have all gone.

He added many other similar details from the recordings.

The judge's decision concerning the tape recording was the following:

> It is inadmissible in court since it is a secret conversation between a woman and her mother and whatever the wife said to her mother is not legally admissible without the agreement of those involved – namely the wife and her mother.

These cases and many others show how new technology has found its way into the divorce procedures of the Druze community. These cases did not only reveal the technologies but also the judge's active role in deciding when and under what conditions these technologies are considered admissible to court and when they are denied admission. The judge took it upon himself to define what is morally appropriate and acted upon his personal evaluation of the evidence submitted.

General Findings

The very detailed data thrown up by the research revealed an abundance of information that goes beyond the limit of this study as, for example, the language used in divorce proceedings and the different methods of conflict resolution that were employed. However, a number of general findings are reported simply to provide the reader with background knowledge of a number of variables. Among these variables were the time it takes for a divorce to be processed at court and the effect of the presence of children.

Time a Case is Kept at Court

A judge, by law, is allowed to keep a case pending as long as he sees room for reconciliation, even when the couples had agreed to the divorce. One court employee told me of a case in which both the husband and wife came before the court asking for divorce. The judge noticed that the couple was friendly and that there was no antagonism among them. They treated each other in a very civilized manner and the only cause for divorce was the fact that their parents seemed to have a negative influence on them. The judge postponed issuing a divorce sentence in their case a number of times, to give them more time to become reconciled. His attempts failed and in the end, he had to divorce the couple but only after giving them plenty of time to reconsider their decision. However, this is not always the case.

The research findings actually revealed the opposite. It was found that 77.4 per cent of the divorce cases brought before the court in the 33 years of the study took less than one year to reach a conclusion. Only 16.9 per cent of the cases remained with the court for a year and 5.7 per cent for more than a year. This reveals that a divorce sentence is quite easily arrived at – especially if the husband and wife had signed a divorce agreement before coming to court. It seems evident that certain factors – the age of the divorcing couple and whether they had children among others – might influence the issuing of a quick decision. Evidently, the time a case spends in court is a factor of the type of divorce brought before the court.

Table 4.17 shows this clearly. Cases that ended in one month were mostly divorces by consent because if a couple comes to court with a signed agreement to divorce, the judge is legally bound to issue a divorce sentence unless there is a legitimate cause not to do so. According to Article 42, a married couple has the right to divorce by consent by announcing, in the presence of two witnesses, their joint agreement and the judge is to issue a sentence accordingly. This might include the judge's evaluation as to the possibility of reconciliation or other factors. It is also clear from the table that contested cases, including those that end in agreement in court and those that do not, generally stay in court for a period of one year or more. Analysis of the cases revealed that extra time was particularly necessary when adjudicators were appointed to try to resolve the conflict since they were required to meet with the two contesting parties, attempt to reconcile their differences and then submit a written report of their efforts to the judge. All this evidently takes time.

The following case gives an idea of how long each stage of the process can take. The wife, born in 1958, and the husband, born in 1952,

Table 4.17 Time Spent in Court vs. Type of Divorce

	1 month	2 month	1 year	More than one year
Consent	343 64.2%	133 24.8%	34 10.1%	5 0.9%
In Court Agreement	9 4.1%	30 13.5%	142 64.0%	41 18.5%
Contested	2 2.9%	3 4.3%	43 62.3%	21 30.4%

were related through the patriarchal line and had married in 1980. The husband brought the case before the court on 22 September 1986. The wife responded with a counter-allegation on 8 December 1986. The husband responded on 24 January 1987. Then the judge assigned two adjudicators and the report from the husband's adjudicator was submitted on 8 February 1988. The report from the wife's adjudicator was submitted on 20 February 1988. Then both the husband and the wife appeared before the court and declared their agreement to a divorce in the presence of two witnesses and the judge issued a divorce sentence on the same day 27 March 1988, one year and five months after the case was brought to court.

A similar period of time elapsed in the next case as a result of the proceedings required by the court. The husband, born 1946, and the wife, born 1951, were married in 1975 and the case was brought before the court by the wife on 18 November 1978. The husband responded with a counter-allegation on 13 December 1978. The wife responded with a statement on 3 January 1979 and the husband submitted a response to her allegations on 10 March 1979. Two adjudicators were appointed and they jointly announced on 10 March 1979 that they had failed to reach a compromise. Then the wife submitted an allegation on 10 October 1979 claiming that the husband was asking her to live in a house that was not suitable and could not be considered a 'legitimate residence'. The judge assigned a security force member attached to the court to carry out an inspection of the house. He did and submitted his report. Although the date of the submission is not available in the records it must have been close to the issuing of the judgment since no other allegation was presented from either side. The judge based his sentence on the report and announced a divorce by fault of the wife on 10 March 1980.

The following case is particularly interesting since the case remained in court for almost two years although it was brought by consent. The man was born in 1939 and the woman in 1944. They had married in 1962 and brought a signed agreement to the court on 7 April 1999. The judge refused to act upon their agreement and delayed issuing a sentence until they made further efforts at reconciliation. He even assigned a psychiatrist to attempt to reconcile the difference and prevent a divorce. A year and six month later the psychiatrist submitted her report. In it she wrote:

> They have been married for 30 years and they have seven daughters. The husband wants to divorce to be able to re-marry and get a son. There is some hope in the two continuing their marriage as the husband still comes back to Lebanon occasionally and stays with the family.

The court records included a family record that revealed that their six daughters were born on the following years: 1970, 1971, 1972, 1975, 1976, 1980 and the man wanted to have a boy although as the records revealed his oldest daughter was 29 years old at that time. Three months later they both appeared in person in the court and insisted on their divorce. Thereupon, the judge was forced to comply and issued a divorce sentence on 9 January 2001.

Effect of the Presence of Children

The research revealed that in 50.9 per cent of divorces issued by the Beirut court between 1970 and 2003, the divorcing couples had children. In 29.9 per cent of divorces, the couple did not have children and in a further 19.2 per cent the presence or not of children was unknown. These findings would indicate that, in statistical terms, the presence of children in a marriage was not a factor in preventing or occasioning divorce during the period of the study, though in a number of cases it delayed divorce.

In the following case the wife actually pointed to the presence of children as the main reason that delayed her request for divorce. The couple, first paternal cousins, had married in 1975. The husband was born in 1945 and the wife in 1960 at the age of 15 years and 10 months. The wife petitioned for divorce through a lawyer on 18 October 1999. The petition read as follows:

> She was forced into a marriage to please her parents. She travelled to live with him and her agony started and lasted for ten

> years during which she was forced to accept a life that she did not want. She never loved him and what added to the predicament was the birth of three children, the oldest of whom is 20. Giving birth was a purely biological process imposed on her by the husband. The children helped in easing the wounds but did not cure them. After ten years, the wife returned to Lebanon and the husband continued working abroad. He would visit the family once a year. The wife continued her duties towards her family but the gap between the two widened which had an impact on the children. The children were able to see their parents living in one house but like strangers and they asked their mother to divorce. The wife had not asked for a divorce earlier, upon returning to Lebanon, because of her parent's intervention as they asked her to try to tolerate the marriage.

This case clearly revealed how the wife continued in a relationship that she did not want because of her children and later also filed for divorce upon their urging. Her parents had played a role in delaying the divorce but once her children were old enough to give their support, she filed for divorce.

Pseudo-divorce

As previously noted, in the course of my research, I came across 236 cases of divorce where the couple, although they had signed a marriage contract, were not actually married because sexual intercourse had yet to take place. These cases were excluded from the divorce sample because they could not be labelled as divorces as such. They require some particular attention. Article 27 of the Druze law takes care of the legal repercussions of such a pseudo-divorce. The article stipulates that

> In the event of a spouse's death or divorce after the marriage is consummated, the entire *mahr* should be paid. In the event of death or divorce before marriage is consummated, half of the *mahr* shall be paid.

The research revealed that almost all (99.2 per cent) of these 236 pseudo-divorces occurred within less than a year of the marriage. What prompted these individuals to go to court and sign a marriage contract only to file for a divorce after less than a year? To answer that question, a one-page questionnaire was prepared and handed out to 125 people. Since the aim of the questionnaire, as explained in Chapter one, was simply to clarify the above point and was not a major part of the research, the sample was not chosen to be representative of the Druze community as a whole, but merely to seek an insight on the matter. The method used was what is known in sociological circles as the snowball effect – I chose a group of people from among my acquaintances and asked each to spread the questionnaire among their own acquaintances. The sample included Druze people of both genders, ranging in age from 18 to 60, people living in Beirut, Aley and villages in the Matn and Chouf areas, self-employed workers and employees, students and housewives. What was remarkable was that, regardless of gender, where they lived, or education, most people answered that they would agree to sign a marriage contract a year before the actual marriage if the husband were an immigrant and had to sort out the paperwork to allow his wife to join him in his country of residence once they were married. A few individuals (11) answered that they would agree to this if the engagement was going to be a lengthy one (more than one year) Out of the 125 respondents, 18 answered that they would agree if the parents wanted it – as is normally the case among very religious families, the *uqqal* or the *sheikhs* of the community.

The fact that the majority of respondents saw the arrangement as right for immigrants is in line with my observation regarding the speed with which immigrants arrange to marry. It is common practice for a Druze man living abroad to return to Lebanon on a one-month vacation and spend his time visiting one house after another, looking for a suitable wife. He is normally accompanied by his parents or other family members. Once he finds someone he likes, he proposes and if accepted, the engagement party is held before he leaves. It is not unusual for the signing of the marriage contract to take place immediately after the engagement party, leaving plenty of time to sort out the paperwork for his wife's move to her new country before he returns to Lebanon for the wedding party. This will have been largely arranged by his parents and his bride and normally occurs one year after the engagement. During that period, he may or may not return to Lebanon on one or more visits.

Saeed's story typifies this pattern of events. He was almost 40 in 2002 and lived in the United States. Still unmarried, he wanted to marry a Druze girl from Lebanon and asked his sisters to find him a wife. They called him and informed him that they had found a suitable girl who was a distant relative. He came to Lebanon during the summer, and visited the girl's house. They liked each other and held an engagement party, signing the marriage contract the same month so that he could start applying for the documents that would permit her to travel with him the following summer after they were actually married.

It seems likely that this is what many of the people who sought early divorces had done. After signing their marriage contracts, the husband returned home. Then the couple found out during their year-long correspondence that they really were not suited to each other. Rather than embark on married life together, they decided to file for divorce. This step was necessary since, among the Lebanese Druze, a marriage contract can only be annulled by a court ruling.

The fact is that for the Druze people, engagement (betrothal) is a very structured affair that is governed by a number of traditions and rules. The Druze Personal Status Law lays down general guidelines to the act of becoming engaged, and to the formal ending of an engagement.[34] One may wonder as to why such relationships should be subject to legal strictures of this kind. The explanation is rooted in the traditional nature of Druze society. Traditionally speaking, engagements were conducted between the parents of the couple and not between the individuals themselves.[35] A groom's parents used to ask for the hand of a bride from her parents and receive an oral promise from them before the actual engagement, which might take place later. In many cases, the husband and wife-to-be might not have actually sat and talked together; in some extreme cases, they might not even have met. The engagement was often an agreement between the parents and not the spouses-to-be and needed a formal framework, which was ultimately provided by the law.

A number of divorce cases I came across in the course of my research were of particular interest in regard to this. One or both parties would claim that they had known nothing about their spouse, at the time of the marriage, other than that their parents thought that he or she would make a 'suitable' spouse. In some cases, a disputant might even claim that he or she had not even set eyes on the spouse before the marriage. The following case sheds more light on how these matters were conducted within a very traditional community.

The husband had migrated to Australia in 1950 and was living there at the time of his marriage in 1959. The couple had spent all their married life in Australia. In 1981 the husband brought a case for divorce before the court because his wife refused to return to Lebanon. His petition through a lawyer ran as follows:

> In 1950, the husband, his mother and brothers left Lebanon to Australia. After some time, his mother suggested that he got married to a girl from Lebanon. His sisters, who were living in Lebanon, picked out a girl and arranged the matter with her parents. The girl and her parents agreed to the marriage and to the idea that the bride would have to travel to Australia. His sisters sent him a letter informing him of the matter along with a photograph of the chosen girl. He agreed to the marriage and to his sisters' choice. He sent a written power of attorney to his brother-in-law to sign the marriage contract. He also sent some money to cover the bride's *Jihaz* (clothing and the like), expenses and a travel ticket. She went to Australia and joined him in his house that he had furnished to be their marital home.

The wife's response began with the following sentence:

> The fourteen-year-old could not disobey her parents when they married her off to a person she did not know and lived in Australia.

In one particular incident told me by an old woman of the *Ajaweed* strata[36] who used to work with her son as a cleaning lady in a school, the extremely traditional nature of wedding in the early 1900s was made very clear to me. The woman had not laid eyes on her husband before the wedding night and was even tricked into marrying him. When his family visited her family to propose, they brought a picture they said was of their son. The woman's father showed her the black and white photograph and told her that since they belonged to a good family and were *Ajaweed* he agreed to the marriage. She consented to her father's wishes and the marriage contract was signed in the absence of the husband who was said to be travelling abroad. The man's father had legal right of proxy and signed on behalf of his son. The woman said that in those days, weddings were not elaborate and when the husband was from a distant area only a few family members would come on the wedding day to take the wife, especially as the journey was made by horse or donkey. Since both husband and wife belonged to the *Ajaweed* strata the husband, as is still customary today, did not accompany his family but waited in his house for his bride to be brought to him. The woman accompanied her husband's family on the journey, and when she met her husband she was horrified. She discovered that they had shown her the picture of his brother and that her husband's face and body was totally mutilated from having been accidentally burned as a child. She cried and objected but could do nothing. She did not have any of her family members with her and she had accompanied strangers on a long journey which jeopardized her honour. To return to her father's house would have been inconceivable and she was forced to accept her situation. When she told me her life story, she was quite old, and her son was in his mid 50s.

The questionnaire also asked: Why do you think that a marriage contract is written before the real marriage? Most of the 125 respondents chose one of two responses: 47 thought that a marriage contract allows betrothed individuals more freedom to go out together and 50 answered that the reason might be related to the fact that there would be less criticism from neighbours and kin when a stranger was seen entering the woman's house. Both responses reveal that the Druze have remained a traditional society in which family matters are highly scrutinized and controlled. One does not expect such practices to have continued in our own times yet, as a member of this community, I cannot help but notice how rapidly engagements and marriages are arranged.

One educated, university graduate, 23 years old, a career woman of the *Ajaweed* strata who lived in the town of Aley, became engaged to a *Sheikh* from a village in South Lebanon only one month after he began visiting her home. They were married two months after their engagement. This woman left her job and willingly moved a long distance away from her parents after marrying a man she had only met three months before. Her comment to me was, 'It is normal. I will get to know him after we marry. He cannot keep coming to our house without us marrying. It just is not right.' Such behaviour is not considered out of the ordinary, although it is more common among the religious group of the *Ajaweed* than among the non-religious.[37]

One cannot help but notice some changes that are already happening. For example, more unmarried women are travelling to find work in the Arab countries. It is true that they normally live with brothers, uncles or aunts, yet, the mere fact that some are allowed to travel on their own is in itself, an indicator of change. Of course, such behaviour is not accepted by everyone, and it is often accompanied by explanations and justifications on the part of the parents and rejection and criticism from relatives. Yet, it seems that the economic factor is indeed influencing the community and prompting change, as the following case reveals.

A female aged 25 left Lebanon to work in Dubai in 2001. Her father was already working there and she lived with him and was later joined by her mother. She found work as a salesperson. She and her family wanted to improve their standard of living and started taking loans to cover the expenses of building a house in their home village in Lebanon. After a while, the father was laid off and was forced to return to Lebanon with his wife. The young woman had to stay on in Dubai alone because she was the only member of the family in work and had to continue to meet the loan repayments. After a couple of months, she too was laid off. Returning to Lebanon was not an option as she had a lot of payments to make, so she applied for a job in Qatar, was accepted and moved to a new country all by herself.

Such experiences, though not yet the norm among the Druze of Lebanon, are definitely becoming more common. Many people in the Druze community do not agree with such behaviour and the elderly denounce it as dishonourable. As one old man in his seventies pointed out to me sarcastically, 'She might as well take up the role of a male and have relations out of wedlock. Who will ever consider her a suitable wife for his son?' Not all Druze react in such a strong manner, however. One woman exclaimed, 'I admire her for the support she is showing towards her parents. But, her parents will die one day and she'll be left all alone. She has not married yet and most likely will not marry in the near future, not until she pays back all the loans. By then she will be over thirty-five and will not be able to find a good husband, if any at all. Pity!'. Even among those who do not perceive the fact that of a girl living alone in a different country as something dishonourable, the reaction is most often one of pity, pointing out the oddity of such behaviour.

Concluding Remarks

The research on divorce revealed that the Druze avoid conflict whenever possible. They consider that the internal affairs of the family belong to the private domain and should be dealt with accordingly, and this was reflected in the overall preference for divorce in consent. A practice that, statistically speaking, remained constant over a period of 33 years. Even when battered women were able to put an end to their plight without the intervention of agencies outside the family, they did so. Court intervention, to these women, was a last resort which is a reflection of desire by the women and family members alike to resolve all conflicts within the family. In general, battered women are pressured by family members and are made to feel as if 'the intervention of law into the inner working of the family . . . is generally experienced as a humiliating experience' (Engle Merry, 2003: 378). Women who in fact take the matter outside the boundaries of the family and approach the court find themselves forced to deal with public humiliation, which as the research revealed, women were not comfortable with. Divorce in itself is viewed as stigmatizing within the community and the further attraction of public attention is not something victims of household violence welcome, since they know that their own morality and value as wives and mothers are being questioned, publically scrutinized and analyzed. The same kind of concern was found by Osanloo (2009) in Iran. 'Indeed the concern with a perception of moral depravity was a major factor that troubled women who got involved in legal issues surrounding private and family matters' (Osanloo, 2009: 145). This concern with how others will perceive their behaviour forces women to hesitate before they approach the court. They only do so when they have the support of other family members such as fathers, brothers and, in some cases, children. Avoidance of public conflict was mirrored in the divorce practices among the Druze which can be seen to be a reflection of the core Druze values of group unity and solidarity.

The concern with group unity and solidarity was further reflected in the judge's decisions and the procedures taken in court. When a divorce case is brought to court the judge imposes several procedures to attempt to avoid the further escalation of the conflict. Court appointed adjudicators, family members, social workers and psychologists were utilized to resolve the conflict. The judge had been forced to impose a sentence on the contesting parties in a small percentage of the cases. This practice had also continued to be dominant during the 33 years under study.

Continuity of various practices related to divorce was evident in the research, but various aspects of the divorce processes witnessed some change. These changes that were observed reflected the socio-economical changes that had occurred in Lebanon during the period understudy. This change may be mostly reflected in the domain of gender, whereby women's increased participation in the labour force transformed their status from non-productive consumers within the house to industrious producer outside the house. This gained economic advantage gave women leverage and an increased ability to negotiate their rights within divorce. More women were asking for custody and visitation rights. In many instances they were able to use their economical productivity to settle these issues with their husbands – forgoing their *mahr* in return for longer custody periods. A change in the judge's sentences related to giving women their rights have also accompanied this change which, if not conclusively, nonetheless, reflects a change in the perception of women by the legal-religious authority, an indicator of change in some values in the community.

To conclude, continuity and change were concurrently observed in the study of divorce. Both were in line with the core values of solidarity and group preservation that are crucial to the Druze community. Continuity of practices reflect the desire of the older generation and the religious strata in the community for a maintenance of traditions that had worked out well for the Druze over a long period of time At the same time, socio-economic changes impose themselves on the community bringing about change, especially among the youth.

CHAPTER 5

MARRIAGE AND DIVORCE: A COMPARATIVE APPROACH

The two social phenomena, marriage and divorce, are among the most important aspect of family life in any society – but at opposite extremes in that marriage begins the process of forming a family whereas divorce marks the breakdown of family life. That is why, to understand fully many aspects of divorce, such as rates of divorce and social trends, it is helpful to compare them similar to factors related to marriage.

Divorce Rates

There are various ways of calculating divorce rates. Some social analysts do so by comparing the number of divorces each year against the number of people of marriage age in a certain population. In the case of Lebanon, this method cannot be applied because there is no recent population census.[1]

Some others simply look at the number of divorces every year and compare the number in one year against the number in another year to assess if there has been an increase or a decrease. A major drawback to this method is that, since it does not account for demographic changes such as population rise and other variables, it produces misleading results. If this method had been utilized in this research it would have led one to jump to the conclusion that divorce has increased among the Lebanese Druze since there were only six divorces in 1970 and 50 divorces in 2003. Such an assumption would be totally false since the number of divorces alone is taken as indicative of the rate of divorce without taking into consideration any other variables related to the nature of the population under study. For example, ten divorces in a village of 500 people are much more indicative of a high/low rate of divorce than ten divorces in a city of 10,000 people.

A third way of analyzing divorce rates is to compare the number of divorces each year against the number of marriages in the same year. This is the method most social analysts employ since it yields results that are as close as possible to the actual reality. Moreover, this method has the advantage of freeing the researcher from the need to rely on a headcount or population census. Utilizing this method in the current research, and taking the two time-intervals 1970–74 and 2000–03 as focal points for comparison, the following results are reached:

1. Rate of divorce in 1970–74=
$$\frac{\text{\# of divorces}}{\text{\# of marriages}} = \frac{84}{75} = 1.12$$
2. Rate of divorce in 2000–03=
$$\frac{\text{\# of divorces}}{\text{\# of marriages}} = \frac{169}{533} = 0.32$$

In other words, for every marriage contracted in 1970–74, there were 1.12 divorces, whereas for every marriage contracted in 2000–03, there were 0.32 divorces. This result would lead to the conclusion that the rates of divorce had decreased rather than increased as most people assume. However, although objectively arrived at, this rate still remains largely misleading since the number of marriages contracted in the 1970s only is compared against the number of divorces in the 1970s; no allowance is made for marriages contracted before the 1970s that ended in this decade. Since the date of the marriage is entered on all the available court records of divorce cases, it was thought that the study would better represent the social reality of the Druze if the date of marriage of divorcing individuals were controlled and limited to marriages concluded between 1970 and 2003, to match the dates of the marriage contracts studied in the part of the research that concerned marriage. While acknowledging that a marriage contracted in 1970 might end up being dissolved in 1990, it was felt that this method of comparison would produce a rate of divorce that reflected more accurately the reality of the Druzes' situation. Table 5.1 represents a summary of the number of marriage contracts and the number of divorce cases (of people who had married from 1970 to 2003) in the sample under study.

The rates reported in the table may be considered, statistically speaking, the most accurate reflection of the actual divorce rates among the Druze under the jurisdiction of the Beirut court. A number of important findings are contained in this table, but before discussing them it is important to draw attention to the very high rate reported for the 1975–79 time-interval. This was 1.92, meaning that for every marriage contract signed in that period there were 1.92 divorces. Such an extraordinarily high rate could not be an actual representation of the social reality of the Druze people especially if we bear in mind that the next highest reported rate during the entire 33 years under study was 0.37 during the 1985–89 time-interval.

A reasonable explanation for the high rate recorded in 1975–79 is that the Lebanese war had started one year before and consequently a very small number of marriages took place during that period, and since the divorce rates were calculated out of the marriages, the result was distorted. The disruptions of the war made it more arduous and dangerous for people to travel to the court in Beirut, as the Druze are required to do to get married. During the war, marriages could be

Table 5.1 Rates of Divorce by Five-Year Intervals

	70–74	75–79	80–84	85–89	90–94	95–99	00–03[2]	Total
Marriage Contracts	75	27	152	132	1114	953	533	2986
Divorce Cases	21	52	55	49	132	190	156	655
Divorce Rates	0.28	1.92	0.36	0.37	0.12	0.19	0.29	0.22

contracted in whichever court was easiest to reach and as people in the Matn and the Chouf areas, normally under the jurisdiction of the Beirut court, could get married in any other court; it can be safely assumed they were married in places such as Aley or Baáqlin. With divorce, the case was a little different. It is true that people's safety was similarly at risk; however, unlike a marriage, a divorce could not be moved to another court. Moreover, with a divorce case it is enough for only the lawyer or the individual making the claim to appear before the judge, whereas marriages require the presence of four witnesses in addition to the couple getting married, and the bride's guardian if under 21. In addition, the signing of a marriage contract is a time of celebration and several family members are usually invited, adding to the number of those putting themselves in danger. All these factors contributed, in one way or another, to decreasing the number of marriages during that period and thus increasing the divorce rate disproportionately.

One particularly interesting finding with regard to the rates of divorce reported in this table concerns those at the beginning and the end of the study. These rates are almost the same. The rate of divorce during 1970–74 was 0.28 compared to 0.29 during 2000–03. If one were to compare only the rates of divorce in these two time-intervals, one would reach the inevitable conclusion that the rates had remained stable over a period of three decades. However, this would be totally misleading since the rates witnessed fluctuations in the intervening periods.

Going back to the analysis of the different rates reported in Table 5.1, one finds that the overall rate of divorce over the whole 33 years was 0.22. The rates fell and rose over the different time-intervals. The lowest rates reported were in the 1990s, falling as low as 0.12 in 1990–94 and 0.19 in 1995–99. Such low rates are explained in terms of the socio-political and demographic nature of Lebanon as a whole and of the Druze people in particular. That 1990–95 time-interval, directly following the end of the Lebanese civil war, was distinguished by a huge return of immigrants from abroad. For the Druze at least, this meant a large influx of immigrant men coming back to the country to find a bride. This had the direct effect of reducing the rate of divorce sharply, simply because the number of marriages increased substantially. The fact is that the number of divorces (132) exceeded the number of divorces in any earlier time interval; however, the determining factor in the decreased divorce rate was the considerable increase in the number of marriages (1,114) during that period, a phenomenon directly related to the end of the civil war.

Another reason might have to do with the fact that it was during the 1990s that obligatory military service was imposed on all males of 18 and one way of avoiding it was to get married since a married man is not compelled to serve in the army. Many young Druze males did just that and got married to escape military service. This ultimately caused quite a sharp decline in the rate of divorce, bringing it down to an average of 0.15 by the second half of the decade.

The above analysis shows that the divorce rate among the Druze has not remained stable over the three decades under study and it is possible to point to fluctuations related to the civil war, its ending and other factors. However, these rates must remain tentative since no one can measure the divorce rate with any degree of certainty without a proper population census, which is not available in Lebanon.

Marriage and Divorce: A Comparison

As well as calculating the rate of divorce, the comparison of marriage contracts against divorce cases also served to disclose any general trends that might act as determinants of divorce or pointers to a higher probability of divorce. Among such pointers were the spouses' age at marriage, the age difference between them, the place of residence of each and their familial relationship, if any. To analyze these factors, the whole sample of marriage contracts was included and tested as a single entity against which to compare the divorce cases. This was found to be the most appropriate statistical method to use as time or change across time was not a variable in this analysis. The aim was to investigate the percentages across the whole sample and check to see if they reflected any patterns that could act as indicators of divorce. As in the previous analysis, only divorce cases of individuals who had married between 1970 and 2003 were included.

Age at Marriage: Marriage vs. Divorce

a. Husband's Age

The preferred marriage age for males throughout the entire period of the sample was from 25 to 34 years, noticeably increasing over the passage of time. The question to be asked in this part of the research is whether the age at marriage for husbands is a determining factor in divorce. In other words, is the age at which a male marries a variable that would determine the likelihood of divorce?

In order to answer this question the ages of husbands who signed marriage contracts in the Beirut court from 1970 to 2003 were compared against the ages of husbands named in divorce cases over the same period. It is important to point out that in certain cases – particularly divorce cases – the date of birth of the husband was missing and thus his age could not be calculated. These cases were excluded from the findings, which explain the discrepancy in numbers between the reported findings in Table 5.2 and the overall number of cases in the whole sample.

The percentages in Table 5.2 clearly reveal a direct relationship between the husband's age at marriage and the incidence of divorce. It was found that 635 (21.3 per cent) of males married between 1970 and 2003 were aged 26 or less. On the other hand, out of the whole sample of divorces during the same 33 years, the percentage of males who had married before the age of 26 was 35.7 per cent. If we compare the two percentages, we find that the percentage of males married before they were 26 was lower (by 14.4 per cent) than the percentage of those from

Table 5.2 Husband's Age by Year-Intervals in Marriage Contracts and Divorce Cases

	Less than 25 years	**26–34 years**	**34–45 years**	**More than 46 years**
Marriage contracts	635 21.3%	1575 52.9%	579 19.4%	191 6.4%
Divorce cases	295 35.7%	375 45.4%	106 12.8%	50 6.1%

the same age group whose marriages ended in divorce. This being the case, there is an increased probability of divorce for a man who marries before the age of 26. Among men who married after the age of 26, the probability of divorce decreases, since the percentage of divorces is lower than that of marriages. The percentage of divorces among men who married at the age of 26 to 34 was 7.5 per cent lower than the percentage of males marrying in that age group over the whole 33-year period. The same result, but with a difference of 6.6 per cent, was reported among males marrying at the age of 34 to 45. The only age group for which equal percentages of marriages and divorces were reported was those who married over the age of 46.

To conclude, the probability of divorce among males marrying before the age of 26 was higher than for other age groups. Among males marrying after the age of 26 the probability of divorce was very small and it was more likely that these individuals would stay married. In this analysis, the age at which males married could serve as an indicator of divorce.

A possible explanation for the above finding may have to do with their financial situation. Young men before the age of 26 are generally not well off, and if the husband is unable to support his wife adequately it may lead to friction and the escalation of conflict between the couple. This variable, the inability to support a wife, was mentioned in several divorce cases.

In one such case, the husband was 22 years old and the wife 16 when they married in 1977. In 1990, the wife petitioned for divorce. The named cause for divorce was the husband's way of life: he was a drug addict and an alcoholic. During the civil war he had belonged to a militia and taken part in fighting. He had been imprisoned for killing three men, a crime that was not pardoned under the general amnesty law passed at the end of the civil war in Lebanon. The men he had killed had been farmers working in the fields and not soldiers or other militia men and because the killings had not been committed in combat the children of the deceased had filed charges against him. In her claim, the wife said that he had never provided for her or for the children. Her own father rented a house for her and her three children, two boys and a girl, and used to give her money. Her husband was never able to find a job and used to spend the money he got from the militia on drugs and alcohol. She had not filed for divorce before because she was afraid of him. They came from the same village and people kept telling her to be patient for the sake of the children – even her parents. After the civil war ended, she filed for divorce since he refused to take his family responsibilities seriously.

Another case, brought before the court during the war in 1986, also pointed to the relationship between early marriage and the husband's failure to provide for his family – the couple had married in 1978 when the husband was 20 years old and the wife 18. The wife cited her husband's inability or refusal to provide a house of her own as the main cause for divorce. In her petition, made through a lawyer, she said she had accepted they were hard-up and that they and their children had to share a house with ten other people, her husband's family and the family of his uncle. All through her marriage, she did not even have a separate room she could call her own. She used to put mattresses on the floor of the living room and sleep there with her children. Her husband would leave her in these living conditions and travel abroad to work. She was left at the mercy of his mother and relatives who treated her like a servant. She hoped things would change but whenever he returned from abroad, and whenever she complained, he would beat her, as would his sister who was also living with them. She put up with everything for the sake of her children, hoping her husband would change with time. Her husband's sister took away her jewellery and both her husband and his sister would beat her when she asked for it. When she asked for a separate residence, she was told by her husband to go back to her parents. She insisted she was willing to remain married to him but only if he provided a separate residence. He was unable to do so and the judge pronounced a divorce.

In some cases, there may be psychological reasons for the failure of an early marriage, such as the immaturity of the husband. He may be over-dependent on his family, allowing his parents, siblings, or other family members to interfere and meddle in the couple's life together, often cited as a cause of conflict and irreconcilable differences in divorces.

One couple had married in 1993 when both were 21 years old. The wife petitioned for divorce in 1999 through a lawyer. She said she had met her husband while he was working in Beirut in a hotel owned by her father. He was in good physical shape but did not have a degree. She had a hearing impairment but was well educated; she had studied in France and could lip-read. She, too, was working in the hotel when they met. He was able to convince her that he loved her but her parents opposed the marriage because he was not able to support their daughter. So he kidnapped her. Her parents soon discovered them but he had already forced himself on her and she was no longer a virgin. They found her crying and in a miserable condition so they had to agree to a settlement.[3] A marriage contract was signed and the husband took his wife to live with his parents on the roof of a building where his father worked as a janitor. She had to sleep on the floor. He did not care about his wife and would spend the money he made from his work in a jewellery shop on physical fitness clubs and muscle-building aids. He kept telling his wife to get money from her parents. After a while, her father took pity on her and rented a furnished apartment for the couple but the husband became abusive towards her, beating her and forcing her to get money from her parents even after their son was born. She hid the beatings from her parents as she was afraid they would stop giving her money. However, after one beating she needed medical care but left on her own in the apartment, she was forced to call her mother for help and so her parents learned of her ordeal. She refused to leave him because she knew he would take her son away but finally he demanded she moved to his village to live in his father's house and then told her he was keeping his job in Beirut and would only visit her at weekends. He issued an ultimatum – either that or divorce. Unable to live apart from her parents, she filed for divorce. The psychological immaturity of the husband was evident in his readiness to spend the money he earned on physical fitness clubs rather than his family.

Psychological immaturity was mentioned in several other cases where the husband was quite young at the time of marriage, and this was especially so when the court had called upon a psychiatrist's services. For example, the psychiatrist's report in a case brought before the court in 1995 drew particular attention to the husband's immaturity.

The couple had married in 1986 when husband was 21 and the wife was 15. She petitioned for divorce on the grounds that her husband was not providing for her and treated her inhumanely. The case documents revealed that for the first five years of their marriage they lived with his parents in Saudi Arabia. Throughout that time, he did not have a permanent job and showed no desire to find one in order to change their living circumstances and end their dependency on his parents. She claimed that she put up with it because she did not want to be labelled by society as a divorcee. When they all returned to Lebanon, she was forced to continue living with his parents but then their economic position changed and they could no longer afford to keep their son's family. So her husband returned alone to Saudi Arabia leaving her with their two children at his parent's house and had not asked about her since. Then, one month before she filed for divorce, he returned from Saudi Arabia and ordered her to return to her parent's house.

Asked to intervene in the case by the judge, the psychiatrist's report said:

> Despite the fact that he is currently 31 years old he is still immature in his behaviour. He does not take his responsibilities towards his family seriously. He did not pay his children's tuition fees at school and only did so when his children were expelled from school and suffered public humiliation. He constantly asks for his parent's opinion on everything and his mother wants to keep an upper hand in all matters and he allows her to do so. He also admitted to beating his wife twice and their sexual relationship is also abnormal. He forces her to have illegitimate sexual practices (anal) when she is menstruating. His parents insulted her in my office and he did not answer them or tell them to stop.

The judge acknowledged that the husband's behaviour was immature and that he was unduly dependent on his parents by pronouncing a fault divorce and ordering the husband to pay his wife a sum of money for the harm and injury he had caused her.

b. Wife's Age

The same analysis of marriage contracts and divorce cases was carried out with respect to the wife's age at marriage and the results reported in Table 5.3.

The data revealed that the percentage of divorces among women who had married before the age of 17 was 27.3 per cent, far exceeding the 10.3 per cent of women who married before the age of 17 during the entire period under study. This difference of 17.0 per cent is very significant and indicates a high probability of divorce among females who married at this age. The same tendency was reported among females who married between the ages of 18 and 20: the percentage of divorces in this group was 25.9 per cent compared with 19.6 per cent of women marrying at this age over the entire period. Though not as high as for the previous group, the difference of 6.3 per cent is still a significant indicator of divorce.

The above findings were reversed when it came to the marriage of women after the age of twenty especially in the 26–30 age group where the percentage of divorces (8.5 per cent) is less than half the percentage of marriages among that age group (19.6 per cent). In other words, the likelihood of a successful marriage, or at least a marriage that does not end in divorce, is rather high for females who marry between the age of 26 and 30, but falls again slightly for woman who marry after 30.

In conclusion, and only for the 33 of the study, the research revealed that the age at which a woman marries is an indicator of the probability

Table 5.3 Wife's Age by Year-Intervals in Both Marriage Contracts and Divorce Cases

	Less than 17 years	18–20 years	21–25 years	26–30 years	More than 30
Marriage contracts	306 10.3%	585 19.6%	1047 35.1%	583 19.6%	461 15.4%
Divorce cases	225 27.3%	214 25.9%	211 25.6%	70 8.5%	105 12.7%

of divorce. Women married before the age of 20 are more likely to divorce than those married after the age of 20. Of course, this is a tentative conclusion only, since divorces may still occur and influence the findings for different age groups. However, it stands correct for the sample under study at the time of the research.

The high number of divorces among women who married at an early age may arise from their immaturity and lack of understanding of what married life entailed. One divorced woman, now in her late thirties, said she was just 16 years old when she married, adding that at that age she did not know what was expected of her:

> I believed I was playing a game of *bayt byout.*[4] I did not even expect the sexual encounter. My mother had not explained anything to me. I was ignorant. My husband explained to me what sex was. I remember that I cried all night. I was just a child and did not know what it meant to get married. It was horrible. Then, his mother and sisters kept interfering and would turn my husband against me if they did not like what I said, wore or even cooked. He used to listen to them and would hit me when I complained. He was 20 years older and I was afraid of him. I could not think of divorce and my parents kept telling me that I had to try not to annoy him. After my third child was born, I could take it no more. I left him but took my two daughters with me.[5] I should not have married at such an early age. If I was older, I would have been able to stand up to his mother and sisters but as a child I did not know what to do or how to behave.

Similar experiences were reported in several divorce cases brought before the court. In one such case, the husband was 32 and the wife was 15 when they married in 1977. In her petition for divorce ten years later, the wife said that the marriage had actually taken place when she was 14 years old and they had waited until she was 15 to officially register the marriage in court.[6] She was half his age but considered marriage as *sotra* (protecting a girl's honour, from the Arabic term *satr* which means to cover the nakedness of the body) and agreed to the marriage one month after they met. As soon as they married, her torments began, caused by his stinginess. When she asked for more money and support he would react by beating and verbally abusing her and she was forced to run away from him on several occasions. She was always made to return by her parents or other relatives who told her to be patient. On one occasion he actually kicked her out of the house because she had given birth to a baby girl, as if she was able to control the sex of the child. On another occasion, her jewellery was stolen from their house and he accused her and her parents of taking it. When he later discovered that one of his own relatives was the thief, he asked her to return. On a third occasion he refused to pay the medical costs of surgery she had to undergo.

The fact that this woman was so young at the time of her marriage made her incapable of standing up to an abusive husband. In another case, a vulnerable 14-year-old wife had been psychologically abused and manipulated by her husband's family. Because the wife was under age, the couple had been forced to delay registering the marriage at the court for a year.[7] The husband, who was 26 at the time, filed for divorce in 1998, after ten years of marriage, claiming that his wife had behaved in such a way as to make their life as husband and wife impossible. The wife stated that when she had married she thought her life would be happy and good. However, her husband took her to live in a very small house next to his parents' and brother's house. He promised her that this arrangement was only temporary until he could build a larger house, but he did not. She was expected to do all the housework for both residences and to clean and cook for all the family. Her life became very hard and when she found she was physically unable to do all the work she told her husband that she wanted to stop – she was married to him alone and should only have to look after her house. Her in-laws were not happy with her complaints and started to plot against her, accusing her falsely of having an extramarital affair. A workman used to come to her house to take water from a tap. She knew that his brother would think the worst of her if he saw the man at her door and so she asked her husband to tell him to stop coming. One day, the man came to fill up with water just as she heard her brother-in-law coming down the stairs of his house next door. Being young and foolish, she asked the man inside and locked the door. The brother found out that the man had gone into her house and told her husband that she was having an affair.

The court investigation proved these allegations to be false. The psychiatrist was asked to intervene and was able to convince the husband that he should ignore his own brother and trust his wife. In her report the psychiatrist claimed that the wife was being manipulated by her in-laws due to her inexperience and had fallen victim to 'psychological trickery'. The husband later gave in to his parents and insisted on the divorce.

Age Difference: Marriage vs. Divorce

The study revealed that in the majority of Druze marriages registered at the Beirut court between 1970 and 2003 the difference in age between husband and wife was 6–10 years, with reported changes over time. To discover whether age had a determining influence on divorce, the percentages for the various age-difference intervals reported in the marriage contracts were compared with the age differences recorded in the divorce cases over the 33 years of the study, as shown in Table 5.4.

The table revealed that the percentages reported for both marriage contracts and divorce cases were almost the same in all age-difference intervals. This implies that the age difference between the husband and the wife was not a strong determinant of divorce and among the

Table 5.4 Spouses' Age Differences in Marriage Contracts and Divorce Cases

	Less than 1	Less than 2	3–5 years	6–8 years	9–10 years	11–15 years	More than 15
Marriage contracts	12.4%	12.9%	18.3%	18.7%	11.3%	17.7%	8.7%
Divorce Cases	12.1%	13.1%	16.9%	15.7%	11.7%	19.4%	11.1%

Druze it was not as important an indicator of divorce as the age of the spouses at marriage. In fact, in the Arab world in general a somewhat large age difference – say, of more than ten years – is not considered unusual. For example, one young man of 23 who had recently graduated from university told me that he wanted to marry someone who was at least ten years younger than he was. His reason was that women age faster than men physically, and he wanted his wife to look young when he is 40 or 50. Because a large age difference is readily accepted among the Druze, as a variable it did not stand as a strong indicator of divorce. Yet this does not mean that people do not divorce because of age difference, as the following case indicates.

The woman was 15 years old and the man 37 when they married in 1968. The case was brought before the court in 1972. The substantial age difference of 22 years came up in the court proceedings. The wife's petition said that the husband's family had tricked a 15-year-old girl into marrying an older man. He made her live in the same house with his mother. They had a son in 1970. Right from the start of the marriage the husband and his mother constantly abused the wife by calling her a maid. They would beat her when she dared to ask them to stop. He would return home at five o'clock in the morning heavily drunk and would beat her if she questioned him. On one occasion she left the house after he had beaten her, but her mother asked her to return to her husband and to be patient to try to avoid divorce. However, his behaviour and his mother's behaviour gave her no choice.

In another case, the actual cause for divorce was directly related to the large age difference. The husband, who at 35 years of age was 17 years older than his 18-year-old wife, was very jealous and his jealousy made him behave irrationally, forcing her to file for divorce after only five months of marriage, in 1972. They were from the same village and belonged to the same patriarchal family. In her petition, through a lawyer, the wife claimed that the husband's mean and violent behaviour and recent threats of murder made life impossible. She asked for divorce as her husband kept claiming that 'his temper was beyond his control'. The husband said that he loved his wife and did not want to divorce her, adding that her parents were poisoning her mind against him. The wife then responded with a further statement that clarified the real cause behind her divorce. She wrote:

> I hereby present the most important causes of disagreement between my husband and myself. On our wedding night, he yelled at me because he claimed that I had not closed the curtains of the hotel room in which we were staying and that the fishermen at sea would be able to see me. He keeps accusing me of flirting with various men including the policeman in the village, the pharmacist, his own nephews, my cousins... and he even forbade me from greeting my relatives by kissing them on the cheeks – even my two-year-old little brother. He does not allow me to open any window in the house. He pulled me by my hair when I greeted my sister's fiancé. He puts sand on the threshold to check for footprints when he returns from work.

She went on to name several other incidents and concluded that his jealousy was unbearable and she wanted a divorce accordingly. The husband continued to insist that he only loved his wife a lot but the divorce was granted as the wife was determined on it.

Place of Residence: Marriage vs. Divorce

There is a general belief among Arabs in general and the Lebanese Druze in particular that to marry within one's village is a guarantee against divorce. Because husband and wife share a similar social background they are less likely to disagree or have conflicts related to the other person's way of life or customs that may lead to divorce. To study whether this was indeed the case, the percentages of spouses coming from the same place and whose marriages ended in divorce was compared against the percentage of spouses coming from the same place in the total sample of marriage contracts registered at the Beirut court. For the purpose of the analysis, the places of residence were categorized as: 1) Same place of residence; 2) Neighbouring places of residence; 3) Different places of residence.

Table 5.5 Percentages of Spouses Coming from the Same, Neighbouring or Different Places of Residence in Marriage Contracts and Divorce Cases

	Same Place	Neighbouring Places	Different Places
Marriage Contracts	25.5%	8.5%	66.0%
Divorce Cases	26.9%	8.6%	64.5%

Table 5.5 shows that the percentages in all three categories were almost the same with regard to marriage contracts and divorce cases over the whole 33 years of the study. In particular, 25.5 per cent of spouses who married between 1970 and 2003 came from the same village, town or city compared to 26.9 per cent of divorces among spouses who came from the same place.

From this we may safely conclude that the fact that husband and wife are from the same village has no bearing on the durability of their marriage. Spouses from the same village, town or city were as likely to divorce as those from different residential areas.

Husband-Wife Relationship: Marriage vs. Divorce

a. Spouses of the Same Patriarchal Family

A widely-held belief among the Lebanese Druze is that if a person marries someone from the same patriarchal family, the likelihood of a divorce diminishes, the assumption being that people who are related through the paternal line are more likely to tolerate each other. The extended patriarchal family acts as a buffer to prevent any conflicts between the two from escalating. To assess whether this assumption was correct or not, the following analysis was carried out: the percentage of spouses coming from the same patriarchal family who married during the 33 years of the research was compared against the percentage of spouses divorced during the same period who also belonged to same patriarchal family.

Table 5.6 shows that the percentages reported in the overall marriage contracts and divorce cases covered in the study were comparable: 17.6

Table 5.6 Percentage of Patriarchally-Related Spouses in Marriage Contracts and Divorce Cases

	Patriarchally related	Not related patriarchally
Marriage Contracts	525 17.6%	2461 82.4%
Divorce Cases	150 18.2%	676 81.8%

per cent of spouses named in marriage contracts were from the same patriarchal family as were 18.2 per cent of spouses who divorced. This indicates that the fact that the spouses belonged to the same patriarchal family did not increase or decrease the likelihood of divorce. The research on marriage, as noted earlier, in fact revealed a decline in the number of marriages between patrilineal cousins among the Druze.

b. Maternally Related Spouses

One of the most common practices when it comes to seeking out a wife for a Lebanese Druze man is for the choice to fall upon a daughter of his mother's sister (that is, his aunt); in other words, the couple is maternal cousins. Such marriages are highly encouraged by mothers who feel that their daughter-in-law will not pose a threat to the unity of her family members. Old Druze women negotiating the marriage of her son to her sister's daughter are often heard saying things like 'At least, that way I'll be sure my daughters will always be welcomed at their brother's house'. They also generally believe that a person's maternal cousin will help the household in bad times and good and not cause conflict within the family. Such marriages are believed to be durable. To assess whether this is the case, the percentage of males married to a maternal relative in the 33-year study was compared against the percentage of males married to maternal relatives who divorced in the same period.

The findings shown in Table 5.7 would seem to indicate that marriage to a maternally-related spouse plays a strong role in maintaining the marriage and renders it more durable. It was found that

Table 5.7 Percentages of Maternally-Related Spouses Reported in Marriage Contracts and Divorce Cases

	Maternally related	Not related maternally
Marriage contracts	711 23.8%	2275 76.2%
Divorce cases	111 13.6%	707 86.4%

divorces among maternally-related spouses represented 13.6 per cent of the total number of divorces and that maternally-related marriages represented 23.8 per cent of all the marriages concluded during the same period. The fact that the percentage of marriages exceeds that of divorces suggests that maternal cousins are less likely to divorce; however, it should not be taken to mean that spouses who are maternally related do not have marriage conflicts. Rather, the maternal relationship ensures that these conflicts are not allowed to escalate into a divorce as the following case study illustrates:

Sami and Dana are maternal cousins – their mothers are sisters. The two families agreed to the marriage when Sami was 20 and Dana was 18. Sami carried on with his education after they were married but Dana had to give hers up as she had two children in quick succession and was busy with them. The two have been married for over twenty years but Dana claims that being married to a maternal cousin is not easy. She says:

> Having an aunt as a mother-in-law is not helpful. She does not appreciate me and keeps nagging Sami about me. No matter what I say or do, his mother is always right. She is my aunt so I cannot say anything bad about her. I cannot even tell my mom when I am upset with my mother in law. She is her sister and would not accept it. Once I had a disagreement with my aunt and my parents knew. They told me to apologize to my aunt and not to create problems in the family. It is hard when, as a female, you cannot rely on your parents for support.

When I asked her if she considered that being married to a paternal cousin was as hard, she answered:

> Not at all. It is true that fathers and uncles would not want any conflict within the family but at least the girl would have the support of her mother. She can rely on her to interfere on her behalf. It is much easier to be married to a paternal cousin than a maternal one.

Limitations of the Comparative Study

Certain aspects of the process of divorce within a particular community cannot be fully understood without making a comparison of marriage and divorce rates. It is true that, due to their ever-changing nature, any attempt to compare social relationships such as marriage and divorce will always have limitations. However, what this comparative study has attempted to do is give an overview that reflects as much as possible the family life and social structure of the Lebanese Druze as revealed in their marriage and divorce rates. The rates used in this study were those for the Druze falling under the jurisdiction of the Beirut court over the 33 years of the research, and while they may point to overall trends among the Druze, the research in no way claims to be descriptive of all Druze everywhere and at all times. Of course one is entitled to project upon the findings, but it is always wise to be cautious in such an attempt since comparative research is always subject to factors that may change with time.

Another limitation is directly related to the political make-up of Lebanon. Leaving aside the civil war which limited access to the court during particular periods of time, the confessional nature of Lebanon's political make-up reflects negatively on any attempt to carry out statistical analysis of rates or trends relating to the population. There is no recent census in Lebanon and a population count is not available. Since the war and the return of parliamentary elections, the Ministry of the Interior has been trying to compile some data regarding those who are eligible to vote; that is, everyone over the age of 21. These numbers are not very helpful if one wants to apply them to marriage and divorce rates because a Druze male in Lebanon can marry at 18 and a female at 16. Thus any attempt to set the rates included in this chapter against a general population count cannot be accomplished. A population census is not something that any Lebanese government can easily undertake since it is likely to create considerable political tension in the country, with some sects claiming they should be given greater parliamentary representation to reflect the true size of their population. The lack of this option, nevertheless, does not diminish the value of what has been attempted in this chapter, which remains the first study of its kind ever made of the Druze. It is the author's hope that further follow-ups will be done on this topic in the future, when maybe population statistics will be available that better reflect the rates of divorce and divorce trends among the Druze in Lebanon.

CHAPTER SIX

THE DRUZE: PERIPHERAL CHANGE

This research on marriage and divorce among the Druze revealed, through its focus on the way these social practices played out in court and in social interactions, parallel trajectories; one of continuity and the other of change. Certain marriage and divorce practices remained remarkably static over a period of 33 years from 1970 to 2003. However, these same years witnessed various social, political and economical changes that influenced both Lebanese society and the Druze community. These changes left an impact on Druze family life, bringing about an alteration in the way marriage and divorce are conducted.

Continuity of certain customs was quite evident in the research findings. A highly conventional aspect of marriage that continued to be observed almost unchanged throughout the 33 years under study was the naming of a sewing machine and bedroom furniture in the dowry specifications of marriage contracts. Similarly, the research on divorce also revealed a high degree of consistency in practices across time; for example, the percentages of divorces that ended in an out of court settlement remained the same, as did the percentages of women who petitioned the court for divorce.

At the same time, the study revealed considerable change with regard both to marriage and divorce in the behavioural patterns of the Druze. Marriage from within the same family decreased significantly. The age of marriage increased for both males and females. Where divorce was concerned, it was observed that women increasingly demanded, and obtained, visitation rights to their children. These developments reflect the socio-economic changes that have shaped Lebanese society in recent decades, and have accordingly modified Druze social practices.

The aim of this study was to examine social change and to understand the nature of the changes that have affected marriage and divorce. Change was observed but so were continuities, and these cannot be explained without reflecting on the values and social make-up of the Druze.[1] In other words, a consideration of the Druze habitus is essential and in particular, their strong belief in freedom, equality and, most of all, the supremacy of the *'Aql*,[2] the mind. For the Druze, the mind is supreme and knowledge is the ultimate aim of all believers. In fact, according to the religion, people reincarnate to gain knowledge and to acquire ultimate wisdom. The supremacy of the *'Aql* is further supported by the Druze emphasis on freedom – both in action, as evidenced in their legal system, and in belief.

Within the legal process, and through the active role the judge performs, freedom of action is emphasized. For example, freedom of action is articulated in the judge's refusal to marry someone unless he hears them give their clear consent. Similarly, when a case of divorce by consent is brought before the judge, he insists on hearing explicitly from both husband and wife that their agreement was given freely and willingly. He also ensures this by stipulating, as is legally required, a period of one month during which the couple may back out of the divorce. On a religious level, freedom is also important. There is no coercion – neither social nor religious. No formal religious behaviour is demanded of the ordinary Druze – there are no structured prayers or any religious obligations (naturally, this does not apply to the religious strata of *Ajaweed*). What is strongly demanded of the individual – and this is the only instance where freedom of choice is not allowed – is that he or she identifies themselves as a Druze. A Druze who fails to do that thereby endangers the sect's internal unity, and will face almost certain social ostracism. It is very easy for the Druze people, as a community, to make someone who, for example, has given their blessing to the marriage of a son or daughter to a non-Druze, feel totally alienated. That person is not invited to weddings and engagement parties. Other Druze people – especially *Ajaweed* – will not visit them, and they are made to feel unwelcome visiting others' houses. The worst blow for those who are ostracized is knowing that no religious *sheikh* will pray at their funeral and that very few people will even consider attending it. Moreover, they will not be granted the religious words of mercy (*Rahma*) upon their death – a stigma passed on to their descendants for generations.[3]

> All we need to recall is that there exist non violent means of coercion which may have the same, or, under certain conditions, even greater effectiveness than the violent ones. Frequently, and in fairly large areas even regularly, the threat of such measures as the exclusion from an organization, or a boycott, or the prospects of magically conditioned advantage or disadvantage in this world, or of reward and punishment in the next, are under certain cultural conditions more effective in producing a certain behaviour than a political apparatus whose coercive functioning is not always predictable with certainty. (Weber, 2005: 57)

So, yes, a Druze is totally free and there is no official religious control – but only if he or she continues to identify themselves as a Druze.

Another important value is that of gender equality, albeit within the limitations imposed by the Druzes' historical presence in the midst of a majority population that does not practice equality. This manifests itself in a legal context in the right of both men and women to petition the court for divorce and in not allowing the husband the right to repudiate his wife. It is also reflected in the fact that women are able to approach the court fully aware of and actively pursuing their legal rights. Nevertheless, equality is not absolute or without boundaries. The boundaries themselves are what define the individual as a Druze. A Druze, whether male or female, enjoys total equality in relation to another Druze but only in as much as he or she 'acts out' their 'Druzeness'. For example, a Druze man who chooses to leave his wife for another woman will be frowned upon by the judge and may be forced to make his wife substantial amends. However, the research made it clear that a Druze man who leaves his wife to marry a non-Druze woman will be highly penalized, not just socially but also legally, and may be viewed as unfit to bring up his children.[4] Once a Druze has jeopardized the internal solidarity of the group he or she is likely to be treated as a second-class citizen, no longer worthy of being a Druze.

Beliefs in reincarnation also define and shape the Druze community. A Druze remains a Druze forever since the soul is 'Druze', not the body, and the soul will reincarnate many times and as a Druze in each life. The choices that one makes in this life shape the outcomes of the next life. Thus a Druze will be held accountable for every deed he or she commits and will have to pay the price for any wrongdoing, not necessarily in this lifetime but during the next life, or the one after. A basic Druze teaching is 'protecting your brother in faith' – *Hofz Al-Ikhwan*[5] – which is understood to mean the obligation to preserve the sect's unity, solidarity and well-being and to readily offer assistance to fellow Druze. If you jeopardize this, you will be held accountable, not just in this life but in future reincarnations. This belief in reincarnation within the sect – a Druze is always born as a Druze – is reflected in the group's practice of endogamy and its rejection of change imposed from outside. The young Druze who feels that many of the traditional practices of the Druze are irrational will not openly question them when in the presence of a religious authority such as the judge of the court, who is a religious *sheikh*. The research showed, for example, that some young Druze considered the mention of sewing machines and bedrooms in the *mahr* as nonsensical, but when confronted with the *sheikh*, they were unable to defend their position and had to give in. It was not simply that he represented the law, it was fact that he combined his legal authority with religious authority that made it very hard for them to question his words. As one young man said, 'We are taught to respect the *Zayy* [i.e. the religious garment worn by a *sheikh*] and as such do not question it.'

Peripheral Change

A Druze is seemingly free to change or adapt any form of behaviour, yet should it come to affecting the sect's internal solidarity, all freedom and elements of choice are set aside. In other words, peripheral change is accepted but any change that touches the structure of the group is condemned. This can be seen at work in the way divorces were decided and marriage choices made. Both took place within a general framework that could not be broken. In divorce, the overriding tendency was to find a way of settling issues by mutual agreement and to avoid the in-court resolution of conflicts. Even when there were irreconcilable differences and it was necessary to bring the matter to court, thus bringing the conflict out into the open where it posed a threat to internal cohesion, it was done in as discreet a manner as possible. Court-imposed divorce settlements were very limited in number and it was common practice to attempt to resolve emerging disagreements in all ways possible, whether through the intervention of family members, court-appointed adjudicators, or even social workers. It was even deemed acceptable to make use of such an apparently 'modern' method of conflict resolution as employing a psychiatrist if it would help to dissipate internal tension. Change and the introduction of new ideas are permissible when they serve the general purpose of maintaining internal solidarity and preserving the structure of the group. However, if change does not serve the purpose of the group, it is rejected. The research showed that there was a certain tension within the community personified in the attempts of the religious judges to maintain the upper hand in defining what is accepted and the efforts – however mild – of younger Druze to break with traditional practices.

To conclude, the changes and non-changes in marriage and divorce that the study revealed, though seemingly contradictory in nature, can be more easily understood when analyzed in terms of how they serve to preserve the ultimate aim of the group – the overall structure that may not be broken or compromised. Within this framework, parts are allowed some margin of manoeuvre, some peripheral change, as long as the structure is maintained. Maton (2008) argues that when people behave in a regular manner – not breaking away from a normative order or from what traditions dictate – they do so because they react to social conditions that are predictable under the force of the habitus. These people are indeed free agents but their freedom is shaped and limited by the structure. He maintains: 'We often feel we are free agents yet base every decision on the assumptions about the predictable character, behaviour and attitudes of others.

Sociologically, social practices are characterized by regularities' (Maton, 2008: 50).

The research revealed a number of changes brought about under pressure from the ever-shifting imperatives of modern living; however, all these changes remained within certain boundaries that preserved the solidarity of the Druze and their identity as such. If one asks an ordinary Druze about their religion, the information elicited would not amount to much, the reason being that religious knowledge is not open or made known to all. Only religious people belonging to the *Ajaweed* strata are exposed to religious teachings. Yet a Druze who is not an *Ajaweed*, while possessing little religious knowledge, owns a very strong sense of self-identification as a Druze. The internal sense of being a Druze that unites the whole community is not religiously taught but is strongly 'felt' and maintained through a number of behavioural signals such as the use of the strongly stressed 'k' in everyday speech,[6] appeal to religious symbols/figures[7] and the prevalence of sacred shrines in their residential localities. In this research, this sense of being a Druze manifested itself in the avoidance of outward conflict in divorce cases and the inclusion of traditional items in marriage contracts. It is these elements, unchanging and 'traditional', that unite the Druze and preserve their structure. However, this does not mean the Druze are static. On the contrary, they do change and react positively to the socio-economic realities that demand change, but they do so while preserving the overall structured unity of the community. Bourdieu (1977) maintains that 'the habitus, the durably, installed generative principle of regulated improvisations, produce practices which tend to reproduce the regularities immanent in the objective condition of the production of their generative principles, while adjusting to the demands inscribed as objective potentialities in the situation, as defined by the cognitive and motivating structures making up the habitus' (Bourdieu, 1977: 78). As such, adjustments in practices are expected but will ultimately result in reproducing the social habitus.

The Legal Setting

Another important research finding relates to the legal setting in which marriage and divorce take place – namely the court, and the active participation of the judge. The judge played an instrumental role both in the marriage and divorce procedures. He actively engaged in regulating the *mahr* when any marrying couple wanted to deviate from the normative practices for its assignation. The judge played an even more active role in divorce cases, trying to abide by what the Druze value most in their religious traditions. He refused to sign a divorce agreement when he was in doubt as to whether both parties had acted freely in bringing the settlement before the court. He offered his own moral interpretations as to what was acceptable or not, refusing simply to implement the law. The judge was also an active agent in shaping and laying out the boundaries of what he defined as appropriate Druze conduct, and when an individual's actions contradicted Druze traditions, he took necessary measures to rectify the situation and punish the offending party. For example, he might delay a divorce, introduce adjudicators, bring in the psychiatrist or social workers, and then give a month for the couple to reconsider their decision before making the divorce final. On the other hand, when the core values of the Druze community were threatened, the judge would quickly divorce a couple and severely punish the culprit. For example, when a Druze man wanted to divorce his Druze wife to marry a non-Druze, the judge penalized him by denying him custody of his children and sentenced him to pay a large sum of money to his former wife. Thus, although the judge was limited by the stipulations of the law, he was able to use his personal judgment to promote the values of the Druze community in rejecting change or changing certain aspects to maintain group solidarity.

Social Change and Solidarity

The research makes it clear that social life among the Lebanese Druze is a very complex web of intertwining elements that seem to control and shape their everyday existence. These elements relate to what the Druze community defines as the most important and salient aspect of their continued existence in Lebanon: being a minority group that continues to survive within a self-perceived image of persecution and a feeling of imminent danger[8] endows the people with a particular attitude toward change and a particular reaction to any forced or imposed changes. Change is perceived as something to be cautious about, if not feared and rejected. This fear of change expresses itself in various social practices such as the rejection of outsiders and the refusal to sell land in their villages to non-Druze, acts that might jeopardize their continuing presence. In marriage, it is manifested in the rejection of marriage outside the group and of a major alteration in traditional practices. In divorce, it is seen in the avoidance of conflict and the attachment to Druze traditions in matters of custody, visitation rights and compensation for injury.

The Druze value their unity as the basic element that has contributed to their continued existence and presence in the Middle East – and particularly so in Lebanon where, during the civil war, they fought in what they perceived to be a battle for their very survival. This highly-valued and preserved group unity and solidarity has shaped their social life and evidently continues to do so. It has manifested itself through an outward rejection of change and an insistence upon group unity and cohesion, while at the same time negotiating the demands imposed by changing socio-economic variables.

The feeling of unity, this Druzeness that the people feel, is not based on a knowledge of the tenets of the faith, nor on an unshakable understanding of the teachings of '*Tawheed*'; neither does it reflect familiarity with the epistles in the Books of Wisdom. This Druzeness is something that transcends, or even bypasses, knowledge in favour of an established sense of identity that is the result of everyday behaviour and practices, backed up by the constant attempts of the elders and the religious *sheikhs* to point out to the young their unique Druze identity.

The sense of Druzeness is further strengthened by the history of the people. As a minority group, the Druze were subject to persecution from the time of the initiation of the Call until it was closed to outsiders and this led them to practice a particular kind of behaviour reflected in their marriage choices and divorce decisions or agreements. As a minority, the Druze display a very strong 'ethnic' feeling that breeds internal solidarity and cohesion. This in turn strengthens the ethno-religious feeling and so on, creating a kind of circular movement that feeds on itself.

This circle cannot be penetrated or broken, or even endangered. It is continually augmented by safeguarding particular practices. The preservation of the group is achieved by emphasizing its internal solidarity of the group, constantly strengthened and renewed by endogamous marriage and by resistance to any change, especially when imposed by

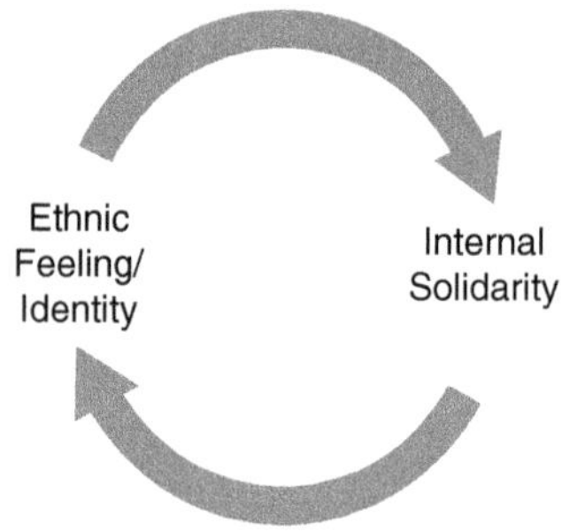

the majorities. Many minority groups find themselves unable to resist such change and in many instances are forced to do so as to cope with the surrounding conditions. The Druze in Lebanon, as the research revealed, did not change essentially. They practiced their particularity, while at the same time preserving their independent existence. This was their condition in Syria and Palestine and even, if in a less pronounced manner, in Jordan. The Druze remained stable because of the great value they attach to their internal solidarity constantly nourished and nurtured by their religious teachings, beliefs and practices.[9]

Lebanon is particular in the sense that it is a country distinguished by the presence of various sects, all of which participate in the political life of the country and in the government. Moreover, a numerical minority – the Christian Maronites – hold the highest rank in government, the presidency (Khuri, 1988: 197–208). In this sense, numerical minorities rule – not majorities as is the case in other countries. Living under such a system, minorities do not feel the need to change or alter.

The Lebanese situation itself compounded the Druze's tendency towards resistance to change. No political pressure – in a direct sense – is exerted by the Lebanese system to force or promote drastic change among the Druze.[10] The peripheral changes that were observed in the research represented people's reaction to the socio-economic changes taking place in Lebanon but did not extend to elements that might touch upon the group's internal solidarity.

APPENDIX A

PERSONAL STATUS LAWS OF THE DRUZE SECT IN LEBANON

The appendix includes a set of the laws guiding marriage, divorce, child custody and maintenance as it was published in the Official Paper (الجريدة الرسمية). These were taken from the internet site of the Druze Courts and they are in the Arabic Language. A translation is also offered.

الفصل الأول: في اهلية الزواج

المادة 1:

تاريخ بدء العمل: 03 /03 /1948

يجوز الخاطب على أهلية الزواج باتمامه الثامنة عشرة والمخطوبة باتمامها السابعة عشرة من العمر.

المادة 2:

تاريخ بدء العمل08/07/1959:

(كما تعدلت بموجب القانون تاريخ 02 /07 /1959)

لاحد شيخي العقل او قاضي المذهب ان يأذن بالزواج للمراهق الذي اكمل السادسة عشرة من عمره ولم يكمل الثامنة عشرة اذا ثبت لديه طبيا ان حاله يتحمل ذلك، على ان يكون اذن احد شيخي العقل او قاضي المذهب موقوفا على إذن ولي المراهق .

المادة 3:

تاريخ بدء العمل08/07/1959:

(كما تعدلت بموجب القانون تاريخ 02 /07/ 1959)

لاحد شيخي العقل او قاضي المذهب ان يأذن بالزواج للمراهقة التي اكملت الخامسة عشرة من العمر ولم تكمل السابعة عشرة اذا ثبت لديه طبيا ان حالها يتحمل ذلك واذن وليها.

المادة 4:

تاريخ بدء العمل 08/07/1959:

(كما تعدلت بموجب القانون تاريخ 02/ 07/ 1959)

اذا اذن احد شيخي العقل او قاضي المذهب بزواج المراهق والمراهقة بدون اذن الولي حق لكل من المراهق والمراهقة ان يطلب فسخ الزواج في مدة ستة اشهر تبتدئ من تاريخ بلوغ السن المبينة في المادة الاولى.

المادة 5:

تاريخ بدء العمل 08/07/1959:

(كما تعدلت بموجب القانون تاريخ 02/ 07/ 1959)

.لا يجوز لاحد اصلا ان يزوج الصغير الذي لم يتم السادسة عشرة والصغيرة التي لم تتم الخامسة عشرة ولا يجوز تزويج المعتوه ولا المعتوهة ولا المريض ولا المريضة بعلة من العلل السارية وهي الامراض الزهرية والجذام والتدرن الرئوي في طور النمو.

وعلى احد شيخي العقل او قاضي المذهب ان يستثبت قبل الاذن بالزواج سلامة الزوجين من العته والعلل السارية بتكليفهما ابراز شهادة صحية من طبيب قانوني ويجوز الاعتراض على هذه الشهادة لدى احد شيخي العقل او قاضي المذهب وقراره بشأنها قابل لطرق المراجعة.

المادة 6:

تاريخ بدء العمل 08/07/1959:

(كما تعدلت بموجب القانون تاريخ 02/ 07/ 1959)

إذا طلبت الكبيرة التي يتراوح سنها بين السابعة عشرة والحادية والعشرين أن تتزوج بشخص فأحد شيخي العقل أو قاضي المذهب يبلغ ذلك لوليها، وإذا لم يعترض الولي في مدة خمسة عشر يوما من تاريخ تبليغه أو اعترض ورؤي اعتراضه في غير محله، إذن أحد شيخي العقل أو قاضي المذهب بزواجهما.

المادة 7:

تاريخ بدء العمل 03/03/1948:

الولي في الزواج هو العصبة بنفسه على الترتيب ويشترط أن يكون مكلفا، فلا ولاية للصبي والمجنون والمعتوه على أحد أصلا.

المادة 8:

تاريخ بدء العمل 08/07/1959:

(كما تعدلت بموجب القانون تاريخ 02/ 07/ 1959)

إذا لم يكن لطالب الزواج ولي أو كان وليه غير حائز الأهلية القانونية فيقوم بالولاية أحد شيخي العقل أو قاضي المذهب أو من يستنيبه لهذه الغاية.

الفصل الثاني: في من هو ممنوع زواجه

المادة 9:

تاريخ بدء العمل 03/03/1948:

عقد الزواج على مزوجة الغير أو معتدته ممنوع وباطل.

المادة 10:

تاريخ بدء العمل 03/03/1948:

ممنوع تعدد الزوجات فلا يجوز للرجل أن يجمع بين زوجتين وإن فعل فزواجه من الثانية باطل.

المادة 11:

تاريخ بدء العمل 03/03/1948:

لا يجوز لأحد أن يعيد مطلقته.

المادة 12:

تاريخ بدء العمل 03/03/1948:

تزوج النساء ذوات الرحم المحرم برجل بينه وبينهن قرابة نسبية ممنوع وباطل. والنساء المذكورات أربعة أصناف:

-1أم الرجل وجداته.

-2البنات والحفيدات.

-3الأخوات وبنات الاخوة والأخوات مطلقا وحفيداتهن.

-4العمات والخالات مطلقا.

المادة 13:

تاريخ بدء العمل 03/03/1948:

تزوج النساء الرجل الذي بينه وبينهن مصاهرة ممنوع وباطل. والنساء المذكورات أربعة أصناف:

-1.زوجات الأبناء والحفيدة.

-2.أمهات الزوجات وجداتهن مطلقا.

-3.زوجات الآباء والأجداد.

-4بنات الزوجات وحفيداتهن.

الفصل الثالث: في عقد الزواج

المادة 14:

تاريخ بدء العمل03/03/1948:

يتم عقد الزواج بالإيجاب والقبول من الفريقين في مجلس العقد بحضور شهود، ويجوز أن يكون الشهود من أصول وفروع الخاطب والمخطوبة على أن لا يقل عددهم عن الأربعة ويجب أن يتم العقد كتابة وأن يوقعه الزوجان وشهودهما، وإذا تعذر حضور أحد الزوجين مجلس العقد يجوز أن يوقعه عنه وكيل مفوض بموجب وكالة خطية مصدق عليها من المختار ومن يقوم مقامه على أن يذكر في التوكيل قيمة المهر أو يترك تعيينه لرأي الوكيل وعلى أن يضم هذا التوكيل إلى العقد.

المادة 15:

تاريخ بدء العمل03/03/1948:

الإيجاب والقبول في الزواج يكونان بالألفاظ الصريحة وكذلك في الخطبة وإشارة الأخرس تقوم مقام العبارة.

المادة 16:

تاريخ بدء العمل08/07/1959:

(كما تعدلت بموجب القانون تاريخ 02/ 07/ 1959)

لا يكون عقد الزواج صحيحا إلا إذا أجراه أحد شيخي العقل أو قاضي المذهب أو من أنابه عنه لإجرائه.

المادة 17:

تاريخ بدء العمل08/07/1959:

(كما تعدلت بموجب القانون تاريخ 02/ 07/ 1959)

يعين أحد شيخي العقل أو قاضي المذهب مأذونا أو أكثر لإجراء عقد الزواج في كل ناحية أو بلدة حسب الاقتضاء وليس للمأذون أن يجري العقد قبل أن يحصل على إذن خاص خطي من أحد شيخي العقل أو قاضي المذهب بذلك.

المادة 18:

تاريخ بدء العمل08/07/1959:

(كما تعدلت بموجب القانون تاريخ 02/ 07/ 1959)

بعد أن ينظم المأذون العقد يرسله إلى أحد شيخي العقل أو قاضي المذهب لأجل المصادقة عليه وتسجيله ويسري مفعول هذا العقد اعتبارا من تاريخ حصوله.

المادة 19:

تاريخ بدء العمل08/07/1959:

(كما تعدلت بموجب القانون تاريخ 02/ 07/ 1959)

على أحد شيخي العقل أو قاضي المذهب أن يسجل هذه العقود في سجل مخصوص ممهورة صفحاته من قبله ومرقمة بالتسلسل. ويعاد العقد إلى صاحبه خلال شهر على الأكثر من تاريخ إيداعه المحكمة المذهبية لتسجيله

الفصل الرابع: في احكام الزواج

المادة 20:

تاريخ بدء العمل03/03/1948:

يلزم مهر الزوجة ونفقتها الزوج منذ إجراء العقد الصحيح ويثبت بينهما حق التوارث

المادة 21:

تاريخ بدء العمل03/03/1948:

ليس للزوجة حق المطالبة بالمؤجل من المهر قبل حلول أحد الأجلين الطلاق أو الوفاة.

المادة 22:

تاريخ بدء العمل03/03/1948:

تجبر الزوجة بعد استيفاء المهر المعجل وإجراء عقد الزواج الشرعي على الإقامة في بيت زوجها إذا كان مسكنا شرعيا وكذا على الذهاب معه إذا أراد الذهاب إلى بلدا أخرى ولم يكن هنالك مانع جدي.

والمسكن الشرعي هو المسكن الذي يمكن أن يسكن فيه أمثال الزوجين.

المادة 23:

تاريخ بدء العمل03/03/1948:

الزوج مجبر على حسن معاشرة زوجته ومساواتها بنفسه والزوجة مجبرة أيضا على إطاعة زوجها في الحقوق الزوجية المشروعة

الفصل الخامس: في المهر

المادة 24:

تاريخ بدء العمل03/03/1948:

المهر هو المال الذي يجب بالزواج ويترتب على الزوج للزوجة بمجرد العقد الصحيح عليها ويعين مقداره

بعقد الزواج وإذا لم يعين مقدار المهر في العقد يحكم القاضي بمهر المثل.

المادة 25:

تاريخ بدء العمل03/03/1948:

يجوز تعيين وتأجيل المهر كلا أو بعضا.

المادة 26:

تاريخ بدء العمل03/03/1948:

لكل من الخاطب أو المخطوبة أن يرجع عن الخطبة من غير أن يلزمه شيء أما فيما يتعلق بهدايا الخطبة فإذا كان الرجوع من جهة الخاطب فلا يجوز له أن يسترد شيئا مما قدمه للمخطوبة سواء أكان باقيا وقت رجوعه أملم يكن. وإن كان الرجوع من جهة المخطوبة وجب عليها أن ترد كل شيء قدمه الخاطب لها، فإن كان قائما ردته بنفسه وإن كان قد هلك في وقت رجوعها ردت مثله أو قيمته ما لم يكن بينهما شرط فيعمل به.

المادة 27:

تاريخ بدء العمل03/03/1948:

إذا توفى أحد الزوجين أو وقع الطلاق بينهما بعد الإجتماع الصحيح يلزم المهر بكامله أما إذا وقع الطلاق أو الوفاة قبل الإجتماع الصحيح يسقط نصف المهر

الفصل السادس: في النفقة.

المادة 28:

تاريخ بدء العمل03/03/1948:

النفقة هي ما ينفقه الإنسان على عياله وزوجته ويشمل الطعام والكسوة والسكنى والتطيب وخدمة الزوجة ذات الكرامة أو العاجزة أو المريضة وهي لازمة الأداء بتراضي الفريقين أو بحكم القاضي.

المادة 29:

تاريخ بدء العمل03/03/1948:

بعد تقدير النفقة يجوز زيادتها أو إنقاصها بحسب تغيير الأثمان أو تبدل حال الزوجين يسرا أو عسرا.

المادة 30:

تاريخ بدء العمل03/03/1948:

إذا امتنع الزوج الحاضر عن الإنفاق على زوجته وطلبت الزوجة النفقة فالقاضي يقدر النفقة حسب حال الفريقين اعتبارا من يوم الطلب وله أن يأمر بإعطائها سلفة عن المدة التي يعينها.

المادة 31:

تاريخ بدء العمل03/03/1948:

إذا عجز الزوج الحاضر عن الإنفاق على زوجته وطلبت الزوجة النفقة فالقاضي يقدر النفقة اعتبارا من يوم الطلب على ان تكون دينا بذمة الزوج ويأذن للزوجة أن تستدين باسمه.

المادة 32:

تاريخ بدء العمل03/03/1948:

إذا ترك الزوج زوجته بلا نفقة واختفى أو تغيب بذهابه لمحل بعيد أو فقد فالقاضي يقدر النفقة اعتبارا من يوم الطلب بعد إقامة البينة على الزوجية والغيبة وعلى كونه مفقودا وبعد تحليف الزوجة بأن الزوج لم يترك لها نفقة وبأنها غير مطلقة ويأذن للزوجة لدى الحاجة بالإستدانة باسم الزوج.

المادة 33:

تاريخ بدء العمل03/03/1948:

إذا أذن القاضي للزوجة المعسرة بالإستدانة عملا بأحكام المواد السابقة واستدانت من قريب تلزمه نفقتها فلهذا القريب حق الرجوع على الزوج فقط. أما إذا استدانت من غريب فللدائن الخيار في أن يطالب الزوج أو الزوجة.

المادة 34:

تاريخ بدء العمل03/03/1948:

اذا كان للزوج الغائب مال بيد الغير أو بذمته وأقر المؤتمن أو المديون بالمال الذي بيده أو بذمته أو أنكر ذلك وأثبتت الزوجة أمام الحكمة المدنية المختصة فبعد أن تقيم الزوجة البينة بالزوجية وتحلف اليمين على أن الزوج لم يترك لها نفقة وبانها غير مطلقة يقدر لها نفقة من ذلك المال أو من ريعه أو من ثمنه اعتبارا من يوم الطلب.

المادة 35:

تاريخ بدء العمل03/03/1948:

لا يسقط المقدار المتراكم من النفقة المقدرة قضاء أو رضاء بالطلاق أو بوفاة أحد الزوجين.

المادة 36:

تاريخ بدء العمل03/03/1948:

اذا تركت الزوجة بيت زوجها بدون سبب مشروع أو كانت في بيتها ومنعت زوجها من الدخول إليه قبل طلب نقلها لبيت آخر تسقط نفقتها مدة دوام هذا النشوز.

الفصل السابع: في المفارقات

المادة 37:

تاريخ بدء العمل03/03/1948:

لا ينحل عقد الزواج بالطلاق إلا بحكم قاضي المذهب.

المادة 38:

تاريخ بدء العمل03/03/1948:

لا تحل للرجل مطلقته أبدا بعد صدور حكم القاضي بالتفريق بينهما.

المادة 39:

تاريخ بدء العمل03/03/1948:

إذا ظهر للزوجة السالمة من عيوب المقاربة قبل أو بعد الزواج أن زوجها مصاب بعلة لا يمكنها معها مساكنته بلا ضرر كالجذام والبرص والزهري وما شابهها، فلها أن تراجع القاضي وتطلب التفريق. فإذا كانت العلة غير قابلة الشفاء فيحكم القاضي بالتفريق في الحال وإذا كان من أمل بزوال العلة فيؤجل القاضي التفريق سنتين على أن يقرر في الحال الفصل الموقت بين الزوجين، وإذا لم تزل العلة خلال هذه المدة ولم يرض الزوج بالطلاق وأصرت الزوجة على طلبها يحكم القاضي بالتفريق. أما العاهات كالعمى والعرج فليست سببا للتفريق.

المادة 40:

تاريخ بدء العمل03/03/1948:

إذا كان الزوج مصابا بالعنة فللزوجة أن تطلب التفريق متى ثبت طبيا أن هذه العنة غير قابلة الشفاء.

المادة 41:

تاريخ بدء العمل03/03/1948:

إذا جن الزوج بعد عقد الزواج وراجعت الزوجة القاضي طالبة التفريق فالقاضي يؤجل النظر، بالطلب مدة سنة وإذا لم يزل الجنون في خلال هذه المدة وأصرت الزوجة حكم بالتفريق.

المادة 42:

تاريخ بدء العمل03/03/1948:

للزوجين أن يفسخا عقد الزواج بالتراضي ويتم هذا الفسخ بإعلانه بحضور شاهدين أمام القاضي الذي يصدر حكما به.

المادة 43:

تاريخ بدء العمل03/03/1948:

إذا حكم على الزوج بجريمة الزنا فللزوجة أن تطلب التفريق وإذا حكم على الزوجة بجريمة الزنا وطلقها زوجها لهذه العلة يسقط عنه مؤجل المهر.

المادة 44:

تاريخ بدء العمل03/03/1948:

إذا حكم على الزوج بعقوبة الحبس لمدة عشر سنوات فأكثر وقضى منها في خمس سنوات متتالية كان للزوجة أن تطلب التفريق في ختام هذه المدة.

المادة 45:

تاريخ بدء العمل03/03/1948:

إذا اختفى الزوج أو تغيب مدة ثلاث سنوات وتعذر تحصيل النفقة منه فالقاضي يحكم بالتفريق بطلب الزوجة.

أما إذا تيسر تحصيل النفقة فلا يجاب طلبها إلا إذا مر على الغيبة خمس سنوات بدون انقطاع وإذا حكم على الزوج الحاضر بالنفقة وتعذر تحصيلها منه مدة سنتين فللزوجة أيضا أن تطلب التفريق.

المادة 46:

تاريخ بدء العمل03/03/1948:

إذا حكم بفسخ زواج امرأة لغيبة الزوج وتزوجت بآخر ثم ظهر الزوج الأول فظهوره لا يوجب فسخ الزواج الأخير.

المادة 47:

تاريخ بدء العمل03/03/1948:

إذا وقع نزاع أو شقاق بين الزوجين وراجع أحدهما القاضي يعين القاضي حكما من أهل الزوج وحكما من أهل الزوجة وإن لم يكن بين أهلهما من توفرت فيه أوصاف الحكم اختار القاضي حكما من غير أهلهما.

المادة 48:

تاريخ بدء العمل03/03/1948:

على الحكمين أن يتعرفا أسباب الشقاق بين الزوجين وأن يجتهدا في إصلاح ذات البين وإذا لم يمكن التوفيق بينهما وكان القصور والإصرار من جهة الزوج يفرق القاضي بينهما ويحكم للزوجة بكامل المهر المؤجل أو ببعضه وإذا كان من جهة الزوجة يحكم القاضي بإسقاط المهر المؤجل كلا أو بعضا وللقاضي أن

يحكم في كلا الحالين على غير المحق من الزوجين بما يستحق الآخر من عطل وضرر.

المادة 49:

تاريخ بدء العمل03/03/1948:

وإذا ظهر للقاضي أن الطلاق لا يبرره سبب شرعي يحكم للزوجة بالعطل والضرر علاوة على مؤجل المهر على أن يؤخذ بعين الإعتبار الضرر المعنوي والمادي.

الفصل الثامن: في العدة

المادة 50:

تاريخ بدء العمل03/03/1948:

مدة العدة أربعة أشهر تبدأ من تاريخ الطلاق او التفريق او وفاة الزوج وعدة الحامل تنتهي بالوضع أو بسقوط الجنين.

المادة 51:

تاريخ بدء العمل03/03/1948:

لا تلزم العدة إذا وقع الطلاق أو الفسخ قبل الإجتماع والمقاربة.

المادة 52:

تاريخ بدء العمل03/03/1948:

تبدأ العدة من تاريخ وقوع الطلاق أو الفسخ أو وفاة الزوج وإن لم تطلع الزوجة على الوفاة.

المادة 53:

تاريخ بدء العمل03/03/1948:

تجب نفقة العدة للمرأة المطلقة على زوجها ولا تجب للمراة التي توفى زوجها سواء كانت حاملا أم غير حامل.

الفصل التاسع: في الحضانة

المادة 54:

تاريخ بدء العمل03/03/1948:

الأم أحق بحضانة الولد وتربيته حال قيام الزوجية وبعد الفرقة إذا اجتمعت فيها الأهلية المطلوبة.

المادة 55:

تاريخ بدء العمل03/03/1948:

يشترط في الحاضنة أن تكون بالغة عاقلة أمينة صحيحة الجسم قادرة على تربية الولد وصيانته وأن لا تكون متزوجة بغير محرم للصغير ولا فرق في ذلك بين الأم وغيرها من الحاضنات.

المادة 56:

تاريخ بدء العمل03/03/1948:

إذا تزوجت الحاضنة أما كانت أم غير أم بزوج غير محرم للضغير سقط حقها في الحضانة وانتقل إلى من يليها في الإستحقاق من الحاضنات فإن لم توجد مستحقة أهلا للحضانة فلولي الصغير اخذه ومتى زال المانع يعود حق الحضانة للحاضنة المستحقة.

المادة 57:

تاريخ بدء العمل03/03/1948:

حق الحضانة يستفاد من قبل الأم فيعتبر الأقرب فالأقرب من جهتها ويقدم المدلي بالأم على المدلي بالأب

عند اتحاد المرتبة قربا. فإذا ماتت الأم أو تزوجت بقريب أو لم تكن أهلا للحضانة ينتقل حقها إلى أمها فإن لم تكن أو كانت ليست أهلا للحضانة تنتقل إلى أم الأب وإن علت عند عدم أهلية القربى ثم لأخوات الصغير وتقدم الأخت الشقيقة ثم الأخت لأم ثم الأخت لأب ثم لبنات الأخوات بتقديم بنت الأخت لأبوين ثم لأم، ثم لخالات الصغير وتقدم الخالات لأبوين ثم الخالة لأم ثم لأب ثم لبنت الأخت لأب ثم لبنات الأخ كذلك ثم لعمات الصغير بتقديم العمة لأبوين ثم لأم ثم لأب ثم خالات الأم ثم خالات الأب ثم عمات الأمهات والآباء بهذا الترتيب.

المادة 58:

تاريخ بدء العمل03/03/1948:

إذا فقدت المحارم من النساء أو وجدت ولم تكن أهلا للحضانة تنتقل للعصبات بترتيب الإرث فيقدم الأب ثم الجد ثم الأخ الشقيق ثم الأخ لأب ثم بنو الأخ الشقيق ثم بنو الأخ لأب ثم العم الشقيق ثم العم لأب فإذا تساوى المستحقون للحضانة في درجة واحدة يقدم أصلحهم ثم أكبرهم سنا.

المادة 59:

تاريخ بدء العمل03/03/1948:

إذا لم توجد عصبة مستحقة الحضانة أو وجد ليس اهلا لها فلا تسلم إليه المحضونة بل تدفع لذي رحم محرم ويقدم الجد لأم ثم الأخ لأم ثم ابنه ثم العم لأم ثم الخال لأبوين ثم الخال لأب ثم الخال لأم ولا حق لبنات العم والعمة والخال والخالة في حضانة الذكور ولهن الحق في حضانة الإناث ولا حق لبني العم والعمة والخال والخالة في حضانة الإناث وإنما لهم حضانة الذكور فإن لم يكن للأنثى المحضونة إلا ابن عم كان للقاضي أن يوليه حضانتها إن رآه صالحا وإلا سلمها لامرأة ثقة أمينة.

المادة 60:

تاريخ بدء العمل03/03/1948:

أجرة الحضانة غير بدل النفقة وكلها تلزم الأب إن لم يكن للصغير مال فإن كان له مال فلا يلزم أباه منها شيء إلا أن يتبرع.

المادة 61:

تاريخ بدء العمل03/03/1948:

إذا كانت أم الطفل هي الحاضنة له وكانت مطلقة او متزوجة بمحرم للصغير أو معتدة له فلها الأجرة وإن لم يكن للحاضنة مسكن تمسك فيه الصغير الفقير فعلى أبيه سكناهما وإن احتاج المحضون إلى خادم وكان أبوه موسرا يلزم به وغير الأم من الحاضنات لها الأجرة.

المادة 62:

تاريخ بدء العمل03/03/1948:

إذا أبت أم الولد ذكرا كان أم أنثى حضانته مجانا ولم يكن له مال وكان أبو معسرا ولم توجد متبرعة من محارمه تجبر الأم على حضانته وتكون أجرتها دينا على أبيه ولها أن تستدين بإذن القاضي إذا كانت معسرة.

المادة 63:

تاريخ بدء العمل03/03/1948:

إذا وجدت متبرة أهل للحضانة من محارم الطفل وكان الأب موسرا ولا مال للصغير فالأم وإن طلت أجرة أحق من المتبرعة أما إذا كان الأب معسرا وللصبي مال أو لا مال له تخير الأم بين إمساكه مجانا

ودفعه للمتبرعة فإن لم تختر إمساكه مجانا ينزع منها ويسلم للمتبرعة وللأم رؤية الولد وتعهده إذا كان الأب موسرا وللصبي مال وكانت المتبرعة غريبة فلا يدفع إليها الصبي بل يسلم لأمه بأجرة المثل ولو من مال الصغير.

المادة 64:

تاريخ بدء العمل03/03/1948:

تنتهي مدة حضانة الصبي عند إتمامه السنة السابعة من العمر وتنتهي مدة حضانة الصبية عند إتمامها السنة التاسعة

ويجبر الب على أخذ الولد. فإذا لم يكن للولد أب أو جد يدفع للقرب من العصبة إذا كان صبيا أما الصبية فلا تسلم لغير محرم فإن لم يكن عصبة يترك المحضون عند الحاضنة إلا إذا رأى القاضي غيرها أولى له منها.

المادة 65:

تاريخ بدء العمل03/03/1948:

يمنع الأب من إخراج الولد من بلد أمه بلا رضاها ما دامت حضانتها فإن أخذ المطلق ولده منها لتزوجها بغريب ولم يكن له حاضن غيرها جاز له أن يسافر به إلى أن يعود حق أمه أو من يقوم مقامها في الحضانة.

المادة 66:

تاريخ بدء العمل03/03/1948:

ليس للأم المطلقة أن تافر بالولد الحاضنة له من بلد ابيه إلى بلد بعيد بغير إذن أبيه وليس لغير الأم من الحاضنات باي حال نقل الولد من محل حضانته إلا بإذن أبيه أو بإذن القاضي إذا لم يكن له أب.

Translation of the Laws

Chapter I: Legal Capacity for Marriage[1]

Article 1: (enforced as of 08/07/1959 and amended by law of 02/07/1959)

The fiancé has the legal capacity for marriage when he reaches eighteen years of age, whereas the fiancée has the legal capacity for marriage when she reaches seventeen years of age.

Article 2: (enforced as of 08/07/1959 and amended by law of 02/07/1959)

Either the Sheikh al-ʿAql or the confessional judge may authorize the marriage of a male teenager who has reached the age of sixteen and not reached the age of eighteen, if it is medically established that he is in good condition for marriage, subject to the authorization of his custodian.

Article 3: (enforced as of 08/07/1959 and amended by law of 02/07/1959)

Either the Sheikh al-'Aql or the confessional judge may authorize the marriage of a female teenager who has reached the age of fifteen and not reached the age of seventeen, if it is medically established that she is in good condition for marriage, subject to the authorization of her custodian.

Article 4: (enforced as of 08/07/1959 and amended by law of 02/07/1959)

If either the Sheikh al-'Aql or the confessional judge authorizes teenagers to get married without the custodian's approval, both teenagers shall be entitled to request the termination of the marriage within six months as of the date they reach the age mentioned under Article I hereof.

Article 5: (enforced as of 08/07/1959 and amended by law of 02/07/1959)

The marriage of a male who has not reached the age of sixteen and/or a female who has not reached the age of fifteen may not be authorized by anyone.

Neither someone insane nor someone infected by any transmissible diseases, which includes venereal diseases, leprosy or someone developing pulmonary tuberculosis can be married.

Before authorizing marriage, either the Sheikh al-'Aql or the confessional judge should establish that neither the husband nor the wife is insane or suffers from any transmissible disease by requesting them to submit a health certificate issued by a legal physician. The aforementioned certificate may be subject to objection either before the Sheikh al-'Aql or the confessional judge and the decision taken in this regard shall be subject to recourse.

Article 6: (enforced as of 08/07/1959 and amended by law of 02/07/1959)

In the event a female adult aged between seventeen and twenty-one requests to marry someone, either the Sheikh al-'Aql or the confessional judge shall notify her custodian. If the custodian does not object within a fifteen-day period beginning on the day of notification, or if his objection is deemed inappropriate, either the Sheikh al-'Aql or the confessional judge shall authorize their marriage.

Article 7: (enforced 03/03/1948)

The custodian in marriage shall be a paternal relative as per the order of kinship, provided that he is legally capable of this. An immature, insane or mad male may not act as a custodian.

Article 8: (enforced as of 08/07/1959 and amended by law of 02/07/1959)

In the event where the seeker of marriage has no custodian or his custodian does not enjoy the legal capacity to assume such a responsibility, then the Sheikh al-'Aql or the confessional judge, or whoever acts on behalf of either of them, shall be the custodian.

Chapter II: Marriage Prohibitions

Article 9: (enforced 03/03/1948)

The marriage of an already married woman is prohibited, as is the marriage during *iddah*[2] period of a divorced or widowed woman.

Article 10: (enforced 03/03/1948)

Polygamy shall be prohibited and a man may not have two wives at the same time, and if he does the second marriage shall be invalid.

Article 11: (enforced 03/03/1948)

No man may remarry a wife he has divorced.

Article 12: (enforced 03/03/2948)

The marriage between a *Mahram*[3] woman and her male relatives shall be prohibited and invalid. *Mahram* women are divided into four groups:

1) Mother and grandmothers;

2) Daughters and granddaughters;

3) Sisters, nieces, and their granddaughters;

4) Maternal and paternal aunts.

Article 13: (enforced 03/03/1948)

The marriage between women and men who are their relatives-in-law shall be prohibited and invalid. These women are divided into four groups:

1) Daughters-in-law and granddaughters-in-law;

2) Mothers-in-law and grandmothers-in-law;

3) Step-mothers and step-grandmothers;

4) Step-daughters and step-granddaughters.

Chapter III: Marriage Contract

Article 14: (enforced 03/03/1948)

A marriage contract is conducted upon the agreement and consent of both parties who should be present in person and in the presence of witnesses related to the engaged parties, on condition that these witnesses are not less than four. The contract must be written and then signed by the marrying couple and their witnesses. If one party could not attend the session, a legal appointee may replace him/her as long as that person has obtained a written legal power-of-attorney that must be ratified by the local *mukhtar*. The written document must include a specification of the *mahr* or a statement that the matter is to be left to the legal appointee to specify. This document should then be attached to the marriage contract.

Article 15: (enforced 03/03/1948)

Consent to marriage as well as to engagement shall be clearly expressed in words; however, in the case of muteness, a signal shall act as an expression of consent.

Article 16: (enforced as of 08/07/1959 and amended by law of 02/07/1959)

The contract of marriage shall not be legal unless concluded by either the Sheikh al-'Aql or the confessional judge, or whoever acts on their behalf in this respect.

Article 17: (enforced as of 08/07/1959 and amended by law of 02/07/1959)

A marriage official is assigned in any region or town by either the Sheikh al-'Aql or the confessional judge to conclude the marriage, but only upon receiving a written authorization to that effect from either the Sheikh al-'Aql or the confessional judge.

Article 18: (enforced as of 08/07/1959 and amended by law of 02/07/1959)

Having organized the marriage contract, the marriage official shall send it to either the Sheikh al-'Aql or the confessional judge for ratification and registration. This contract shall be effective as of the date of its conclusion.

Article 19: (enforced as of 08/07/1959 and amended by law of 02/07/1959)

Either the Sheikh al-'Aql or the confessional judge shall register these contracts in a special record sealed by them and numbered in order. The contract shall be returned to the concerned party no later than a month after it is lodged at the religious court for registration.

Chapter IV: Marriage Provisions

Article 20: (enforced 03/03/1948)

The husband shall cover his wife's *mahr* and support her from the time the legal contract is concluded, and inheritance rights shall be established between them.

Article 21: (enforced 03/03/1948)

The wife shall not be entitled to request the deferred portion of her *mahr* before the coming of one of these ends: either divorce or death.

Article 22: (enforced 03/03/1948)

After receiving the advance portion of the *mahr* and the conclusion of the legal marriage contract, the wife should stay at her husband's house if it is a legal residence and accompany him to another country unless prevented by a serious deterrent. The legal residence is the place where people of the same social class as the married couple can live.

Article 23: (enforced 03/03/1948)

The husband should fairly treat his wife and consider her his equal, and the wife should also obey her husband in terms of the legitimate marital rights.

Chapter V: The *Mahr*

Article 24: (enforced 03/03/1948)

The *mahr* is the amount of money which is due upon marriage and shall be paid by the husband to his wife once the legal contract of marriage is concluded. The amount of *mahr* shall be specified in the marriage contract; otherwise, an amount similar to that assigned to a female of the same social class shall be decided by the judge.

Article 25: (enforced 03/03/1948)

The *mahr* may be totally or partially specified and totally or partially deferred.

Article 26: (enforced 03/03/1948)

The fiancés shall be entitled to withdraw from the engagement without any obligations. However, with regard to engagement gifts, if the fiancé withdraws, he may not retrieve any gift offered to his fiancée whether it still exists or not. If the fiancée withdraws, she should return all gifts offered to her by her fiancé. If gifts still exist, they must be returned as they are; if they are worn out at the time of her withdrawal, she must replace them with gifts that are similar or have the same value, unless otherwise agreed to by the fiancés.

Article 27: (enforced 03/03/1948)

In the event of a spouse's death or divorce after the marriage is consummated, the entire *mahr* should be paid. In the event of death or divorce before marriage is consummated, half of the *mahr* shall be paid.

Chapter VI: The Support

Article 28: (enforced 03/03/1948)

The *support* is the amount of money spent by a man on his children and wife. It covers the costs of food, clothing, housing, medication, and services for dignified, disabled or ill wives. The *support* is mandatory, as agreed by both parties or as decided by the judge.

Article 29: (enforced 03/03/1948)

Once estimated, the *support* may be increased or reduced in accordance with price changes or solvency of spouses.

Article 30: (enforced 03/03/1948)

In the event where the husband refrains from spending on his wife and the latter requests *support*, the judge shall estimate the *support* in accordance with the couple's financial situation as of the day of request, and may order him to pay it in advance.

Article 31: (enforced 03/03/1948)

In the event where the husband fails to spend on his wife who requests *support*, the judge shall estimate the amount of *support* as of the day of request, provided that this amount is considered as a debt owed by the husband, and the wife shall be entitled to take a debt in his name.

Article 32: (enforced 03/03/1948)

In the event where the husband leaves his wife without *support* and disappears or goes to a remote place or is missing, the judge shall estimate the amount of *support* as of the day of request, after establishing that the couple is married and that the husband is missing, and after taking a statement under oath from the wife that her husband did not leave her any *support* and that she is not divorced. When the need arises, the wife may borrow in the name of her husband.

Article 33: (enforced 03/03/1948)

In the event where the judge authorizes the insolvent wife to borrow pursuant to the articles hereinabove and she borrows from a relative who is legally responsible for her *support*, the latter shall be entitled to have recourse against the husband only. If she borrows from a stranger, the creditor may have recourse against the husband or wife.

Article 34: (enforced 03/03/1948)

If the absent husband had entrusted or lent money (*maal*) to others and if the trustee or debtor recognized this or denied this fact but the wife was able to establish this before a civil court, and she can then prove her marriage and give a statement under oarth that her husband did not leave any *support* for her and that she is not divorced, then the *support* shall be estimated from that money, it proceeds or its price[4]. The *support* is to be calculated starting from the day the request is made.

Article 35: (enforced 03/03/1948)

The cumulating amount of *support* shall not decrease *de facto* or *de jure* as a result of divorce or death of a spouse.

Article 36: (enforced 03/03/1948)

In the event where the wife leaves her husband's house without a legal cause or stays at her house and prevents her husband from entering before making a request to be transferred to another house, the *support* shall decrease throughout the period of the wife's disobedience (*noshouz*).

Chapter VII: Divorce/Separation

Article 37: (enforced 03/03/1948)

The marriage contract shall not be terminated by divorce unless the confessional judge renders a judgment in this respect.

Article 38: (enforced 03/03/1948)

A man does not have the right to remarry his divorced wife after the judge renders the separation judgment.

Article 39: (enforced 03/03/1948)

In the event where the wife, who is in a good health, notes, before or after marriage, that her husband suffers from a defect that prevents them from living together as it presents a danger to her health, such as leprosy and venereal diseases, *inter alia*, or any disease of a similar nature, she may resort to the judge and request separation. If the defect is incurable, the judge shall immediately render a judgment of separation, but if there is hope that the defect may be cured, the judge shall defer separation for two years provided that a temporary separation is decided. If the defect remains during that period and the husband does not accept to divorce her, and if the wife insists on her request, then the judge shall render a decision of separation. Defects such as blindness and lameness shall not constitute reasons of separation.

Article 40: (enforced 03/03/1948)

In the event where the husband suffers from impotence, the wife shall be entitled to request separation if it is medically established that the impotence is incurable.

Article 41: (enforced 03/03/1948)

In the event where the husband becomes insane after marriage and the wife requests separation before the judge, the judge shall defer the examination of the case for a year; if the husband remains insane during that period and upon the wife's insistence, a judgment of separation shall be rendered.

Article 42: (enforced 03/03/1948)

The husband and wife shall amicably terminate the marriage contract in the presence of two witnesses before the judge who shall render a judgment in this respect.

Article 43: (enforced 03/03/1948)

If the husband commits adultery, the wife can request separation. If the wife commits adultery and is divorced by her husband for that reason, her right to the deferred portion of *mahr* shall abate.

Article 44: (enforced 03/03/1948)

In the event where the husband is sentenced to imprisonment for ten years or more and five consecutive years of that period elapse, the wife shall be entitled to request separation at the end of that period.

Article 45: (enforced 03/03/1948)

In the event where the husband disappears or is absent for three years and the wife is unable to get *support* from him, the judge shall render a decision of separation upon the wife's request. If the wife was able to receive *support*, her request shall not be met unless the husband has been away for five consecutive years.

If a present husband is sentenced to grant the *support* but refrains from doing so for a period of two years, the wife shall also have the right to request separation.

Article 46: (enforced 03/03/1948)

In the event where a woman's marriage is terminated as a result of her husband's absence and she gets married to another man but her first husband appears again, her second marriage shall not be terminated.

Article 47: (enforced 03/03/1948)

In the event of a dispute or discord between husband and wife, where either of them refers the case to the judge, the judge shall appoint an adjudicator from the husband's family and another one from the wife's family. If none of their relatives has the legal capacity to be an adjudicator, the judge shall appoint a non-relative adjudicator.

Article 48: (enforced 03/03/1948)

Both adjudicators should learn about the reasons of discord between husband and wife and seek to repair the relationship. If the couple could not be reconciled and if the husband is guilty of the shortcoming and insists on his request, then the judge shall render a decision of separation and grant all or part of the deferred *mahr* to the wife. If the request is made by the wife, the judge shall decide to abate all or part of the deferred *Mahr*. However, in both cases, the judge decides what harm or damage should be paid to the wronged party.

Article 49: (enforced 03/03/1948)

In the event where the judge considers that divorce is not legally grounded, he may decide to have the husband pay damage and harm to the wife in addition to the deferred *mahr* provided that the moral and physical damage are taken into consideration.

Chapter VIII: *Iddah*

Article 50: (enforced 03/03/1948)

The *iddah* shall be of four months as of the date of divorce, separation or husband's death. For pregnant women, the *iddah* shall end with the delivery of the child or with abortion.

Article 51: (enforced 03/03/1948)

The *iddah* shall not apply in the event that divorce or termination of the marriage occurs prior to intercourse.

Article 52: (enforced 03/03/1948)

The *iddah* shall begin as of the date of divorce, termination of the marriage or husband's death even if the wife did not know about the death.

Article 53: (enforced 03/03/1948)

The *iddah support* shall be paid to a divorced woman and not to a widowed woman, whether pregnant or not.

Chapter IX: Custody

Article 54: (enforced 03/03/1948)

The mother shall be more entitled to child custody and responsible for the upbringing of children upon contracting of the marriage, and after separation if she has the required legal capacity.

Article 55: (enforced 03/03/1948)

The female custodian should be adult, wise, loyal, in good health and capable of raising and preserving the child. She should not be married to a *non-Mahram* for the child, and there shall be no difference in this regard between the mother and other female custodians in this respect.

Article 56: (enforced 03/03/1948)

In the event that the female custodian, whether she is a mother or not, is married to a *non-Mahram* for the child, her right to custody shall abate and be transferred to an entitled custodian, as outlined below. If the entitled custodian does not appear to satisfy the conditions for custody, the guardian shall take the child until the deterrent disappears and the right of custody is restored to the entitled custodian.

Article 57: (enforced 03/03/1948)

The right of custody shall be first granted to the mother and her female relatives. Custodians from the mother's side shall be given priority over custodians from the father's side when they have a similar degree of kinship with the child. If the mother dies, is married to a relative or does not satisfy the conditions of custody, her right shall be transferred to her mother. If the latter is not present or does not have the legal capacity for custody, her right shall move to the father's mother, and then to the child's sisters with a priority given to a sister followed by a maternal stepsister and then a paternal stepsister. The right shall then move to the sisters' daughters by giving priority to a sister's daughter followed by the daughter of a maternal stepsister, and then to the child's maternal aunts by giving priority to the direct aunts followed by a maternal step-aunt and then a paternal step-aunt. The right shall then move to the daughter of a paternal stepsister followed by the brother's daughters, and then to a paternal aunt by giving priority to the direct aunts, followed by a maternal step-aunt and then a paternal step-aunt, then to the mother's maternal aunts followed by the father's maternal aunts, and then to the paternal aunts of mothers and fathers in order.

Article 58: (enforced 03/03/1948)

In the event where female *Mahram* are absent or do not have legal capacity for custody, the right of custody shall move to paternal relatives as per the order of inheritance whereby priority shall be given to the father followed by the grandfather then the brother, then it shall move to the stepbrother, then to the brother's sons, then to the stepbrother's sons, then to the uncle, then to the step-uncle. If persons eligible for custody have an equal degree of kinship, priority shall be given to the most adequate and then to the oldest.

Article 59: (enforced 03/03/1948)

In the event where paternal relatives are absent or do not have legal capacity for custody, the custody of the girl shall not be granted to them but to a *Mahram* with a priority given to the maternal step-grandfather, then to the maternal stepbrother, then to his son, then to the maternal step-uncle, then to the direct maternal uncle, then to the paternal step-uncle followed by the maternal step-uncle. The daughters of uncles and aunts shall not be entitled to the custody of boys but only of girls, and the sons of uncles and aunts shall not be entitled to the custody of girls but only of boys. If the girl does only have a paternal cousin, the judge shall grant the right of custody to her cousin if he is deemed adequate; otherwise, the judge shall grant that right to a religious and trustworthy woman.

Article 60: (enforced 03/03/1948)

Custody fees are different from *support* and they should all be paid by the father if the child has no money; otherwise, the father shall not be obliged to pay unless he volunteers.

Article 61: (enforced 03/03/1948)

In the event where the child's mother is the custodian, is divorced or married to a *Mahram* or in her *iddah*, she shall receive custody fees. If the female custodian does not have a place to accommodate the child, the father should provide them both with accommodation. If the child in custody needs a servant, his father should fulfill his needs if he is solvent, and all custodians other than the mother should receive the custody fee.

Article 62: (enforced 03/03/1948)

In the event where the mother of the child refuses a free-of-charge custody and if the child does not have money and his father is insolvent, and if no *Mahram* volunteers, the mother shall be obliged to take the child into her custody and his father would owe the custody fees to the mother, and the latter shall be entitled to borrow, in the event of insolvency, as per the judge's authorization.

Article 63: (enforced 03/03/1948)

In the event where a female volunteer, from the child's *Mahrams*, is eligible for custody and if the father is solvent and the child has no money, then priority in custody shall be given to the mother even if she is receiving custody fees. If the father is insolvent and the child has or does not have money, the mother shall choose between a free-of-charge custody and granting custody to the female volunteer. If she does not make the first choice, the child shall be taken from her and custody shall be granted to the female volunteer while maintaining the mother's right to see the child. If the father is solvent and the child has money and the female volunteer is a stranger, custody shall be given to the mother with custody fees even if such fees will be paid from the child's money.

Article 64: (enforced 03/03/1948)

The boy's period of custody shall end at the age of seven and the girl's at the age of nine. The father shall be obliged to take the child. If the child is a boy who has no father or grandfather, his custody shall be granted to the closest paternal relative; whereas for girls, the right of custody shall not be granted to non-*Mahrams*. If there are no paternal relatives, the boy shall stay with the female custodian unless the judge decides that there is a more eligible custodian.

Article 65: (enforced 03/03/1948)

The father shall not be allowed to take the child out of his mother's country without the latter's authorization as long as the mother is still the custodian. If the divorced father takes the child away from his mother because she got married to a non-*Mahram*, and if she is the only custodian, then the father may travel with him until the right of custody is restored to his mother or to any custodian substituting her.

Article 66: (enforced 03/03/1948)

The divorced mother shall not travel with the child in her custody to a far away country without his father's authorization, and a custodian other than the mother shall not be entitled, in any way whatsoever, to move the child from his place of custody without the authorization of the father, or the judge if the child has no father.

The website address is:

www.druzepersonalstatus.gov.lb
(date of access: Thursday, 26 April 2012)

APPENDIX B

SAMPLE OF MARRIAGE CONTRACT

The following is a copy of the wedding contract signed at the Druze Court.

هامش

الجمهورية اللبنانية
القضاء المذهبي الدرزي

عقد زواج

الرقم: ____________
رقم السجل: ____________
رقم الصفحة: ____________

محكمة ____________ الدرجة الاولى

الفريق الأول

	الاسم واسم الاب والشهرة	اسم الأم	تاريخ ومحل الولادة	محل الإقامة ورقم السجل
الزوج				
الوكيل				
الشاهد الأول				
الشاهد الثاني				

الفريق الثاني

	الإسم واسم الأب والشهرة	اسم الأم	بكر ام ثيب	تاريخ ومحل الولادة	محل الإقامة ورقم السجل
الزوجة					
الوكيل					
الشاهد الأول					
الشاهد الثاني					

المهر

المعجل	
المؤجل	

الشروط الخاصة

بسم الله الرحمن الرحيم والصلاة على نبيه الكريم. اما بعد، وبناء على الاذن الصادر عن ....
.... بتاريخ .... رقم .... فقد اجريت عقد زواج
الفريقين المبين اسم كل منهما أعلاه اللذين اتفقا بإيجاب وقبول واصبحا بحكم هذا الصداق زوجين شرعيين
متمتعين بحقوق الزوجية المعتبرة شرعا والمرعية دينا وقانونا، وقد نظم هذا العقد بحضور الشهود الموقعين
وفقا للأصول والحمد لله بدءا وختاما. حرر في

الزوجة　　　　الزوج　　　　مجري العقد

شهود العقد والتعريف والوكالة　　　　اجزناه وصدقناه

Lebanese Republic	Number: _______
Druze Sectarian Judiciary System	Registration number: ______
_________ Court of first Appeal	Page number: ___________

Marriage Contract

First party

	First, father's and family name	**Mother's name**	**Place and date of birth**	**Place of residence and registry number**
Husband				
Custodian				
First witness				
Second witness				

Second party

	First, father's and family name	**Mother's name**	**Virgin or not**	**Place and date of birth**	**Place of residence and registry number**
Wife					
Custodian					
First witness					
Second witness					

Mahr

Muqadam	
Paid dowry	
Mu'akhar	
Deferred dowry	

Special Conditions

In the name of God the merciful and praise to his noble prophet. In accordance with the permission issues by __________ on ____________ number __________, I have concluded the marriage of the two parties mentioned above who agreed in consent and acceptance and have become in accordance to this contract legally married and enjoy the marital rights that are considered legitimate in accordance to religion and law. This contract was concluded in the presence of the undersigned witnesses and in accordance with traditions. Thanks to God in the beginning and end.

Written on

The husband	The wife	Person who concluded the marriage contract

Contract, identification, and power of attorney witnesses

Concluded and ratified

APPENDIX C

ROLE OF THE ADJUDICATOR

This document, written in Arabic, was given to me by Mr. Fuad Hamdan, a trainee judge at the time I was doing my research. He had prepared the paper as an introduction for those appointed to the role of the adjudicator. The following is an English translation of the document:

The role of the adjudicator in attempting to resolve conflict:

> When the case presented before the court is based upon conflict and disagreement between the spouses the judge appoints, in accordance with Article 47 of the Druze Personal Status Law, two adjudicators. These are chosen from the families of the spouses or from other, non-family members, whom the judge considers capable of resolving the conflict between the spouses. The people are selected after each of the spouses names his/her adjudicator.
>
> The role of the adjudicators is to identify the causes of the disagreement between the spouses and try to resolve the conflict. They should bring the spouses together in one place and invite other people to attend whose presence would, in their opinion, be helpful.
>
> If it proves impossible for the adjudicators to bring the couple together, they should carry on with their efforts by listening to each spouse alone in turn.

Should agreement be reached between the spouses, the adjudicators are to write down the terms of the agreement and submit it to the judge.

In cases where the adjudicators fail to resolve the conflict, each should submit a detailed written report to the judge setting out their efforts. They should describe the way discussions evolved, their opinions on the matter, their suggestions as to the cause for the marital conflict and the extent to which each party should be held responsible for the escalation of the conflict.

The report must be clear and precise so that the judge can rely on it as an accurate summary of the efforts made by the adjudicators to work together and cooperate in preserving the marriage institution wherever possible.

The legal references:

1. Articles 47 and 48 of the Druze Personal Status Law
2. Article 338 to Article 342 of the Law of Principles of Shari'i (religious law) Courts

APPENDIX D

DIVORCE CASE OF MAN MARRYING A NON-DRUZE

This is a copy of a case hand copied from the court records during the process of data gathering. It is provided as an example of a case whereby the judge was sympathetic to the woman as the man took another wife.

ورود: ٢٧/١٠/٩٩
المستدعية:
ضد:
موضوع: نفقة

عقد زواج: ٣٠/٩/١٩٦٩ (مطلقة)
الدرج: ١٢ حزيران ١٩٨٥

الاولاد: ١٢ اذار ١٩٨٦
[illegible]
معجل: ٧٠٠ ل.ل [illegible] خياطة
مؤجل: ١٠٠٠ ل.ل

استحضار الزوجة ٢٧/١١/١٩٩٩
طلبها نفقة: رزقنا ١٣ ولد . تزوجت ويقيمون معي في المنزل الزوجي
. ومنذ شهر شباط ١٩٨٨ ترك زوجي المنزل ولم يعد ولم يؤمن نفقة .
لذلك اطلب نفقة

رد الزوج ٢٨/١٢/١٩٩٠

فور زواجي في ١٩٦٨ اكتشف ان زوجته ليست بكر رغما انه ذلك ما وضعته في
كتابة عقد الزواج اذ انه اكتشف انه كان متزوجا بامرأة كانت متزوجة ولها طفلة.
وكتمت الامر عنه بحجة الرياء. انطلت حيلتها عليه ولم تكن له في اي يوم سندا
بل عبثت في بيتي فسادا واصبحت الالسن تلوك قصص الزوجة واعمالها.
قدم لها كل ما استطاع من حقوق وجلس في ظل ظروف صعبة جدا الا انها بدأت تتغير تجاهه
وبدأ يظهر رفضها لواقعها حيث ازدادت تعنتا وسوءا وبدأت تروي الاوضاع له في اقل الامور
وبالنتيجة توتر العلاقة. حتى اصبحت تخرج من المنزل في غيابه ولا تعود الا قبل عودته
بحجة زيارة الاصدقاء رغم انه منعها ذلك. وانتهى الامر بالهجمة عليه اذ هجمت
عليه وطردته من منزله بكل شراسة. هذا عدا عن ميلها الا نجال لذكره وهي
الان ترتدي ثوب البراءة امام المحكمة. بالتالي هي ليست فقط ناشزا بل سيئة النية
بتقويها بهذه الدعوى بهدف النيل من زوجها والتي لا اساس لها من الصحة.

بالتالي هي المذنبة في التفريق وبطلب اعلان تفريق على مسؤوليتها وعدم وجوب نفقة لها

رد الزوجة: ٢٢/٤/٢٠٠٠

في تصويب الوقائع يذهلني ان تهون عليه عشرة ٢٠ عاما قضيتها في الذل صابرة
على عائلتي حيث كنت احمل في الخياطة لادفع لقمة العيش بعدما اذاقني المر.
قبل زواجي به كان على علم ويقين انني متزوجة وان زوجي توفي ولي ابنة وبرغم
ذلك اصر على زواجه بي رغم معارضة اهله ووالدته بالذات التي كانت ترغب بتزويجه
من شقيقتي ولكنه صمم على الزواج بي وظننت انني بقبول ذلك اهرب من
ظلم خالتي زوجة ابي الا انني هربت الى ما هو اسوأ... ثم تم زواج ابنتي من
ابن خال زوجي بسعي من والدته التي تأكدت من حسن تربيتي لابنتي وحسن سلوكي
لذلك سعت الى هذا الزواج حتى ان شقيقتي خطبت ثم تزوج شقيقة زوجي
في ذلك الوقت اي سنة ١٩٦٩ كان زوجي لا يعمل وكنت اصرف عليه وعلى المنزل من عملي
في الخياطة وعلى الاولاد. رفضت طلب المساعدة من اهلي لان زوجي كان مشغولا في عمله في
الاحزاب حيث انتمى الى تنظيم فلسطيني فكان يتغيب طويلا عن المنزل من دون ان اتجرأ
على سؤاله. كنت اصبر خوفا على اولادي ولعدم رغبتي العودة الى منزل زوجة ابي حيث عانيت الاهانة
وكنت اؤمن اغراض المنزل تحت القصف وهو بعيد عني.
بقي الامر حتى سنة ١٩٩٠ حيث طلبت وتوسطت لاحصل له على وظيفة في شركة Pepsi وقبل
العمل. الا ان القدر كان لي بالمرصاد حيث تعرضت لحادث سيارة سنة ١٩٩٥ بسبب عدم
قدرتي على استمرار الخياطة مما اضطر الاولاد لطلب المال من والدهم الذي كان يرد عليهم
بالضرب وكم مرة ضربني واهانني امام الناس. وكان كلما طلب اولادي ستره يرميها
بوجهه ونعله. كان هدفنا كل الكحول ويتحرش بكل النساء حتى بنات جيراننا
للزيارة حيث تحرش بجيراننا واصدقاء ابنتنا وكنت اشاهد كما علي ان اخفي ما زوده الشيء
حاملة او يقلب الطاولة ويرحل. طلب منا ترك المنزل والرحيل ولكننا رفضنا عندما ترك
المنزل حيث قال انه عاش من دون اهله وسيتخلى عنا ايضا. ارسلنا كثيرا من الناس
للمحاولة ردعه ولكنه رفض وردد امام كثيرين انه طلقني حتى اخذ مصاغي ومقدمه هدية
لزوجته الثانية وعلمت انه تزوج امرأة اخرى من الطائفة الشيعية.

+ رسالة من ابن شقيقه يعلمني انه تزوج بأخرى

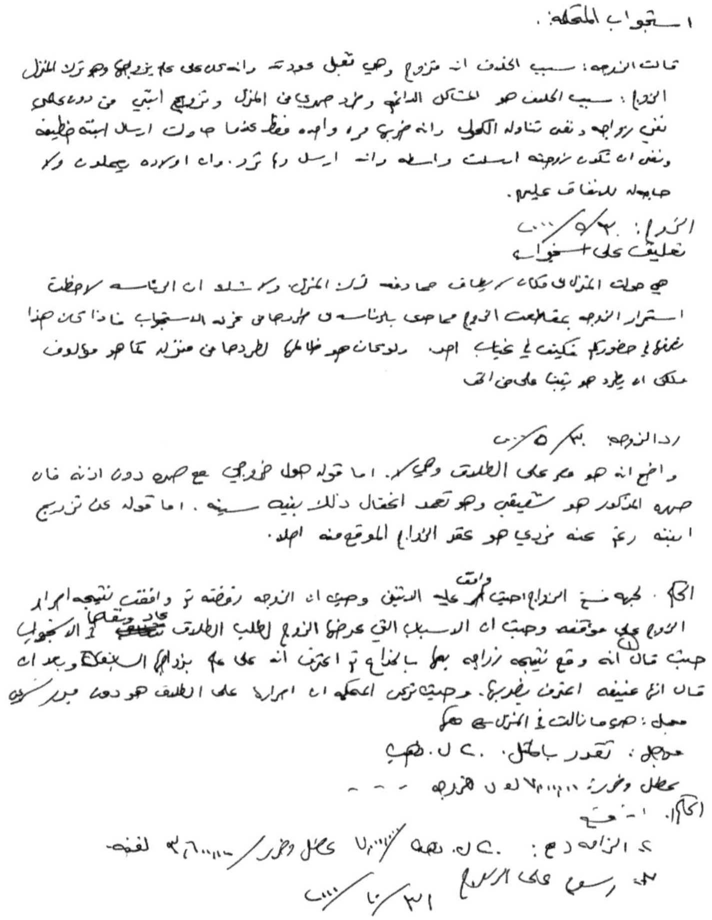
استجواب المحكمة:

قالت الزوجة: سبب الخلاف انه متزوج وهي تقبل عودته وانه كان على علم بزواجي وهو ترك المنزل
الزوج: سبب الخلاف هو المشاكل الدائم وطرد صهري من المنزل وتزويج ابنتي من درزي على
نفي زواجه ونفى تناوله الكحول وانه ضربها مرة واحدة فقط عندما حاولت ارسال ابنته خطيفة
ونفى ان تكون زوجته اسلمت واسمه وانه ارسل لها ثم ... وان اولاده يعملون ولم
حاجة للانفاق عليهم.
الثلاثاء: ٢٣/٥/٢٠٠٠
تعليق على استجوابه
هي حولت المنزل الى مكان لرفاق هادفه ترك المنزل ولم يثبت ان الرئاسة لاحظت
استقرار الزوجة بمقاطعة الزوج ما حصل بالرئاسة ان طردها من غرفه الاستجواب فاذا كان هذا
تصرفه في حضوركم فكيف في غياب احد. ولو كان هو ظالما لطردها من منزله كما هو مألوف
ممكن ان يطرد هو ثيابا على حق الله

رد الزوجة: ٣٠/٥/٢٠٠٠
واضح انه هو مصر على الطلاق وهي لا. اما قوله حول ضربها مع صهره دون اذنه فان
صهره المذكور هو شقيقه وهو تعهد الاحتفال ذلك بنيه سنيه. اما قوله عن تزويج
ابنته رغم عنه من درزي هو عقد الزواج الموقع منه اهلا.

الحكم: لجهة فسخ الزواج حيث لم يوافق عليه الطرفين وحيث ان الزوجة رفضته ثم وافقت نتيجة اصرار
الزوج على موقفه وحيث ان الاسباب التي عرضها الزوج لطلب الطلاق عاد ونقلها في الاخير
حيث قال انه وقع نتيجة زواجه بعمل بالخارج ثم اعترف انه على علم بزواج السابق وبعد ان
قال انه عنيفة اعترف بضربها. وحيث ترى المحكمة ان اصرار على الطلاق هو دون مبرر شرعي
محل: هو ما زالت في المنزل هي هكذا
مؤجل: تقدر بالحل. ل.ل. شهريا
معطل وحرز: ٢٠٠٠٠٠٠ ل.ل. للزوجة - - -
الحكم: ان فسخ
٤ الزوجة دفع: ل.ل. نفقة ١/٧/٢٠٠٠ حتى تاريخ ٦٠٠٠٠ ل.ل لنفقه
رسوم على الزوج
٣١/١/٢٠٠٠

Case Description

The names and residential details of the people in this case have been changed to protect their identity.

The following case was brought before the court in 1999. It started off as an action for maintenance and support case brought by the wife against her husband but ended in divorce.

The couple had married in 1969. Hind, the wife, was born in 1941 and her husband was four years younger. The two did not come from the same area and they were from different families and not maternally related. The witnesses to the marriage contract were not related to either of the couple's paternal or maternal families, which normally points to the fact that they were marrying without their families' agreement.

The wife's original petition submitted to the court on 27 July 1999:

> We had three children Rana, Tamer and Rita. Rita is married and Rana and Tamer are living with me in the marital home. My husband left the house[1] in February 1999 and has not returned since and is not providing maintenance, which is why I am making this demand.

The husband's counter-statement submitted through a lawyer on 28 December 1999:

> As soon as he married in 1969, he discovered that his wife was not a virgin although she had indicated as much in the marriage contract. He discovered the woman he had married had been married before and had a daughter. She had kept the fact hidden from him and tricked him into marrying her. She had never supported her husband and was vicious. People started talking about his wife's wilful behaviour. He had offered her the best he could in terms of a roof over her head and clothing, supporting her in extremely difficult circumstances but her attitude towards her husband began to change. She began to make their life together impossible. She disobeyed him more and more and refused to listen to him, even on the slightest matters. She then began to leave the house without his permission. She would leave while he was out and would return before he did, being absent all day, claiming that she was visiting friends although he had told her not to. The situation got worse and worse until it ended with her assaulting him, forcing him leave the house. She kicked him out. This is just a little of what she did. She is now presenting herself before the court as an innocent woman. As such she is not just a *nashez* but has ill intentions towards her husband as her petition to the court reveals. Her sole purpose is to attack her

> husband and the case itself has no basis. She is the one responsible for the couple's separation and thus I request a divorce that pronounces her guilty and ask that the maintenance case be dismissed.

The wife's response:

> Setting the facts straight: It amazes me that thirty years of our living together would be so easy for him to ignore. Thirty years that I spent living in humiliation in order to preserve my family. I used to work as a tailor to provide food for my family after he made my life wretched. Before I married him, he knew that I was previously married, had a child and that my husband had died. Despite that, he insisted on the marriage although his parents disagreed, especially his mother who wanted him to marry my sister. But he was determined and I thought that by marrying him I would escape the miserable life I was living with my stepmother who was mistreating me. Instead, I ended up jumping straight out of the frying pan into the fire. Later on, his mother acted as matchmaker to arrange a marriage between my daughter and his maternal cousin. This came about because she could see I had brought my daughter up properly and my reputation was good. My brother even married his sister. At that time, in 1969 when we got married, my husband was not working and I spent the money I earned from my work on keeping him and my children. I refused to ask for help from anyone as my husband was busy with his political work after he joined a Palestinian organization. He would be absent from home for long periods of time and I did not dare ask him about his whereabouts. I was long-suffering because I feared for my children and because I did not want to return to my stepmother's house and her mistreatment. I even had to go out under fire [during the civil war] to try to get the things we needed for the household, but he never cared.
>
> That continued until 1990 when I begged people to get him a job with the Pepsi Company and he agreed to work. However,

> fate was against me as I was involved in a car accident in 1995, which forced me to give up my work as a tailor. My children had to ask their father for money but he responded by beating them, and he constantly struck me and humiliated me in front of other people. Whenever the children asked him for anything, his reaction would terrify us. He had become an alcoholic and used to hit any woman who came to our house until people stopped visiting us altogether. He even used to hit my daughter's friends. If the food that accompanied his drinking was not to his liking, he would push the table over and rush out. Finally he ordered me and the children to leave the house but we refused so he went, saying that he had lived without his parents for a long time and could easily live without us. We sent many people to try to persuade him not to leave but he refused to come back and he started saying in front of other people that he had divorced me. He even took the gold that was part of my dowry and gave it to his second wife who is a Muslim Shi'i woman.

Accompanying the wife's statement was a letter from the husband's brother attesting to the fact that his brother had actually married another woman.

The court then asked both parties to appear before it for questioning. In her examination the wife said that the reason for the conflict was that he had married another woman. She agreed to continue with the marriage, adding that he knew she had been married before and that he had left the house of his own accord and had not been made to leave. The husband insisted that the reasons for the break-up were the constant fights and the fact that his brother-in-law forced him to leave the house. Also his wife had married off his daughter without his consent. He denied he was an alcoholic and said that he had only beaten her once after she attempted to set up his daughter's elopement. He denied that his wife had sent people to mediate between them and the fact was that he had sent some people but she had not responded to their attempts. He also said that his children worked and did not need maintenance.

The husband then submitted his comments on the court examination on 30 May 2000:

> {His wife} made the atmosphere in the house unbearable, which was why he left. There can be no doubt that the judge had noticed how his wife kept interrupting during the questioning session as he had ordered her to be removed from the court room. If that was the way she behaved in the presence of a judge, it can be only too easily imagined how she at home when no one else was around. If he had been cruel and unjust, he would have kicked her out of the house as is the common thing in the community. The fact that it was he who was forced to leave shows how things really were.

The wife's comments, also submitted on 30 May 2000:

> It is clear that it is he who wants to divorce and not I. As for his claim that I left the house with his brother-in-law (i.e. the husband of his sister), I want to point out that he maliciously omitted to mention that that man is my own brother and not a stranger, and the fact that he intentionally left out this detail is proof of his ill intentions. As for his claim that I married off his daughter against his will, I merely point out that the marriage contract was signed in his presence and he in fact signed it as one of the witnesses.

The sentence:

> With regards to the request for divorce: Since both agreed to the divorce and since the wife was forced to agree in light of the husband's insistence, and since the husband made certain claims but then went back on them, claiming not to have known that she was married before but then saying he had, and since the husband claimed that she was violent but then acknowledged that he had hit her, the court finds that the husband's insistence on divorce {through the wife's fault} is without legal substance.

Her pre-paid dowry is still with the wife and remains her right.

Her deferred dowry is valued at 20 gold liras.

Damage is evaluated at 7,000,000 LBP, this sum to be paid by the husband to the wife.

Sentence:

1. Divorce.
2. The husband has to pay: 20 gold liras, 7,000,000 LBP in damages and 3,600,000 LBP as maintenance and support.
3. The legal fees to be paid by the husband. Dated: 31 October 2000

APPENDIX E

DIVORCE CASE INVOLVING A SOCIAL WORKER APPOINTED BY COURT TO HELP SPOUSES

This case is one of the cases hand copied from the court records during the data gathering. It is provided as an example of the kind of work done by a social worker appointed by the court to resolve the conflict.

ورود: ٢٠/٦/١٩٩١

المستدعية:

عليه:

موضوع: نفقة وفسخ زواج

عقد الزواج: ٣٠ ايار ١٩٧٨

الزوج محسنة الاعور/ ميشال ٩٣٧

[illegible]

الزوجة: / عنبزوطه ٢٨/٦/١٩٥٧

مهر

معجل: ١٠٠٠٠ ل.ل قطعة نقود

مؤجل: ١٥٠٠٠ ل.ل

استحضار الزوجة ٢٠/٦/١٩٩١

لقد تزوج زوجي مرتين قبلا وكلتا الحالتان باءتا بالفشل

١- تزوج من امرأة برازيلية نتج عنها ابنة تخلى عنها ووالدتها.

٢- التي رافقت الامرين وانتهت الزواج

اما هذا فليس بافضل من سابقته بسبب ممارسة الزوج التي هي اقل ما يقال انها في غاية الدهور والتعالي

الزوجة حاولت ان تتخطى بعض الخلافات الا ان ظلمه وتسلطه الى ان بلغ حد التقص من اذى جسدي ونفسي

- الاذى المادي: حرمها معجل مهرها + منع المعروف عنها وعن اولادها مما اجبرها الاستعانة باهلها على انشاء محل تجاري واقامت دورات في الرسم.

- الاذى جسدي: ضرب باقسى الادوات كالسيف والركل..

- ايذاء نفسي: غياب لمدة طويلة ثم العودة فقط للتسلط والضرب.

... حتى اخيرا شرع في تناول سمعة زوجته الى ان طردها من المنزل.

مع تفهم وساطة المصلحين

رد الزوج: تعرفت على زوجتي العائدة من فنزويلا في وقالت انها لم تتزوج. استعجل
اهلي وتزوجنا. قبل الزواج بيومين قالت لي انها كانت متزوجة بفنزويلا من شاب
درزي سوري وانها طلقته و لدى اهلي. وافقت على الزواج بها مع انها صرحت
امام القاضي انها بكر.

بعد ايام من الزواج جاءني تهديد من الشاب الدرزي الذي لحقها الى لبنان ولم يكن
قد طلقها. ولم تعره اهتمام وطلبت من اهلها اجراء معاملات طلاق منه
ويمكن جلب مستندات تثبت ذلك. هذا افقدني بعض ثقتي بها ولكني استمريت
بحياتي معها مع انها منذ الليلة الاولى تحدثني عن زوجها بطريقة لا يقبلها رجل واقولها للمحكمة
اذا اقتضت الحال.

- بما انها عاشت خارج لبنان تختلف تقاليدنا وترتبط من اهلها وقدمت لها ما تطلبه
ورزقنا اولاد وعندما ساءت احوال البلد فاخذت تتأفف من كل شيء ظننت انها
افتقدت اهلها فارسلتها لهم الا انها عادت بعد شهر لتقنعني ببيع الأثاث
المنزل العقارات والذهاب الى اهلها رفضت اولا ثم بسبب الاحوال ولانها
قالت ان اهلها عندهم مصانع للعمل وافقت وهاجرنا. ولكن بسبب
خلافات بيني وبين زوجات اشقائها اصبح العيش تحت سقف واحد فقال
لنا اهلها ان نعود. فكانت النتيجة خسارة مادية فادحة. ولكني بقيت اصبر.
اما بالنسبة الى زواجي السابق فصحيح الا اني لم اكن اعامل زوجاتي بعنف
- اما زوجتي البرازيلية رفضت العودة الى لبنان بعد وفاة والدي.
- اما الثانية فكان بسبب صحي لانها لم تجري فحوص قبل الزواج.
- معاملتي لزوجتي: كيف انجبت ثلاثة اولاد مني اذ لم اكن جيداً؟ ثم هي لا تجرؤ على
شيء. وتخاف من الوحدة حاولت اجبارها على الحب ولكني لم اوفق وعادت تطلب
السفر الا انني لم اوافق لانه عندي ابنتان لا اريدهما ان يتربيا في الغربة
وكانت قاسية على الاولاد الذين بسبب ضربها لهم يهربون من المنزل ويلجأون
الى المحل التجاري وكانت تستعملهم للضغط علي.
جربت كل طريقة لتغيير رأيها وارسلتها الى المعهد الفني للتعلم الرسم والاشغال اليدوية
واصبحت محترفة وفاجأتني ذات يوم بانها جمعت كل شيء
وعادت لاهلها.
ثم تركت المنزل بحجة اجراء اوراقها ولم تعد. وطلبت السفر الى والدها زاعمة ان
امها توفيت ولم اقبل فلاحقتني وشتمتني وذهبت الى منزل اختها ورفضت العودة

وحاولت الام ان ادم [illegible] البلده رفضوا التدخل كما كانت قد طلبت.

رد الزوجة: انه يشك بزوجته وباجبارها التشهير لاثبات شكه. ويضرب ويستعمل السلاح للتهديد فليس عزيبا ان يرتكب جريمة. تكرار.
هو لا يعود لضربها من قبل اقاربها بل هو هو.

رد الزوج: لم اضربها ابداً طوال المنزل. - رعاية الاولاد: لا احرمهم منها بل هي لا تعتني بهم حتى استاذ وجودهم في المنزل. وبسبب تركها هي تدهور الوضع المادي بعد ما - المحل ليس لي.

[illegible]

تقرير الاخصائية الاجتماعية عن السيدة [redacted] ١٩٩٦/٥/٢٧
بعد لقائي بالاثنين تبين
١- عدم صحة ادعائاته بحسن معاملتها.
٢- شكه قاتل. ٣- اتهامه الدائم لها بالخيانة ووضع علامات وشارات لمعرفة اذا تركت المنزل. ٤- تهديدها بالسلاح وتستفيق من نومها على ضرب.
٥- تأثر بوالده وكيف كان يعامل والدته. ٦- خشيته على اولادها منه اقترحت وضعهم ببيت اليتيم حيث تعمل لضمان حمايتهم ٧- طلبت بشكل ملح رؤية السيد خاصة الشيخ [illegible] الا انه رفض وشوه صورتها امامهم.

تقرير كتبه تحليله: [illegible] عن الزوج: رجب رجب [illegible] / ابع مالية [illegible] حرياته ونظراته. وكل من اولاده ما [illegible] عن الزوجه على [illegible] - - - تقف عقود [illegible] تعلم [illegible]
[illegible]

وبعدان وافقا على طلاق رضائي عاد عنه الزوج
في الجلسة العلنية ٢١/١٠/١٩٩٦
الحكم: للأم ٣ اولاد يبقوا في عهدة والدهم على ان تأخذهم امهم كل اسبوع من مساء الجمعة الى السبت في المدارس وفي العطل [illegible] الى الاحد.

[illegible]
٤/١/[illegible]

Case Description: Social Worker Psychiatrist Evaluation.

The names and residential details of the people in this case have been changed to protect their identity.

The spouses' families come from the same residential area but the wife had been born and had lived for a long time outside Lebanon. They were not maternally related. The witnesses to the marriage contract included only one individual from the wife's family, which suggests that both sets of parents were opposed to the marriage.

The marriage contract was signed in 1978 when Aref, the husband, was 41 and his wife Majida was 21. It was she who brought the case before the court asking for maintenance and divorce.

The wife's petition, drawn up by her lawyer and presented to the court on 20 November 1991:

> Her husband had been married twice before and each of his previous marriages had ended in failure. He had married first a Brazilian woman and had a daughter with her whom he had abandoned. He then married another woman who had had to suffer a lot, and that marriage too had ended in divorce. This marriage was in no better condition because of the husband's behaviour which can only be described as contrary to tradition and proper decency. She had tried to surmount some of the difficulties between them but his authoritarianism was causing her extreme physical and psychological pain:
>
> (1) Economic harm: He denied his wife access to her dowry and refused to give her and her children an allowance, which had forced her to seek help from her parents. She was obliged to open a shop and give painting lessons to support herself.
> (2) Physical harm: Her husband used to beat her with hard objects including a whip and would kick her.
> (3) Psychological harm: He would be absent for long periods and on his return would hit her and insult her. He had recently begun to tarnish her reputation before kicking her out of the house.

All attempts at reconciliation had failed.

The husband's response:

> I met my wife who had returned from Venezuela in 1978 and she said that she would go back to Venezuela if she did not marry. I loved her and married her. Two days before the actual marriage she told me that she had been married before to a Syrian Druze in Venezuela and that she had divorced him. Because I loved her, I agreed to go through with the marriage although she had said before the judge that she was a virgin.
>
> Some days after the marriage, I received a threat from the Druze boy she was married to who had followed her to Lebanon. He had not divorced her. She did not care about him and asked her parents to proceed with a divorce case. I can bring documents to testify to this if required.
>
> As she had lived outside Lebanon, I taught her the values and norms of our community and I tried to bring her closer to my parents and provided all her needs. We had children. When conditions became bad in the country, she began to nag and I thought she was missing her parents so I sent her to them but she returned one month later and started on me to sell the house and furniture and all my land and go with her to join her parents. At first I refused, but then because of the situation in Lebanon and because she had told me her parents owned factories and I could work for them, I agreed. Then, because of her constant fights with her brothers' wives, life under fire became more bearable than life with her family and her parents told us to return to Lebanon. My financial losses were huge but I stayed with her because I loved her.
>
> As for my previous marriages, it is true that I was married twice but I was never violent towards either of them. My Brazilian wife refused to return with me to Lebanon after my father died, and as for my second divorce, it was down to health reasons as we had not carried out the necessary medical checks before the marriage.
>
> Regarding my treatment of my wife – how did we have three children if I was as horrible as she describes? She is very impatient

> and is always afraid and I do not blame her and I tried to keep her away from the war but could not. She wanted us to leave Lebanon but I refused because I have two daughters and I do not want them to live in a strange community. She was very harsh with the children and would beat them for no reason whatsoever and they would run away from her and come to my shop because they are afraid of her. She would use them to try to exert pressure on me. I tried everything I could think of to make her change her mind and I even sent her to an art institute to learn crafts and painting and she became an expert at that. One day she left the house taking all her things with her, which surprised me a lot. She created rows with my parents and left the house to go to one of her relatives and has not returned since. She demanded to leave Lebanon claiming that her mother had died but I refused to let her go so she insulted me and departed for her sister's house and has refused to return. I have tried my best to get her to return but the village notables refused to interfere as she had asked them not to.

The wife's response (through her lawyer):

> He doubts his wife and resorts to magic to prove his suspicions that she is betraying him. [The statement then repeats much of what was mentioned in the original petition.] He constantly beats her and threatens her with weapons. It is not surprising that he denies everything. When he came to her sister's house, he did not ask her to return but beat her.

The husband's counter-statement:

> I never forced her to leave the house. As for the children, I did not deny her the right to see them but she does not care about them and never did, even when she was at home. She left home for financial reasons because of the deterioriating economic situation after the war and the shop is not hers.

A social worker, appointed to evaluate the case, reported as follows:

> After meeting the two it became clear that his protestations that he treats his wife properly are incorrect.
>
> He mistrusts his wife a lot and is deeply suspicious of her. He constantly accuses her of cheating on him and places marks and signs to detect whether she has left the house. He uses weapons and she often wakes up to his beatings. The man is largely influenced by his father and the manner in which he used to treat his mother. She was afraid for her children's lives and suggested that they be placed in the Druze Orphanage where she works to protect their lives. She demanded to see her children but was denied that right, especially her little daughter. The husband gave the children a distorted image of their mother.

Report of the mediating committee:

> The husband thinks ill of his wife and he beats her. He accuses her of going to inappropriate places and looking at people in an inappropriate manner. He heard from his children that their mother was planning to leave and travel abroad. There is no trust between the two and no way through which an agreement could be arrived at. We advise that the two divorce.

Both parties agreed to a divorce settlement but after the husband refused to go along with it, the judge issued the following sentence:

> The three children are to remain with their father. The mother may have the children once a week from Friday evening until Saturday evening during school time and until Sunday evening during holiday weekends and vacations.
>
> The two are divorced.
>
> Each party exonerates the other of any further responsibility.
>
> Dated: 4 November 1992

APPENDIX F

DIVORCE CASE BROUGHT BEFORE THE COURT BY HUSBAND

This is a case brought by the husband before the court. It is one of the cases hand copied from the court records during the data gathering process.

Name: .... الإسم :

Date: / / التاريخ / /

ورود: ٢٠/١٠/١٩٨١

مستدعي:

مستدعى عليه:

موضوع:

عقد زواج: ٣ ش ١٩٥٦

مولود

مولودة سنة

مقدم: ٥٠٠٠ ل.ل. مصاغ + ماكنة خياطة سنجر + تخت تواليت خزانة

مؤخر: ٥٠٠٠ ل.ل.

استفسار من الزوج ضد الزوجة: ٢٠/١٠/١٩٨١

المدعي متزوج .... ومنذ تاريخ زواجهما والزوجان على خلاف مستمر حتى ان الخلاف طال اقارب الزوج الذين لا يدخلون بيته بسبب تصرفات زوجته. فهي تتفوه بالسباب والشتائم من اقل الاشياء تحدث [illegible] حتى ولو صادر من ابنتها وعلى مسمع الجيران ولا تريد ان يكون لزوجها اي سلطة عليها او اي تدخل بشؤونها وذلك موضوع انتقاد حتى من اولادها.

وكان الزوج صابراً متفاديا للفضيحة مع العلم انها اقدمت على تزويج ابنتها من شاب مسيحي بدون رضى والدها. علاوة منذ ثلاثة اشهر تركت البيت الزوجي دون علم زوجها واولادها وتغيبت مدة ٤ ايام غائبة ثم ذهبت بعدها الى بيت اهلها .... ان اولادها هددوا بترك المنزل اذا ما عادت والدتهم اليه وهذا جزء مما يحصل ولا نريد ان نزيد. ولذلك نطلب الطلاق.

→

Name: .... : الإسم
Date: / / / / التاريخ

لائحة جوابية على ادعاء مقابل مقدم من الزوجة ضد الزوج ٣٠/١٢/١٩٩١

اولاً: لجهة تصحيح الوقائع: قبل الرد على ما جاء في الاستحضار لنا ملاحظات عامة حول الوقائع التي حاولت الجهة المدعية تشويهها بايجاز محاولة منع النيل من كرامة الزوج والتضليل للمحكمة لنيل مآربها بالطلاق من الزوج التي حرمت نفسها لتغيير طريق زوجها

ثانيا: السر في شرعية الزواج: « « «

ثالثا: في الواقعة الاجتماعية: تم الزواج بعد سنة من الخطوبة التي زينت له الدنيا بالرياحين والزهور نظراً لمكانة والده الذي كان من المشايخ الكرام

- في الحياة الزوجية: لقد كانت الحياة سعيدة وانجبت له ٣ بنات، وكان آخرهم مولود سنة ١٩٦٣ وكان هو يعمل

وبعد ان تملك المدعي عليه بالدرك واصبح ميسور الحال وبعد ان تحسن وضعه المادي فتحسن وضعه في شركة حيث اصبح مسؤولين .١٠ و ١٥ الف اصبح سيئ العشرة ويعطل حياة العائلة بحيث يغيب لايام ثم لاشهر ويعود ليصطحبهم في رحلة لينسوا الاهمال وهذا ما كان يحدث.

وحينما اصبحت ابنته في عمر الورود احبت اسا ب من غير الدروز فكان الاب مرحبا بالفكرة حتى تزوجته وعندها رفضت الزوجة الزواج وغادرت المنزل لمدة وقضتها مع اهلها وهو تقضي الصيف ذلك في في منزل صهره ولكي تعود المياه الى مجاريها اعتذر من الزوجة واعادها الى المنزل واخذها برحلة الى فرنسا.

لم تكن الزوجة تعلم انه اخذ يدبر لها المكيدة ويزرع الكراهية في نفوس اولادها بالتعاون مع الصهر الجديد وزوجته الملعون.

وبعد عودتهما من فرنسا اخبرها انه سيشتري لها سيارة وسيعلمها القيادة في مكتب وحصل ذلك ولكنه استغل المرض ليطلق اشاعات حولها وحول تصرفها و اولادها كانوا يسمعون اوامره لانه يهدد بحرمانهم من الارث.

ثم في احد الايام طردها من المنزل بمساعدة الاولاد الذين غيروا

Name: .... الإسم :
Date: / / التاريخ / /

اقفال المنزل ~~[illegible]~~ ولم تشأ ان تزعج احدا ولم تخبرهم بل ذهبت
الى منزل صديقتها ومكثت ٣ ايام ثم عادت الى المنزل فلم يفتح لها احد وعلمت
انهم في عند صهرهم وعادت ثم عنها الى منزل ذويها في
ومرت الايام والشهور ولم يتصل بها احد حتى تبلغنا استحضار الدعوى متأخرة لم
حيثه

لذلك نطلب: بانه لا يريد الصلح الطلاق على مسؤوليته / نفقة / الحقوق الزوجية / عطل وضرر

استحضار من الزوجة ضد الزوج في ١٩٨٦/٢/١٥
عند سؤالي اذا ما كنت ارغب في اصلاح ذات البين . تقدمت [illegible] ...
ليكون حكما ونطلب مواجهة

اضافة ١٩٨٦/٤/٨
طالما قد عقدا زواجهما ... وبما انهما يرغبان في انهاء العلاقة وبتراكم بعضهما
ويطلبان اصدار حكما بالطلاق

الحكم: الشيخ محمد دراج
ارادة ذمة
عجل ١٢/١٠/١٩٨٦

Case Description: A Case Brought Forth by the Husband

The couple came from two different residential areas. They were married in 1956 and the husband petitioned for divorce in 1981. The marriage contract was not available in the court records so there is no information as to whether the two were maternally related, whether the parents of either was present, or whether they agreed to the marriage. The husband's petition for divorce drawn up by a lawyer and submitted in court on 20 October 1982:

> ever since their marriage the husband and wife have fought continuously until the rows even involved the husband's relatives who will not enter his house because of his wife's behaviour. She constantly curses and cusses for the least noise or disturbance even if it was her daughter who caused it, and in full hearing of all the neighbours. She does not want her husband to have any kind of authority over her and refuses to let him interfere in any of her activities. Even her own children criticize her for this.
>
> The husband put up with things because he wanted to avoid a scandal, although she agreed to their daughter's marriage to a Christian without seeking his approval. Moreover, three months ago, she left the house without telling her husband or her children and was absent for four days. After that she went to her parent's house . . . The children have threatened to leave home if their mother returns and this is just a part of what was happening and we will not go into further detail. That is why the husband is asking for divorce.

The wife's counter-allegations and statement submitted on 30 December 1982:

> First: To correct the allegations made by the husband, and before responding in detail to his statement, we have a number of general points to make regarding the facts he has tried to twist. To summarize, he has attempted to attack his wife's honesty and to mislead the court with the sole purpose of obtaining a divorce

from the wife who has burned herself out like a candle to light the way for her husband.

Second: The secrecy in the legality of marriage[1] …

Third: With regard to the social facts: The marriage took place after a year's engagement during which the husband presented himself in the best fashion possible since his father was a well-known and respected sheikh. As for their married life, it was a happy one, and they had three children. The last child was born in 1963 while the husband was working as an assistant pilot. Then the husband inherited land and became very rich. His financial situation improved still further after he became a pilot for Middle East Airlines with an income of ten to fifteen thousand Lebanese pounds, but he became bad-tempered and disrupted their family life. He used to be absent for days and weeks on end and on his return he would take the family away on a trip outside Lebanon so they would forgive and forget his behaviour.

When his daughter became an adult, she fell in love with a Christian man. Her father welcomed the relationship. But the wife opposed the marriage and so she left home and went to live with her parents for a while. The husband, meanwhile, spent the summer in his son-in-law's house. To allow things to settle down, the wife returned to her husband after he apologized to her and took her on a trip to France.

The wife had no idea that he was planning and scheming against her. He told her that he would teach her how to drive and would buy her a car. She agreed and he registered her at a driving school but then started making up stories about the places she was going to and people she was meeting. In obedience to their father, the children also started fabricating stories because they were afraid that if they did not do so he would disinherit them.

Then one day he kicked her out of the house with the help of his children and his son-in-law and they changed all the locks. She did not want to disturb her parents so she went to her friend's (a woman) and spent three days there. Then she went back home but no one allowed her in so she went to her parent's house. Days and months passed and no one contacted her until she received the court notice and was made fully aware of his ill intentions.

That is why we request that the sentence of divorce be pronounced against him and that he pays his wife all her rights along with damage and maintenance.

A request by the wife submitted on 15 February 1982:

> When asked whether I wanted to reconcile with my husband I offered the name of Sheikh XXX as my representative and I request a confrontation with the husband.

Agreement signed by both husband and wife on 8 April 1982:

> Since they were married and since they desire to put an end to the relationship and each party clears the other of any obligation, they ask that their divorce be pronounced.

Sentence issued on 21 October 1982:

1. Divorce.
2. Each party freed of its obligations to the other.
3. Fees to be paid by the party who brought the case before the court.

APPENDIX G

MARRIAGE CEREMONIES AMONG THE *AJAWEED*

The weddings of the *Ajaweed* – the religious strata among the Druze – are different from those of the *juhhal* – the non-religious strata. The purpose of this appendix is not to describe the whole wedding but to point out to the reader the different practices of the *Ajaaweed.*

The first difference is the bride's and groom's outfits on the wedding day. The bride does not wear a white bridal gown. In fact she wears the same kind of clothes that she would wear on any other regular day: dark coloured black or navy blue long sleeved shirt or jacket with an ankle length wide skirt (very few wear dresses). They also do not take off their white thick *mandeels.*[1] The only thing that distinguishes their outfit is that it is new – particularly tailored or bought for that day. *Ajaweed* women, of course, wear no jewellery and no makeup, neither on their wedding day nor on any other day.[2] The groom *sheikh*, along the same lines, does not wear a suit. He wears the clothes that he normally wears – a dark coloured *sirwal* (baggy pants) and a white, beige or dark coloured shirt. Colourful shirts are not worn at any time by the *Ajaweed.*

Another distinctive characteristic of the *Ajaweed* weddings is that the *sheikh* does not accompany his family members to the house of his bride. He stays at his house or his parent's (wherever the guests would be later received) and waits for his family to return with his bride. When they return, men and women are normally separated and the receiving of guests is done separately. Chocolates and sweets are offered to all guests but the *Ajaweed* make sure they buy their sweets from shops that do not use any alcohol in their recipes – preferably from a shop owned and run by a *sheikh*.

APPENDIX H

DESCRIPTION OF THE COURT

The Druze Court of First Appeal is located on the first floor of an otherwise residential building in Wata Al-Mosietbeh area in Beirut. A huge sign placed on the façade of the building's first floor clearly publicized 'The Personal Status Court of the Druze Sect – First Court of Appeal' in the Arabic language. Above the sign, there was a big Lebanese flag which is characteristic of official public offices in Lebanon.

The main entrance of the apartment opened to a small hall that led from the far right side to a long corridor. The entrance also contained three doors. The door on the right led to an office; the door on the left led to a small kitchen; and the third door facing the entrance led to the court room. The long corridor that extended from the right side of the entrance led to three offices – two were working areas for court employees and the third was dedicated to storing the court records. The room included a photocopying machine, one bureau and iron shelves that lined the walls. The court documents were stacked on these shelves in large plastic files each containing several cardboard files that each held one case (divorce, custody, inheritance ...). This room was where I spent long hours going through the files and copying divorce cases and later photocopying marriage contracts which were kept in the same room

Entering the court room from the mail door, one stands facing the judge's bench. To the right of the entrance there is a series of leather seats against the wall and in front of the judiciary bench there were four rows of leather seats. To the left of the room, there was a small desk next to a door. The desk contained a drawer in which the court's bailiff kept several white thin veils called a *mandeel.* He would give (lend) one *mandeel* to any female who enters the court room without one.[1] The door next to the desk, led to the judge's chamber. The door opened to a conference room that contained a leather couch and two armchairs and an oval conference table. The conference room was connected to the judge's office by a door. The judge's office contained office furniture: a large desk, bookshelves and some leather armchairs.

On a normal day, the people who had some work in the court would directly go to whichever office they had official business with or would wait in the court room whether they were there to see the judge or for a court session.

APPENDIX I

OTHER CAUSES FOR DIVORCE MENTIONED IN COURT RECORDS

With the analysis of the previous part dealing with the cause for divorce mentioned by either contending parties, only the most divorce – determining cause (primary cause) was mentioned and coded as the first cause for divorce. However, each divorce case, especially contended ones, included more than one cause. For the purpose of the study, three causes were coded and these shall be revealed in the following parts.

a. Wives' Causes of Divorce

There were many causes for divorce mentioned by women but only the most recurring causes shall be mentioned. Among the most mentioned causes were household violence and non-sustenance. It is expected that these two causes would be the most mentioned since these are considered 'legally' permissible causes for asking for divorce on behalf of women without the woman losing her right to the *mahr* in its deferred form. Out of the total 829 divorce cases (these are the cases whereby the wife mentioned a cause – cases in which the wife was absent were excluded), 559 cases were in consent which leaves 270 cases that include a cause for divorce mentioned by the wife. The following numbers, therefore, should be compared against 270 as the sum number of contended cases. It was found that the wives in 118[1] cases mentioned violence as a cause for divorce and non-sustenance was mentioned in 146 cases. In 30 cases, a husband's infidelity was mentioned as the cause of disagreement that led to divorce. In 62 cases, the cause for divorce mentioned by the wife was the reality that her husband particularly asked his wife to leave her house and in 18 cases threats by the use of gun were mentioned.

b. Husbands' Causes of Divorce

The research revealed that the most common cause for divorce mentioned by the husband was *noshouz*, which means that the wife had left the marital house without a legitimate cause, although as mentioned previously *noushouz* referes to any sort of disobedience to the husband. A husband mentioned a cause for divorce, other than in agreement or no cause due to absence, in 218 cases. *Noshouz* was mentioned in 147 cases out of these 218 cases. This is normal and expected since, according to the Druze law, a husband is not forced to pay his wife maintenance, or to give her the delayed *mahr*, if *noshouz* was proven. Other causes for divorce mentioned by the males were wife's parents' intervention (in 43 cases), wife's cheating (in 28 cases) and a wife's inability to bear children (in 20 cases). Evidently, many other causes for divorce were mentioned, but in fewer occurrences than the above mentioned cases.[2]

GLOSSARY

Ajaweed (أجاويد) : the class of religious men and women among the Druze

Al-Bayada (البياضة) : a religious retreat for the very pious

Al-Estitar Bilma'louf (الإستتار بالمألوف) : conceal under or in the familiar – meaning to act in accordance with whatever is accepted by the majority of the population so as not to be persecuted

Al-Ghaiba (الغيبة) : literary, meaning the absence

'Aqida (عقيدة) : belief

'Aql (عقل) : the mind

Baklaweh (بقلاوة) : a traditional Lebanese sweet (also found in Syria) offered at celebrations especially weddings and engagements parties

Dabkeh (دبكة) : a traditional Lebanese dance

Da'i (داعي) : the preacher or a person who calls onto people to join the new faith

Al-Du'a (الدعاة) : plural of Da'i

Da'wa (الدعوة) : the call to the new faith

Dyafeh (ضيافة) : all sorts of food and drink offered to guests

Haram (حرام) : religiously sinful

Hikma (حكمة) : wisdom

Hodoud (الحدود) : the limits, used to refer to the five hodoud of the Tawheed faith each one denoting a colour of the Druze star flag representing one of the first five heralds of the faith

Hofz al-Ikhwan (حفظ الإخوان) : one of the pillars of the Tawhid faith, meaning to safeguard your brothers in faith

Ibra' Zima (إبراء ذمة) : to forsake any right you might have with another person

Ikhraj Qayd 'A'ileh (إخراج قيد عائلي) : the personal particulars of a family which would include a list of the names and details or birth and residence of the man, his wife and dependents

Ikhraj Qayd Fardi (إخراج قيد فردي) : the personal particulars of an individual

Jihaz (جهاز) : the clothing, accessories and special items bought by the groom for his bride

Jismani (جسماني) : meaning the physical body as opposed to the spiritual; another word used to refer to the Druze of the non-religious strata

Juhal (جهال) : used to refer to the common Druze, literally meaning the people who are ignorant in matters of the faith

Junblatti (جنبلاطي) : belonging to or having allegiance to the Junblat family

Jwayid (جويد) : a word used to refer to the religious man

Kalousah (قلوسة) : a small white hat worn by religious Sheikhs

Khalieh (خلية) : etymologically it means a cell but the term is used to refer to a hall built by members of a family or a village in which public events like weddings, funerals, celebrations etc. are held

Khalweh (خلوة) : the place for religious worship among the Druze

Kutub al-Hikma (كُتب الحكمة) : the religious books that the Druze abide by, meaning Books of Wisdom

Mahr (مهر) : dowry, money paid by the groom to his bride upon signature of the marriage contract

Mandeel (منديل) : a white veil worn by Druze women, thick in the case of the religious strata of Ajaweed and thin in the case of the non-religious strata among the Druze

Ma'zoun (مأذون) : a person who is allowed to conduct marriage contracts

Mithaq (ميثاق) : a covenant that a Druze individual wrote when he/she adopted the faith

Mu'ajjal (معجل) : the part of the mahr that is the legal right of the wife to be paid by the husband upon the signature of the marriage contract

Mu'ajjal (مُؤجل) : the part of a mahr that is delayed, to be paid by the husband to the wife upon divorce or when he dies upon which the amount is taken from the husband's inheritance

Muhakkem (مُحكم) : an adjudicator appointed by the court to try to understand the conflict between the husband and wife, to try to reconcile the two or at least resolve the conflict and then submit a report to the judge

Mukaddam (مُقدم) : paid dowry, part of the dowry that is paid before the actual marriage

Mukhtar (مختار) : an elected representative in residential areas (villages or neighbourhoods in towns or cities) who gives certificates of residency, birth and death etc. to the people in the location he/she represents. It is normally a trustworthy individual who is known and knows most people in the area he/she represents.

Muwahhid (موحد) : a male believer in Tawheed

Muwahhida (موحدة) : a female believer in Tawheed

Muwahhidine (موحِدين) : followers of the Tawhid faith/the Druze

Nafaqa (نفقة) : the money a man spends on his dependants

Nashez (ناشز) : a woman who practises noushouz

Noshouz (نشوز) : when a wife leaves her house without due cause

Qadi (قاضي) : the judge

Qati'a (قطيعة) : the term derivers from the verb qat'a which means to cut and here it refers to the female who is cut off or no longer attached to a male through marriage

Ra'is al-Qalam (رئيس القلم) : the head of the registration office at the court

Rahma (رحمة) : the words spoken at a deceased's funeral to ask for God's mercy

Sayyid (سيد) : a religious title held by the descendants of the prophet and in the case of Sayyid Abdullah it was bestowed because of his religiosity

Shari'a (شريعة) : the religious legal code of behaviour

Sheikh al-'Aql (شيخ العقل) : a political appointee considered the sect's representative before the state

Shirwal (شروال) : baggy pants worn by the males of the religious strata

Sitt (ستّ) : lady or respected woman

Sotra (سترة) : etymologically meaning to be covered and is used to refer to a woman whose honour is protected through marriage

Talaq bil taradi (طلاق بالتراضي) : divorce in agreement

Taliq (طالِق) : a word uttered by the Muslim when he wants to divorce his wife – literally meaning you are divorced

Taqiyya (تقية) : hiding behind what is accepted so as to avoid conflict

Taqlid (تقليد) : customs

Taqammus (تقمص) : etymologically from the word qamees meaning blouse or shirt and the Druze believe that the soul changes from one body to another, like a person changing shirts. The word means reincarnation

Tawheed (توحيد) : the name of the new faith – Druze – literary meaning Unitary

Tolbeh (طُلبة) : the occasion at which a man's parents ask for a bride's hand

'Uqqal (عُقال) : the religious class among the Druze, literary meaning the people who are endowed with wisdom or who take decisions

Wakeel (وكيل) : one who has the power of legal representation

Yazbaki (يزبكي) : referring to one belonging to or holding allegiance to the Arislan family

Yistaktir bi kheireh (يستكتر بخيره) : to be very thankful and grateful to someone for a good deed

Zayy (زيّ) : costume, and it is used to refer to the religious attire worn by those belonging to the religious strata

NOTES

Chapter 1. Introduction

1. Nicolas, William *Your Research Project: A Step-by-step Guide for the First Time Researcher* (London, Sage Publications, 2001: 21) points out six features a sociologist must take into account as he formulates his research problem or thinks of a topic to be the center of his sociological research. These six features are. 1. The research should be of great interest to the researcher; 2. The problem should be significant – of some importance to society; 3. It should be delineated. The problem should be properly defined or named; 4. A researcher should be able to obtain the information needed for administering the research; 5. A researcher should be able to draw conclusions related to the problem; 6. A researcher should be able to state the problem clearly and concisely.
2. On 8 May 2008 the city of Beirut witnessed clashes between the politically antagonistic factions of 'March 8' led by the Shi'i Hizbullah and 'March 14' led by the Sunni al-Mustaqbal party. Junblat, the Druze leader, was at that time an active player in the March 14 faction and when the skirmishes extended to Druze areas, the Druze people took up arms and fought the Shi'is in what they also referred to as a 'war of existence'.
3. For an insight into the experiences of the Druze community in the United States, see Azzam, Intisar *Change For Continuity: The Druze in America* (Beirut, Entreprise Universitare dÉtude et de Publication, 1997).
4. At that time there were two officially recognized Sheikh(s).
5. Refer to Articles 17, 18, & 19 of the Druze Law – Appendix A.
6. Tonnies divides society into two types – Gemeinschaft and Gesellschaft. Societies belonging to the first type, Gemeinschaft, are characterized by a high level of interpersonal relationships, intimacy and communality. In such communities, the 'whole personality of the individual tends to be involved, and in each of them the claims of the social unity upon the individual tend to be nearly total' (Nisbet, Robert and Perrin, Robert *The Social Bond* (New York,

Knopt, 1977: 98). What distinguishes this type is the presence of a strong feeling of internal cohesion and collective identity. In such communities, people are subordinated to the will of the group and personal wishes and desires are subdued and not allowed expression.

The second type of social units is termed Gesellschaft, distinguished by emphasis on the part. Relationships are loose and do not demand loyalty or commitment to the general rules of a society. Individuals are evenly linked together and the focus is on personal motivations (Nisbet and Perrin: *The Social Bond*: 99). The individual, not the whole group, is the focal point. Objective individualistic relationships predominate in such societies: people are more individualistic in their choices and make up their own minds concerning their personal affairs with complete disregard to society as a whole (Azzam: *Continuity for Change*: 2-3).

7. The influence of the media is becoming more and more influential in the Arab world. Abu-Lughod, Lila 'Islam and Public Culture: the politics of Egyptian television serials' *Middle East Report: Power, Mass Media and the Middle East*, 180 (January - February, 1993: 25–30) looks into the influence of the medial in Egypt describing its importance in the life of Egyptians.
8. For more on urbanization see Anderson, Nelis *Urbanism and Urbanization* (Leiden: Brill, 1964)
9. Riles, Annelise, 'Models and Documents: artifacts of international legal knowledge' *The International and Comparative Law Quartely*, 48/4 (October 1999: 805-25) undermines the importance of their documents and their analysis. Messick, Brinkley, 'Written identities: legal subjects in an Islamic state' in M. Mundy (ed.) *Law and Anthropology* (Burlington, Ashgate publishing Company, 2002) also relied on the study of legal documents as a method to construct subjective identities in an Islamic state.
10. This court was established in 2008/2009. Before that all people residing in the Matn area of Lebanon referred their legal matters to the Beirut court. Out of habit, some still do so. During the years covered in the research, the Beirut court was responsible for the whole Matn area.
11. The following table shows the distribution of the areas from which the wife came from in divorce cases and the table reveals that the people coming before the Beirut court are from different areas in Lebanon.

Beirut	Aley	Chouiefat	Chouf	Matn	Babda	Gharb/ Shahar	South	Syria	Outside Lebanon	Other	Total
60	33	64	242	298	77	70	36	77	79	30	1066
5.6%	3.1%	6.0%	22.7%	28.0%	7.2%	6.6%	3.4%	7.2%	7.4	2.8%	100%

12. For an idea on how the copying of the divorce cases was carried out see Appendixes D, E, and F which provide three samples of the hand copied material that was done in the court.
13. Thanks are due to the Honourable Judge Sheikh Nsouh Haydar for his support and understanding regarding this matter. I was given permission to photocopy the records but due to their huge size and the delicate nature of the older records in particular, as many were on the verge of tearing apart, it was most suitable to use a high-resolution camera to photograph the records. This ensured that the records were not compromised.
14. Of course, certain documents were missing and we cannot deny the fact that some cases might have been totally misplaced or lost especially since the courthouse was moved from the old courthouse in Saqiet el-Ganzeer area to the Jinah area in Beirut.
15. The marriage contract provided information regarding date of birth, place of residence, place of birth, and names of witnesses of each spouse. It also includes a detailed description of the *mahr*
16. See Appendix C to clarify the role of the adjudicator
17. I refer to this case later as an introduction to the discussion of divorce.
18. For example, as a Druze belonging to the non-religious group, I have very limited information as to what happens during the special prayer evening held on Thursdays. The information is derived from what people of the religious strata tell me. I am not allowed to attend such prayers and as such cannot conduct any direct observation.

Chapter 2. The Druze

1. The question of whether the *Tawhid* should be referred to as a faith or as a religion is an ongoing debate among Druze scholars. I have followed Dr. Sami Makarem's – a well known authority on the topic – in opting for faith. However, if one chooses to consider that a religion is a sum of beliefs and conceptions about God and the universe then the Tawhid may be referred to as a religion.
2. The five Hudud might be compared to prophets in other religions; however, they further represent the five cosmic principles of *al-'Aql* (the Mind), *al-kalima* (the Word), *al-nafa* (the Soul), *al-sabiq* (the Former) *and al-tali* (the Latter). These cosmic principles are essential to the faith and are assumed to be present at all times but choose to make their presence felt whenever they wish to – as they did during the establishing of the faith. Each is represented by a colour and these five colors (white, blue, yellow, red and green) make up the Druze star or flag.

3. The Islamic religious interpretations include the different Islamic discourse that was dominant under the Fatimid Caliphate – an era that abounded in allegorical interpretation of the Quran. It was within this highly active intellectual atmosphere that Al-Hakim announced the Tawhid faith as the pinnacle of religious knowledge. See Al-Khoury, Fouad *Imamat Al-Shaheed walmamat al-Batal: al-tanzeem al-dini lada al-tawaif wa al-aqaliyat fi al-a'lam al-arabi* (Beirut, Markaz dar al-jamia't, 1988).
4. See Bennett, Anne 'Reincarnation, Sect Unity and Identity among the Druze' *Ethnology*, 45 / 2 (Spring 2006: 87–104). It offers an explanation of how reincarnation strengthens the internal unity of the sect.
5. For more on freedom and ethics see Laidlaw, James, 'For an Anthropology of Ethincs and Freedom' *Journal of Royal Anthropological Institute*, 8 (2002: 311-32).
6. It is believed among the Druze that every individual who believed in the new faith at the beginning of the *Da'wa* wrote a vow upon himself and this is referred to a *Mithaq*. This is explained elsewhere in the chapter.
7. Evidently, here the reference is not to the strata of *Ajaweed* who are expected to meet once a week at the religious *khilwa* – religious gathering place – but other than that are not expected to conduct any prayer in front of others. They spend a lot of time daily reading from the Book of Wisdom but they do so in the privacy of their homes, normally setting a room apart for that purpose. The non-religious are not expected to carry out any of this religious behaviour.
8. Attempts at reflecting this equality were evident in the manner through which the law was formulated but still the law remained short of rising up to the equality ordained by the Books of Wisdom. This lack in equality is due to the effect of the predominant Sunni tradition under whose jurisdiction the Druze lived under the Ottoman rule. Men and women are not treated equally by Islamic rule and this was the social situation among the Druze, although is a less pronounced manner.
9. Being a Drzue myself I was able to get some religious knowledge by reading religious texts and asking some religious men for information – though this was not an easy a task to accomplish.
10. Their website is: www.ads.com.
11. For more details on the process and on the qualities of a person who is allowed to join the strata of *Ajaweed* see Al-Asa'ad, Naseeb *Kashf al-Sitar: bahthun mouathaqun fi mazhab al-tawheed -tarikhahou, falsafatehi, a'aqaidih, shkhsiatihi* (Dimashq, Mouasasat A'laa al-dine liltiba'ati was al-tawzi', 2004) pp. 306–307
12. See Khuri, *Imamat Al-Shaheed*: 293–295 for different ranks among the Druze Sheikhs

13. Lately, televisions have been found in many *Ajaweed* household but they insist that they use the television to watch news.
14. Funerals are public events among the Druze. When a person dies, his/her family send obituaries to many Druze village – any village the extended family might have friends in or in-law from. The obituary is announced over a loud microphone in each village, and people from each village gather and go to the funeral of the deceased. The more people attending, the higher esteem the deceased and his/her family is socially awarded. The number of *Ajaweed* – males and females – attending a funeral also reflects on the social status of the deceased and the deceased's family.
15. For more on gender among the Druze see Azzam, Intisar *Gender and Religion: Druze Women* (London, Druze Heritage Foundation, 2007).
16. Some of these modifications include women's right to ask for divorce and inheritance laws that allow freedom of testation among other.
17. For more information on the topic see Abu-Husayni, Abdul Rahim, *The View From Istanbul: Lebanon and the Druze Emirate in the Ottoman Chancery Documents, 1541–1711* (New York, Center for Lebanese Studies in association with I.B.Tauris Publications, 2004).
18. Bourdieu points to this aspect of the law that allows judges to offer their personal interpretations which 'causes a *historization of the norm* by adopting sources to new circumstances, by discovering new possibilities within them, and by eliminating what has been suspected or become obsolete. Given the extraordinary elasticity of texts, which can go as far as complete indeterminacy or ambiguity, the hermeneutic operation of the declaration (judgement) benefits from considerable freedom.... To varying degrees, jurists and judges have at their disposal the power to exploit the polyemy or the ambiguity of the legal formulas by appealing to such rhetorical devices as restriction (narrowing) ... extensions (broadening)... and a whole series of techniques like analogy and the distinction of letter and spirit which tend to maximize the law's elasticity, and even its contradictions, ambiguities and lacunae' (Bourdieu, Pierre "The Forces of law: Towards a Sociology of the Judicial Field" in M. Mundy (ed.) *Law and Anthropology* (Burlington, Ashgate Publishing Company, 2002: 130-31).
19. Such an active role is played by judges in other situations. For example Messick (1993) points out that 'According to both Shafi'i and Zaidi manuals, except in hudud cases, where evidence must be presented, a judge can give judgment based on his own knowledge ('ilm) of events, and, when the evidence of witness is presented, he can accept or reject it on the basis of his own judgment ('ilm) of the justness or unjustness of the person in question, without requiring further verification of their character' (Messick,

Brinkley *The Calligraphic State: textual domination and history in a Muslim society* (Berkley, University of California Press, 1993: 176).

20. Druze law allows the children of a deceased man or woman to take the place of their dead parent and inherit the part that was the deceased's right, of course following the intestate laws of inheritance which gives a male twice the amount received by females, in accordance with Islamic tradition. This is called the right to *khalafiya*. With regard to marriage, Druze law does not permit polygamy as Islamic law does. Druze law also differs from Islamic law in that it grants equal rights to men and women in asking for divorce. Druze law does not allow a divorcee to re-marry the ex-spouse as other Islamic sects do. Divorce is final.
21. *Al-Bayada* is an area in the South of Lebanon that is the house to a sanctuary for the most religious among the Druze. The *Ajaweed* of the *Bayada* spend their whole time devoted to studying the religious scriptures and practice an austere way of life.
22. 'On the eighth of July year 1945 a Druze elite of religious men, legalists, notables and intellectuals met at the house of Dr. Aref Al-Rayess and after reading the suggested Personal Stratus Law for the Druze sect that was published in the Safa newspaper number 2788 on 22 June 1945, they elected a committee composed of Ali Faqih, Hani Ali Raydan, Ahmad Saab, Fandi Hamadeh, Hani Baz, Dr. Aref Al-Rayess and Bashir Al-Awar. The committee was asked to study the law and suggest any alterations and additions it sees fit to introduce to make the law more in line with the Druze customs and traditions' (Taqii Al-Dine, Slieman and Abou Chakra, Nayel *Nizam al-Mowahedine Al-Dorouz Al-Ijtimaa': fi sijil al-ahkam al-mazhabiat lil qadi Ahmad Taqqi Al-Dine, 1866 – 1870* (Beirut: Dar Isharat lil Tiba'at Wa Al-Nashir Wa Al-Tawzee', 2000: 10). Some changes were suggested and introduced in to the law.
23. For more information on the historical presence of the Druze see Sa'di, Sa'ad *Moujam al-sharq al-awsat: siyasat, tarykh, goqraphia, mazahib, wa tawaif*, (Beirut, Dar Al-jeel, 1998).
24. This ethnic identity is strongly felt among the Druze, not just in Lebanon, but also among those of the occupied territories. However, some writers doubt whether this phenomenon is a case of ethnic affirmation or, in reality, one of ethnic manipulation whereby political leaders play on the ethnic identity to further promote their own goals or aims. This separate ethnic identity promotes the goals of some politicians who seek to strengthen it by simply playing upon the internal identity of the sect. This is carried out basically by the Israeli government. For more information on the topic, read Kaufman, Ilana 'Ethnic Affirmation or Ethnic Manipulation: The case of the Druze in Israel' *National and Ethnic Politics*, 9 (2004) pp. 53–81

25. Marriage within the sect is strong among all the Druze and not just those residing in Lebanon. The Druze of the occupied Golan Heights stand as a profound example of those practices, whereby a Druze male from the occupied territories chooses his wife from the Syrian part. The bride crosses the border at the risk of not seeing her family again. For more information on the topic see Mitnick, Joshua 'Druze Wives Hope to Reclaim Old Ties' *Christian Science Monitor*, 99 / 222, (2005) p.7.
26. Still the case especially outside Lebanon.
27. It is worth pointing out that when a Druze male marries a non-Druze, his offspring are registered as Druze. The same does not happen when the mother is a Druze who has married outside the sect. This fact points to the patriarchal nature of the community, which is willing to overlook a misdemeanour if committed by a male but not if by a female.
28. It a common expression among members of the community that cousins are less likely to divorce when married. Old people are generally heard to say, 'Who will preserve her (referring to a female) better than her cousin.'
29. For more information on the topic refer to Dajani, Nabil *Disoriented Media in a Fragmented Society: The Lebanese Experience* (Beirut: American University of Beirut, 1992).

Chapter 3. Marriage among the Druze

1. Such practice is common in all *tolbeh* celebrations among the Druze. Sometimes the groom's mother also brings a gift of gold that she offers to the bride after the acceptance of the request.
2. The number of people present at a *tolbeh* is largely a function of family size and the house of the bride. The number might be less than twenty but rarely exceeds sixty. Although I attended one *tolbeh* where the number surpassed 160, this is a rare occurrence.
3. On an economical level, many youngsters refuse to pay so much money on a celebration that they consider serves no purpose other than informing the community of their status as engaged. One young female said, 'I'd rather spend the money on furniture for my house or in preparing for the wedding.' This attitude is becoming more common among the younger generation. Another reason was given by a young twenty four years old female. She said, 'I refuse to stand in the midst of all people only to display to those what my groom got me as gold gift. The idea makes me feel as if I am an object being decorated.' Such comments further points to a change in women's attitude as they refuse to think of marriage as an exchange – a thing which the older generation accepted more willingly. For example, one old woman said,

'He is going to take our daughter (referring to her granddaughter), the least he should pay in return is the cost of engagement party.'

4. Normally, the oldest male of each subdivision of a family is invited.
5. *Khalieh* – derived etymologically from the word for a cell – is a large building consisting of one or two huge halls which is paid for by all the members of one family who use it for all public events including marriages, engagements and funerals. They have come into popular use because the increased size of village populations makes it impossible for a single house to hold a large number of people.
6. In more traditional villages, the males enter before the females.
7. Sweets and chocolates to be offered to guests.
8. The *dabkeh* is traditional Lebanese dancing that is often accompanied by high spirited singing and the playing of traditional music that include the *mizmar* or *the mijwiz* (wind instrument – blown with the mouth like a flute) and a *derbakeh* or *daf* (percussion).
9. The sum differs depending on what the groom can afford.
10. As a general guideline, the judge prefers that 12 to 15 people from each family be present during the marriage contract signing so as not to overcrowd the court building. This often creates tensions among family members since those who are not invited often feel left out.
11. Such a lunch is always held after the signing of the marriage contract but it could take place either in a restaurant or at the groom's parents' house.
12. When a Druze male marries, it is still the common practice that all members of the village are invited to the wedding. For females, representative members of the different village families are invited, rather than the whole village.
13. It is considered unsuitable for any of the bride's family members to participate in the dancing as it would reflect that they are happy for their daughter's departure. They ought to be sad and not enjoy the dancing and celebrations.
14. The older brother may be replaced by a grandfather or an uncle depending upon the availability and age of the brother. If the father was dead, an uncle or grandfather would replace him at the bride's side.
15. The bride is expected to cry at her wedding day and those who do not are accused of being 'happy to leave the house of their father because they were treated badly by the parents!'
16. This is not necessarily done by the father. Any older person can do it and in some instances the groom is told how to behave before the wedding and follows the instructions accordingly.
17. Rice symbolizes prosperity and procreation.

18. In some wedding parties, guests may not leave early and as such the bride and groom are forced to leave before the guests announcing the end of the celebrations – especially when they are restricted, time wise, by the hotel or restaurant in which they are holding the function.
19. Ahmad's salary amounted to a little less than three thousand dollars per month. For men working in Lebanon, the cost of a wedding are by far more troublesome, although may not be as high as Ahmad's wedding. Tamer, one young man I know was working at a hotel in Lebanon at the time he got married. His salary was six hundred dollars. His wedding costs were as follows (only the wedding): $1,000 bridal gown, $1,000 dyafeh, $150 his suit, $100 card, $400 floral decorations, $600 dance group, $600 video and pictures. He did not hold a dinner party and the bridal car was a gift from his uncle. The total cost was $5,450. Evidently, the costs and the bride's expectations vary with the income of the groom. Many Druze old men and women insist that what is being done in weddings in contemporary times does not reflect the Druze traditions. Singing and dancing, in the past, were done by relatives and friends, as was the food served during dinners or lunches which was also cooked by relatives and friends.
20. Sheikh al-'Aql is the head of the sect before the state. He is considered the highest authority among the Druze in matters that engage the sect in relationships with other sects and the Lebanese state. He is also the head of the *majlis Mazhabi* – the religious council – which controls matters pertaining to the sects *awqaf* – the money and property belonging to the sect. He is not, however, the highest religious authority. The religious authority is voted to the position by the *Ajaweed.*
21. Among the Druze a *ma'zoun* is simply a person who has the *izn* which means the permission to do something, in this case sign a marriage contract.
22. The courts are in Beirut, Aley, Matn Baaqlin, Rashaya and Hasbaya.
23. The *mukhtar* is a person elected by the people of a certain village or residential area to carry out the registration of births and deaths within that area. This person should have a good knowledge of all the people within the area and functions as a trustworthy figure who is able to ensure the validity and legality of certain documents.
24. These are the author's translations of the articles.
25. This principle was clarified in the second chapter and it allows the Druze to act in accordance with the social accepted norms if following their own norms and traditions might place them in danger.
26. The guardian is the father but in cases the father is deceased or absent the court appoints another male – normally the grandfather or the father's brother – as a guardian.

27. Other cultures have different terms for the allocation of a certain amount of money or goods that are given to the parents of the brie for various reasons. Among the Tswana, this amount is referred to as bogadi. They consider the bogadi as a thank you gift to the parents of the bride who have taken care of her for that time and allowing the groom to marry her. Other explanations are offered such as 'a compensation to the wife's parents for the loss of her services, and others that it is a sort of register of the marriage showing that the cohabitation of the man and woman showing that the cohabitation of the man and woman meets with the full approval of their respective families, but the main function of the bogadi is to transfer the reproductive power of a woman from her own family into that of her husband' Schapera, Issac, 'A handbook of Tswana law and custom' in Sally Falk Moore (ed.) *Law and Anthropology: a reader* (Malden, Blackwell Publishing, 2005: 82).
28. This is a difference between Druze and other Islamic sects.
29. A Druze wife is legally allowed to refuse to join her husband in a residence that is not labelled as *shari'* which means legally accepted without being a *nashez*.
30. Druze resident in the United States have yearly meetings to bring the Druze community together but which indirectly also serve as appropriate settings for spouse selection.
31. Author's explanation in parenthesis.
32. For more information on the topic see Harik, Judith *The Public and Social Services of the Lebanese Militias* (Oxford, Centre For Lebanese Studies, 1994).
33. For more information concerning the laws and obligations surrounding the engagement, marriage contract and wedding ceremonies see the case at the beginning of this chapter.
34. For more on the status of women and marriage in the Arab world see Al-Si'dawi, Nawal *Dirasat A'n al-marati wa al-rajoul fi al-moujtama' al-arabi* (Beirut, Al-mouasasa al-arabiati lildirasati wa al-nahri, 1990). The author points out that the marriage of females in the Arab world is not a matter of choice but more of a *de facto* reality since an unmarried woman is looked down upon and pitied. Mundy, Martha *Domestic Government: kinship, community and polity in North Yemen* (London, I.B.Tauris Publishers, 1995) p. 101) points out the young age at which both men and women marry in Yemen where 90 per cent of women marry by the time they reach twenty and 90 per cent of men by the time they reach 25.
35. See law articles three and four in the Appendix A.
36. This case reflects the importance associated with virginity and the direct connection between virginity and honour, not just among the Lebanese Druze but in the Arab world at large. For more on the importance of virginity and

its association with honour see Katherin Zoepf, 'A Dishonourable Affair: Chastity and Honour Killing in Syria' in S. Khala and R. Khalaf (eds.) *Arab Society and Culture: An essential reader*, (London, Saqi, 2009: 15–166).

37. During the war, many families convinced their girls to marry at an early age (17 or 18) if the groom was an immigrant. They saw marriage to a migrant as one way through which they could ensure their daughter's safety – get out of the country and escape the civil war. Many such females did not hold wedding parties but would travel to their husband's place of residence after the marriage contract was signed by a legal representative on behalf of the groom.
38. Passing through the old souk I counted 13 religious men who were owners of the shops. The total number of shops in the section of the old souk I counted was 56.
39. Mundy's research revealed that economic ability reflects directly on a male's marriage potentials. 'A poor may have to work for several years before he possesses a home or means to marry, whereas among landed families a man's first marriage is his parent's gift' (Mundy: *Domestic Government*: 101).
40. In Egypt's low income communities, the age gap increased between husband and wife because 'women want to start family early and men of their age can't' (Hoodfar, Homa, 'In the Absence of Legal Equity: Mahr and marriage negotiation in Egypt low income communities' *Arab Studies Journal*, 6-7/2-1, (Fall 1998 – Spring 1999), p.105).
41. Among the Druze, it is the man who has to cover the costs of the marriage, including the wedding ceremony, the furniture, the bride's *jihaz*, the house and any other costs incurred in the marriage process. It is even the practice among some families to expect the groom to start supporting his bride from the beginning of the engagement.
42. Among the Druze, the law allows for freedom of testation and my research Tarabey, Lubn *Testate and Intestate Succession among the Lebanese Druze* MA Thesis, Department of Social and Behavioral Sciences, American University of Lebanon, Beirut, Lebanon (1998) on this topic revealed that Druze do not bequeath their immovable property such as land and homes and, therefore, the possibility of favouring in-kin marriage to prevent division of property does not largely apply.
43. This old man had two of his sons married to cousins, and two of his daughters married to men from the same family (in the village, of course). It seems that he favoured in-kin marriages regardless of how easy it would be to marry outside the village or otherwise.
44. See appendix B for a sample of the marriage contract.
45. In marriage contracts, the term bedroom appears written in the space allocated for the specification of the *mahr*. I asked how this is legally evaluated

and the answer was that the bedroom refers to the following: a double sized bed with its mattress, two bedside tables, a chest of drawers or any other piece of furniture that replaces this item and a closet. In case of divorce, the wife takes the bedroom the couple had been using or is given it value in money.

46. I recall that my mother had such one machine but she did not use it a lot. My grandmother on the other hand, did use her sewing machine a great deal.
47. From my own observations in the community, very few young girls know how to use a machine.
48. The next chapter looks in to the practice of divorce and in these cases it becomes evident that in cases of divorce a judge would evaluate the economic worth of the sewing machine and would have the husband pay the wife the sum of money as part of her *mahr* to which she is entitled upon divorce.
49. Bedroom, as a term, is used here to refer to a double bed and a closet and other wooden furniture expected to be present such as bedside tables. If other items such as a mattress and linen are intended to be included they would be explicitly mentioned in the contract.
50. There is no law that requires that the judge to be a sheikh but this has been the usual practice. One judge trainee at the time I was working in the court told me that once he was assigned the post of 'judge' he would immediately dress as a sheikh and seek to become one. Of course, this is not obligatory and, Nouhad Hariz, former head of the Supreme Court – the highest position within the Druze legal system – was not a sheikh although he used to wear the religious attire of a sheikh when he was representing the Druze sect at official meetings with other sectarian leaders in Lebanon and whenever he served at the judicial bench. All judges are in fact expected to dress in their religious attire when they appear in court.
51. According to Max Weber, there are two kinds of contracts: one referred to as purpose contract and the other as status contract. A purpose contract is one that has a specific end or purpose normally economic in nature. Status contracts, on the other hand, are contracts that 'determine a person's status as child, father, wife, slave, master, clansman, fellow warrior, protector. . . Marriage, for example, is evidently a status contract, and obviously Weber knew that it continues to exist in modern society' (Stewart, Frank, 'Archaic forms of contract in Max Weber's theories in Arab and Somali customary law' in Ron Shaham (ed.) *Law, Custom and Statute in the Muslim World* (Leiden, Brill, 2007: 134–135).
52. See Betts, Robert *The Druze*, (New Haven, Yale University Press, 1988).
53. This is also used by Khuri as the title of his book. See Khuri, Fuad *Being a Druze* (London, Druze Heritage Foundation, 2004).

54. The use of the *mahr* as a tool is dealt with in the next chapter. On another level, Homa Hoodfar (1998-99) explains how *mahr* negotiations have become more and more important in Egypt where the amount specified varies depending on the social status of the bride. In low income communities women negotiate their *mahr* and insist on getting it before the marriage because they realize it would be all they would get from their husbands as they cannot expect much after the marriage (Hoodfar: *In the Absence*: 99-111).
55. It was clear in the research concerning divorce (see chapter 6) that the judge nowadays calculates the purchasing value of money at the time the contract was signed and assigns a sum equal in purchasing value at the time of divorce.
56. The effect of residence may reveal itself in the amount – not kind – of *mahr* specified. However, this requires special study that goes beyond the limits of this research since such an attempt would require an analysis of the monetary value of the Lebanese pound and the gold lira in each of the 33 years of the study, and would serve as a subject of a different study.

Chapter 4. Divorce among the Druze

1. Or a detailed description of the court offices see appendix H.
2. If I did not have my own *mandil*, which is a thin white veil, he would provide me with one. He keeps a stack in his desk and would hand these out to women who did not have one. Once, he gave one to a woman who was wearing an t-shirt instructing her to cover her shoulders with it. When I first started visiting the court, he told me that on days when the judge was in the court and when I wanted to attend the sessions or needed to talk to the judge, I had to cover my hair with the *madil*. There was also a sign on the bulletin board in the main entrance that instructed all those entering the court room to be decently dresses. This meant no shorts, open shoes and sleeveless shirts for men and no short skirts and sleeveless tops for women. The note further instructed women to abide by the Druze tradition of wearing a *mandil*. When I worked at copying records, I did not wear my *mandil* and was not asked to. The Druze women wear the *mandil* during funerals, morning and when any religious prayer is being recited such as during the signing of a marriage contract.
3. This man was married to his father's brother's daughter who was three years older than him. His wife, he claimed was becoming obsessively jealous. She had attacked him a number of times and he was finding it hard to deal with her and wanted to get a divorce. He told me that he had married at an early age, 23, and that he was an orphan – both his parents had died when he was

a child. His uncle, his wife's father, brought him up. His uncle did not have a son and asked him to marry his daughter so the inheritance would not go outside the family.

4. This equality is emphasised in the religious scripture (see Chapter two) and the history of the faith, but has been weakened by the Druze's practice of *taqiyya* and their interaction with Sunnis whose religious traditions differ from the Druze with regards to women's equality.
5. One old Druze woman was walking along a narrow street in her village when she noticed her ex-husband coming towards her. She quickly turned her face away and looked at the wall. He passed behind her without even looking in her direction. She continued on her way only after the sound of his footsteps had vanished.
6. For more on the practice of repudiation according to Islamic tradition and the role of other religious authorities such as a *mufti* see Vogel, Frank, 'The complementarity of ifta' and qada': three Saudi fatwas on Divorce' in M.K. Masud, B. Messick and D. Powers (eds.) *Islamic Legal Interpretation: muftis and their fatwas* (Cambridge: Harvard University Press, 1996) and Messick, Brinkley *The Calligraphic State: textual domination and history in a Muslim society* (Berkley, University of California Press, 1993).
7. See Appendix C for more on the role of the adjudicator.
8. The rights that the husband had under these conditions were not to surrender the mahr to his wife and further claim harm and injury. In my research, the husband had not claimed harm and injury in any case.
9. See chapter one for clarification of what is meant by pseudo-divorce.
10. Attempts have been made by a number of legalists and women activists among the Druze to change the custody law so as to ensure that children of divorcees are not separated. In one case, the current judge has actually ruled that the all the children stay with their mother until the youngest girl is nine, after which the father has care of them all.
11. Such out of court procedures were described by Messick, Brinkley, 'Provincial judges: the Shari's judiciary of mid twentieth century Yemen' in Ron Shaham (ed.) *Law, Custom and Statute in the Muslim World* (Leiden, Brill, 2007) as parallel to state imposed legal authority and hence entailing the same degree of authority.
12. The following table reveals the exact distribution.

Decision of adjudicator	In favour	Against	Total
Wife's adjudicator	29	4	33
Husband's adjudicator	23	10	33

13. It is worth pointing out that no female has been appointed to act as adjudicator – at least in the cases covered in the research. However, when a psychiatrist's assistance was sought, or when a lawyer was appointed by the judge to try to resolve the conflict, they were females.
14. Refer to Appendix E for an overview of the case in which the social worker was involved.
15. Smoking is something that the strata of *Ajawid* are not allowed to do.
16. This lawyer says that her role is to try to resolve the conflict in as friendly a manner as possible. She told me she has even resolving a conflict without divorce. The husband and wife were both educated and loved each other but they lived next to his mother who interfered in everything and caused problems. The lawyer convinced him to find another residence and they resumed their marriage. However, she said she is not always as successful. She also informed me that the judge, who is a religious sheikh, does not want to hear details of cases involving jealousy or betrayal, and he prefers to refer such cases to her to submit a written report.
17. I know of one case where the woman left her husband upon hearing from her neighbor that he was saying to some people in the village square that he had divorced her. She later married another man. Neither her first marriage nor her second were registered in court, as was the case with her divorce. The woman died ten years ago at the age of 96.
18. The normal *mahr* is in the range of US $3000–$4000, equal to the cost of their travelling expenses and/or money lost through time off work.
19. In most male Druze wills, there is mention of the *Qati'a* and she (or they) is most often allocated some kind of property to protect her against need in case she remained unmarried or was widowed. For more reference on the topic see Tarabey, Lubna *Testate and Intestate Succession among the Lebanese Druze,* MA Thesis, Department of Social and Behavioral Sciences, American University of Lebanon, Beirut, Lebanon, 1998.
20. Mir Hosseini (2006) mentions this morality crises that judges face particularly in divorce cases. (Mir Hosseini, 'Muslim Women's Quest for Equality: Between Islamic law and feminism' *Critical Inquiry*, 32/4 (Summer 2006), p. 653).
21. At the present time $1= 1,500L.L. So 7,000,000 L.L. is about $3,500. The minimum wage in Lebanon was raised up this year (2013) to about $500 per month. It was $300.
22. An agreement made between Walid Junblat, Nabih Berri and Elli Hobeika, leaders of Lebanon's three main militias, in 1985 in Syria to put an end to the war. It was never put into effect and fell apart the following year. [See eg. http://www.mongabay.com/history/lebanon/lebanon-the_tripartite_accord.html].

23. The predominantly Druze Progressive Socialist Party (PSP) led by Walid Junblatt.
24. The marriage contract that was available with the divorce case did not include the name of her father as the witness to the marriage. Instead her paternal uncle was present with a note that he was acting as her legal guardian since her father refuse to come.
25. See Azzam, Intisar *Gender and Religion: Druze Women* (London: Druze Heritage Foundation, 2007: 57-66).
26. Household violence continue to be a problematic issue in Lebanon as there is no law that protects females from family violence. There are current attempts by feminist groups and NGOs to exert public pressure on the parliament to reconsider the laws but so far all attempts have proven unsuccessful. The police rarely interfere and when they do they only ask the husband to promise not to continue with the violent behaviour. The case is not different in many Arab countries and is not much better in western countries. For example, Sara Beck and Donileen Loseke studied how police dealt with family violence and they discovered that violence to women by family members was largely ignored or treated lightly, which was not the case when violence was inflicted by a non-family member. Furthermore, they noticed a general unwillingness to define women who suffer from household violence as victims, adding that in many cases women who were subjected to family violence refused to follow up on the legal procedures. (Beck, S. and Loseke, D *"Handling Family Violence: Situational Determinants of Police Arrest in Domestic Disturbance"*, in Macauley, Stewart et al., (eds) *Law and Society: Readings on the Social Study of Law* (New York, W.W. Norton and Company, 1995: 25–58).
27. Other causes included psychological violence, meanness, showing disrespect, having psychological problems, failing to welcome guests properly. . . They were grouped into one category because each of these reasons cropped up in one or two cases only and were not susceptible to statistical handling.
28. Someone who practices *noshouz*, which etymologically means a high place. In this instance it is used by religious law to refer to any woman who disobeys her husband's commands, refuses to accompany him to his legal residence, refuses to care for her husband and children, mistreats her husband, uses verbal abuse, and refuses to have sexual relations with her husband.
29. In fact, it is this unwillingness on the part of many females to reveal intimate details of what they consider to be shameful or inappropriate behaviour, such as unacceptable sexual conduct, that denies many women their legal rights. Shame prevents them from revealing details that would be legally beneficial to them.

30. For example, a large number of individuals belonging to the Halabi family from Bshamoun in Mount Lebanon migrated during the civil war to Canada. All have taken up residence in Toronto and live in close proximity to each other. They hold funerals and weddings, celebrate births and religious celebrations together. I know of five siblings (three brothers and two sisters) who live in the same building. They appear to have taken Bshamoon to Toronto.
31. The husband can, according to the Lebanese law, prevent his wife and children from traveling outside the country by arranging for a prevention order to be placed in the airport. A wife can practice the same right but through a court decision whereas a husband does not need a court decision.
32. Among the strata of the *Ajaweed*, a religious male may not marry a non-religious females, but a religious female may do so as in the case of this woman.
33. The judge relies in his judgment on evidence provided by litigants to the court brought from reliable sources such as a doctor's certificate, trustworthy individuals in the community such as a *mukhtar* or well known religious sheikh, as well as technological evidence such as recordings. However, in all instances, the evidence is evaluated by the judge who decides when to accept or reject evidence. Sara Vincent-Grosso 'An ethnography of evidence in a Tunisian divorce court' in Maaike Voorhoeve *Family Law in Islam: Divorce, Marriage and Women in the Muslim World* (London: I.B.Tauris, 2012) examines divorce in Tunisia and the turmoil women face in providing documented proof in the court and the method through which the documents they provide is evaluated and treated.
34. Articles number 1 and 26. Their translation is the following.

    Article 1 stipulates: A male who has completed 18 years and a female who has completed 17 years are allowed to get engaged.

    Article 26 stipulates: Each engaged person is allowed to go back on an engagement without being under any legal obligation. As for the matter of gifts exchanged between the engaged parties, if the breaking of the engagement was from the male, then he has no right to claim his gifts whether these were still present or not. However, if the breaking of the engagement was from the females, then she has to return all that she had received as gifts. If these gifts were still present, she has to return them. If these were used and no longer present, then she has to return similar gifts or their price.
35. The most recent one I personally know about took place thirty five years ago. It was an agreed upon marriage between a man and his father's brother's daughter – agreed to by their parents i.e. the brothers.
36. For more on the nature of *Ajaweed* marriage refer to Appendix G.

37. It is important to clarify that signing the marriage contract, among the religious strata and the non-religious strata, does not make sexual relationships socially accepted. Sexual relationships only become acceptable after the wedding party though during times of war these parties were not held a small dinner would be held at the home of the groom to announce the transition of the couple into marriage life. Signing the marriage contract makes it more socially acceptable for the *sheikh* to visit the house of his bride.

Chapter 5. Marriage and Divorce: A Comparative Approach

1. 'According to available data, the Druze make up about 6.5% of Lebanon's total population of 3,506,000. In other words, there are approximately 228.000 members of the sect in the country' (Azzam, Intisar *Gender and Religion: Druze Women* (London: Druze Heritage Foundation, 2007: xxiii).
2. The reader should be aware that this interval covers four years, not five, because 2003 was the date chosen to end the data-gathering from the court.
3. The marriage contract was not signed by any member of the wife's family which shows that they were opposed to the marriage
4. *Bayt byout* ('mummies and daddies') is a game played by little children where they act out married life. A girl plays at being a mother and a boy plays at being the father.
5. She worked in a school and could afford to take care of her children. When the daughters reached the age of nine their father requested that they live with him. They were unwilling and would make problems for him with his second wife so that he was forced to return them to their mother each time he attempted to have them at his house.
6. It is not permitted to marry a girl under the age of 15 and most (not all because some judges feel morally obliged to marry a girl who had lost her virginity either willingly or not willingly) judges refuse to sign a marriage contract involving such a young girl even if her parents are present and agree to it. Many people find a way around the law by registering an agreement at a local notary office and waiting until the girl is 15 to approach the court.
7. Nassar, Nagle, 'Legal Plurality: reflection on the status of women in Egypt' in B. Dupret, M. Berger and L. Al-Zwaini (eds.) *Legal Pluralism in the Arab World* (The Hague, Kluwer Law International, 1999) clarifies how in Egypt laws that limit age of marriage for females are cheated. The people claim that the girl was not officially registered at birth and did not have an identity card. Then an age certificate would be produced upon a doctor's examination and witnesses testimonies. The author points that 'Many of these certificates are obtained by fraud and falsification of the data of the age

certificate itself... Though clearly a criminal act, the practice of 'age certificate' is neither rejected nor frowned upon by the social standards, nor is it expressly regarded as social threat' (Nassar, *Legal Plurality*: 196).

Chapter 6. The Druze: Peripheral Change

1. Sorokin offers an explanation of such seemingly contradictory behavioural manifestations in terms of what he termed as the 'logico-meaningful integration of culture'. He particularly explains the matter in the following manner:
   '... the ordering element is not uniformity of relationship between the fragmentary variables, but identity of meaning or logical coalescence. Hidden behind the empirically different, seemingly unrelated fragments of the cultural complex lies an identity of meanings which brings them together into consistent styles, typical forms and significant patterns....' (Sorokin, 1973: 23).
   As such, if one is able to identify the logico-meaningful relationship between seemingly different aspects one would be able to better explain the social reality of a culture.
2. The whole religion was centered on this last idea. *Al-'Aql*, in its spiritual form, was the first cosmic principle to radiate or emanate out of God and out of *al-'Aql al-koli* (the total or whole Mind), all reality came to exist.
3. An important part of the Druze funeral is the part in which the deceased Druze is taken in the coffin to the cemetery. Before the coffin is placed inside the structure, normally a small room, built for the dead, the Druze religious men, the *sheikhs*, assemble around the coffin that is placed on the ground to pray. They afterwards say *allah yorhamou* or *yourhama* which means 'may God have mercy on him/her. This utterance of words of mercy – *al rahma* — is highly regarded among the Druze and associated with having a good reputation. Withholding the *rahma* is a stigma that accompanies the deceased's family.
4. Refer to the chapter on divorce and particularly to the case in which the judge upon hearing that the man had married a non-Druze, ordered the husband to pay a large amount of money and to leave the house, which was legally his, for his x-wife and his children to reside in until the marriage of all female children. Such a judgement would not have been cast had the man left his wife for another Druze woman, as other cases revealed. By marrying a non-Druze, this man stopped being a Druze and did not deserve to be treated as such.
5. Refer to *The Druze and Their Faith in Tawheed* by Anis Obeid, 2006 specifically to chapter 5 (pp. 95–169) for more on the tenants of the faith – although Dr. Sami Makarem in his book *The Druze Faith*, 1974 refuses to consider these as Tenants of the faith. To him, they are the characteristics (Khisal) of a *Muwahhid*.

6. The pronunciation of the strong 'q' is characteristic of the Druze, especially those living in villages. It is so characteristic of the Druze that people in Lebanon recognize the Druze from their speech.
7. There are a number of religious symbols/figures that the Druze appeal to at times of stress or crises. They resemble the five *hooud* which the Druze assume are present at all times. When a Druze says out loud the words *ya moulieh al-'Aql* or *ya abou-Ibhrahim*, he/she is appealing to religious figures. It resembles a Christian calling out the name of Mary or Jesus Christ and a Muslim the name of Mohammad.
8. There are numerous accounts of historical persecution from Sunni Muslims. We still hear accounts of how Druze individuals working in Saudi Arabia are constantly subject to harassment from local religious authorities – the *moutaweh* – who consider them 'without a religion' – as one informant told me. Moreover, if one considers the reaction and behaviour of the Druze – both commoners and religious men – on 7 May, 2008 and how they carried arms and fought against the Shi'a in what they considered a fight for survival, one cannot fail to recognize the their continued feeling of being under threat.
9. For detailed information as to how certain religious practices group the Druze together refer to Khuri's book *Being the Druze* and particularly to the chapter entitled 'There are no Free-Floating Druze' which details how the Druze appearing free in their religious practice are in reality always under control in their social behaviour without this control being felt in a structured manner, but is nonetheless strongly felt.
10. The case of the Druze in Jordan does not fully fit this description as they are not acknowledged as a separate sect and thus do not enjoy the same kind of freedom that the Druze in Lebanon enjoy.

Appendix A

1. The laws have been translated by Ms. Nadine Ayoub.
2. *Iddah* refers to the period during which a woman may be suspected of being pregnant. During this period, a woman should not marry so that if she was pregnant, the father of the child could not be a matter of debate.
3. *Mahram* refers to people with whom a person must not marry or have sexual intercourse with.
4. In the Arabic language the term *maal*, though meaning money, is used to anything that has value like money. A plot of land, a water well, or animals are part of a person's *maal* and hence the article specifies that a wife can get support from the value of the *maal*.

Appendix D

1. This means the house that she had been living in with her husband – most likely rented or owned by the husband.

Appendix F

1. The lawyer includes a set of claims about how marriage life should be sacred and the relationships and details should remain part of the sacred relationships and as such a secret.

Appendix G

1. The mandeel that the Ajaweed wear is not the same kind of thin whilte mandeel that the juhhal Druse women wear when they are in court (see chapter four – introduction) or are in the presence of a judge. The Ajaweed mandeel is thicker and larger. It is not just dapped on the hair but wrapped tight around the hair and covering the ears as well. Some women cover their mouths and the very religious even cover their noses showing only their eyes. The mandeel often drops to more than half their back.
2. Some may wear some Arabic kohl in their eyes – inside the eyelids.

Appendix H

1. This was referred to in the introduction to chapter four and further developed in the endnote relating to that section.

Appendix I

1. Here percentages are not used because they might be misleading to or misunderstood by the reader as the total would not add up to a hundred per cent since each case may mention more than just one cause.
2. For example, in one instance referred to under the section – time a case is kept at court – the husband's reason for divorce was wanting to have a son.

BIBLIOGRAPHY

Abu-Husayni, Abdulrahim *The View From Istanbul: Lebanon and the Druze Emirate in Ottoman Chancery Documents, 1541–1711*, (New York, Center For Lebanese Studies in Association with I.B.Tauris Publications, 2004)

Abu-Lughod, Lila 'Islam and Public Culture: the politics of Egyptian television serials' *Middle East Report: Power, Mass Media and the Middle East*, 180 (January - February, 1993), pp. 25–30

Alamuddine, Nura and Starr, Paul *Crucial Bonds: Marriage Among the Lebanese Druze* (New York, Caravan Press, 1980)

Anderson, Nelis *Urbanism and Urbanization* (Leiden, Brill, 1964)

Atashe, Zeidan *Druze and Jews in Israel: A Shared Destiny* (Brighton, Sussey Academic Press, 1995)

Azzam, Intisar *Gender and Religion: Druze Women* (London, Druze Heritage Foundation, 2007)

——— 'Druze Women: Ideal and Reality' in Kamal Salibi (ed.) *The Druze: Realities and Perceptions* (London, Druze Heritage Foundation, 2005) pp. 95–104

——— *Change For Continuity: The Druze in America* (Beirut, Entreprise Universitare d'Étude et de Publication, 1997)

Babbie, Earl *The Practice of Social Research* (California, Wadsworth Publishing Company, 1992)

Barakat, Halim *The Arab World: Society, Culture and State* (California, University of California Press, 1993)

Bennett, Anne 'Reincarnation, Sect Unity and Identity among the Druze' *Ethnology*, 45 / 2 (Spring 2006) pp. 87–104

Berger, Maurits 'The Shari'a and legal pluralism: the example of Syria' in B. Dupret, M. Berger amd L. Al-Zwaini (eds.) *Legal Pluralism in the Arab World* (The Hague, Kluwer Law International, 1999)

Berk, Sara and Loseke, Donileen 'Handling Family Violence: Situational Determinants of Police Arrest in Domestic Disturbance', in Stewart Macaulay,

Lawrence Friedman and John Stookey, (eds) *Law and Society: Readings on the Social Study of Law* (New York, W.W. Norton and Company, 1995) pp. 25–58

Betts, Robert *The Druze*, (New Haven, Yale University Press, 1988)

Bourdieu, Pierre 'The Forces of law: Towards a Sociology of the Judicial Field' in M. Mundy (ed.) *Law and Anthropology* (Burlington, Ashgate Publishing Company, 2002)

——— *The Logic of Practice* (Cambridge, Polity Press, 1990)

——— *Outline of a Theory of Practice* (Cambridge, Cambridge University Press, 1977)

Cohen, Robin and Kennedy, Paul *Global Sociology* (New York, New York University Press, 2000)

Dajani, Nabil *Disoriented Media in a Fragmented Society: The Lebanese Experience* (Beirut, American University of Beirut, 1992)

Dupret, Baudouin *Adjudication in Action: An Ethnomethodology of Law, Morality and Justice* (London, Ashgate Publishing Company, 2011)

——— 'Sexual Morality at the Egyptian Bar: Female circumcision, sex change operations and motives for suing' *Islamic Law and Society*, 9/1 (2002), pp. 42–69

——— 'Legal pluralism, normative plurality and the Arab World' in B. Dupret, M. Berger and L. Al-Zwaini (eds.) *Legal Pluralism in the Arab World* (The Hague, Kluwer Law International, 1999)

Dupret, Baudouin, Maurits Berger and Laila Al-Zwaini (eds.) *Legal Pluralism in the Arab World* (the Hague, Kluwer Law International, 1999)

Engle Merry, Sally 'Legal Pluralism' *Law and Society Review*, 22/5 (1988), pp. 869–96

——— 'Rights Talk and the Experience of Law: implementing women's human rights to protection from violence' *Human Rights Quartely*, 25/2 (May 2002), pp. 343–81

Evlanger, Howard, Elizabeth Chambliss and Marygold Melli 'Participation and Flexibility in Informal Process: Cautions from the Divorce Context' in Macauley, Stewar et al (eds.) *Law and Society: Readings on the Social Study of Law* (New York, W.W. Norton and Company, 1995) pp. 119–128

Falk Moore, Sally (ed.) *Law and Anthropology: A Reader* (Malden, Blackwell Publishing, 2005)

——— 'Certainties undone: fifty turbulent years of legal anthropology, 1949–1999' in Sally Falk Moore (ed.) *Law and Anthropology: A Reader* (Malden, Blackwell Publishing, 2005)

Ferrie, Jean-Noel 'Norms, law and practices: the practical obstacles that makes it impossible to separate them' in B. Dupret, M. Berger and L. Al-Zwaini (eds.) *Legal Pluralism in the Arab World* (The Hague, Kluwer Law International, 1999)

Fitpatrick, Peter 'Law and Society' in M. Mundy (ed.) *Law and Anthropology* (Burlington, Ashgate Publishing Company, 2002)

Giddens, Anthony *Sociology*, fifth edition (Cambridge, Polity Press, 2006)

Goode, William *World Changes in Divorce Patterns* (New Haven, Yale University Press, 1993)

——— *World Revolution in Family Patterns*, (New York, Free Press, 1963)

Grenfell, Michael (ed.) *Pierre Bourdieu: Key Concepts* (Durham, Acumen, 2008)

Harik, Judith *The Public and Social Services of the Lebanese Militias* (Oxford, Centre for Lebanese Studies, 1994)

Hoodfar, Homa 'In the Absence of Legal Equity: Mahr and marriage negotiation in Egypt low income communities' *Arab Studies Journal*, 6–7/2–1, (Fall 1998–Spring 1999), pp. 98–111

Kaufman, Ilana 'Ethnic Affirmation or Ethnic Manipulation: The case of the Druze in Israel' *National and Ethnic Politics* 9 (2004) pp. 53–81

Kelly, Tobias 'Docuemented Lives: fear and the uncertainties of law during the second Palestinian Intifade' *Journal of Royal Anthropological Institute*, 12 (2006), pp. 89–107

Kessing, Roger and Stratherm, Andrew *Cultural Anthropology: A Contemporary Perspective*, 3rd Edition, (Fox Worth, Harcourt Brace College Publishers, 1998)

Khalaf, Samir and Khalaf, Rozanne (eds.) *Arab Society and Culture: an essential reader*, (London, Saqi, 2009)

Khuri, Fuad *Being a Druze* (London, Druze Heritage Foundation, 2004)

——— 'Aspects of Druze Social Structure: There are no Free Floating Druze', in Kamal Salibi (ed.) *The Druze: Realities and Perceptions*, (London, Druze Heritage Foundation, 2005)

Laidlaw, James 'For an Anthropology of Ethincs and Freedom' *Journal of Royal Anthropological Institute*, 8 (2002), pp. 311–32

Layish, Aharon *Marriage, Divorce and Succession in the Druze Family: A Study Based on Decisions of Druze Arbitrators and Religious Courts in Israel and the Golan Heights*, (Leiden, Brill, 1982)

Macauley, Stewart and Friedman, Lawrence *Law and Soceity: Reading on the Social Study of Law* (New York, W.W. Norton and Company, 1995)

Makarem, Sami *The Druze Faith*, (New York, Caravan Books, 1974)

——— 'The Druze Faith' in Kamal Salibi (ed.) *The Druze: Realities and Perceptions* (London, Druze Heritage Foundation, 2005) pp. 1–8

Masud, Muhammad Khalil, Brinkley Messick and David Power (eds.) *Islamic Legal Interpretation: muftis and their fatwas* (Cambridge, Harvard University Press, 1996)

——— 'Muftis, fatwas and Islamic legal interpretation' in M.K. Masud, B. Messick and D. Powers (eds.) *Islamic Legal Interpretation: muftis and their fatwas* (Cambridge, Harvard University Press, 1996)

Maton, Kall 'Habitus' in Michael Grenfell (ed.) *Pierre Bourdieu: Key Concepts* (Durham, Acumen, 2008)

Maxwell, Joseph *Qualitative Research Design: An Interactive Approach*, 2nd edition, (Thousand Oaks, Sage Publications, 2005)

McQuarie, Donald *Readings in Contemporary Sociological Theory: From Modernity to Post-modernity* (New Jersey, Prentice Hall, inc., 1995)

Meltzer, Bernard and Petras, John 'The Chicago and Iowa School of Symbolic Interaction' in *Symbolic Interaction: A Reader in Social Psychology*, 2nd edition, (Boston, Allyn & Bacon, 1972) pp. 43–57

Messick, Brinkley 'Provincial judges: the Shari's judiciary of mid twentieth century Yemen' in Ron Shaham (ed.) *Law, Custom and Statute in the Muslim World* (Leiden, Brill, 2007)

——— 'Written identities: legal subjects in an Islamic state' in M. Mundy (ed.) *Law and Anthropology* (Burlington, Ashgate publishing Company, 2002)

——— *The Calligraphic State: textual domination and history in a Muslim society* (Berkley, University of California Press, 1993)

Mir-Hosseini, Ziba *Marriage on Trial: A Study of Islamic Family Law*, (London, I.B.Tauris Publishers, 1993) (c.2000)

——— 'Muslim Women's Quest for Equality: Between Islamic law and feminism' *Critical Inquiry*, 32/4 (Summer 2006), pp. 629–45

Mitnick, Joshua 'Druze Wives Hope to Reclaim Old Ties' *Christian Science Monitor*, 99/ 222, (2005) p. 7

Mnookin, R. and Kornhauser, L. 'Bargaining in the Shadow of the Law: the case of Divorce' in Macauley, Stewart at al. (eds.) *Law and Society: Readings on the Social Study of Law*, (New York, W.W. Norton and Company, 1995) pp. 119–99

Muakasa, Sahar *Comprehensive Bibliography of the Druze Religion* (New York, The Druze Research and Publication Institute, 2004)

Mundy, Martha (ed.) *Law and Anthropology*, (Burlington, Ashgate Publishing Company, 2002)

——— *Domestic Government: kinship, community and polity in North Yemen* (London, I.B.Tauris Publishers, 1995)

Nassar, Nagle 'Legal Plurality: reflection on the status of women in Egypt' in B. Dupret, M. Berger and L. Al-Zwaini (eds.) *Legal Pluralism in the Arab World* (The Hague, Kluwer Law International, 1999)

Nicolas, William *Your Research Project: A Step-by-step Guide for the First Time Researcher* (London, Sage Publications, 2001)

Nisbet, Robert and Perrin, Robert *The Social Bond* (New York, Knopf, 1977)

Obeid, Anis *The Druze and their Faith in Tawhid* (New York, Syracuse University Press, 2006)

Osanloo, Orzoo *The politics of Women's Rights in Iran* (Princeton, Princeton Uniersity Press, 2009)

——— 'Islamico-civil "rights talk": Woman, subjectivity and law in Iranian family law'. *American Ethnologist*, 33/2, (2006), pp. 191–209

Prothro, Edwin and Diab, Lutfy *Changing Family Patterns in the Arab East* (Beirut, American university of Beirut, 1974)

Riles, Annelise 'Representing in-between: law, anthropology and the rhetoric of interdisciplinarity' in M. Mundy (ed.) *Law and Anthropology* (Burlington, Ashgate Publishing Company, 2002)

——— 'Models and Documents: artifacts of international legal knowledge' *The International and Comparative Law Quartely*, 48/4 (October 1999), pp. 805–25

Ross, Lawrence 'Settled Out of Court: the Social Process of Insurance Claims Adjustment', in Macauley, Stewart at al. (eds.) *Law and Society: Readings on the Social Study of Law* (New York, W.W. Norton and Company, 1995) pp. 104–11

Schapera, Issac 'A handbook of Tswana law and custom' in Sally Falk Moore (ed.) *Law and Anthropology: a reader* (Malden, Blackwell Publishing, 2005)

Shaham, Ron (ed.) *Law, Custom and Statute in the Muslim World* (Leiden, Brill, 2007)

Stewart, Frank 'Archaic forms of contract in Max Weber's theories in Arab and Somali customary law' in Ron Shaham (ed.) *Law, Custom and Statute in the Muslim World* (Leiden, Brill, 2007)

Sorokin, Pitirim *Social and Cultural Dynamic: Fluctuation of Forms of Art*, vol.1, (New York, American Book Company, 1937)

Tamanaha, Brian 'The folly of the "social scientific" concept of legal pluralism' in M. Mundy (ed.) *Law and Anthropology* (Burlington, Ashgate publishing Company, 2002)

Tarabey, Lubna *Testate and Intestate Succession among the Lebanese Druze* MA Thesis, Department of Social and Behavioral Sciences, American University of Lebanon, Beirut, Lebanon (1998)

Thomson, Patricia 'Field' in Michael Grenfell (ed.) *Pierre Bourdieu: key concepts* (Durham, Acumen, 2008)

Turner, Stephen *Social Theory and Sociology: The Classics and Beyond* (Cambridge, Blackwell Publishers, 1996)

Vincent-Grosso, Sara 'An ethnography of evidence in a Tunisian divorce court' in Maaike Voorhoeve (ed.) *Family Law in Islam: divorce, marriage and women in the Muslim world* (London: I.B.Tauris, 2012)

Vogel, Frank 'The complementarity of ifta' and qada': three Saudi fatwas on Divorce' in M.K. Masud, B. Messick and D. Powers (eds.) *Islamic Legal Interpretation: muftis and their fatwas* (Cambridge, Harvard University Press, 1996)

Voorhoeve, Maaike, *Family Law in Islam: Divorce, Marriage and Women in the Muslim World* (London: I.B.Tauris, 2012)

Weber, Max 'The economy and social norms' in Sally Falk Moore (ed.) *Law and Anthropology: a reader* (Malden, Blackwell Publishing, 2005)

Woodman, Gordon 'The idea of legal pluralism' in B. Dupret, M. Berger and L. Al-Zwaini (eds.) *Legal Pluralism in the Arab World* (The Hague, Kluwer Law International, 1999)

Yngvesson, Barbara 'Inventing Law in Local Setting: Rethinking Popular Legal Culture' in Martha Mundy (ed.) *Law and Anthropology* (Burlington, Ashgate Publishing Company, 2002)

Zoepf, Katherine 'A dishonorable Affair: Chastity and Honor Killing in Syria' in S. Khalaf and R. Khalaf (eds.) *Arab Society and Culture: an essential reader* (London, Saqi, 2009) pp. 159–66

Reports

ESCWA *Impact of Social and Economic Changes on the Arab Family: An Exploratory Study* (New York, United Nations, 1992)

——— *Women and Men in the Arab Region: A Statistical Portrait* (New York, United Nations, 1999)

Arabic References

Abu Tourabi, Jamil *Men hom al Mouahidine al Druze? Nahsatahoum al-Tarikhiya, tamoudo'ihim al-geographi, 'akidatahoum al-dinniyat, d'adatahoum watakalidihoum, nidalahoum al-watani wa al-qaoumi, ashhar u'lamihoum* (Dimashq, Dar A'laa al-dine lilinashr wa al-tawzieh wa al-tarjamat, 1988)

Al-Awar, Saji'h *Al-ahwahl al-Dirziat: i'lman wa igtihadan*, (al-moualif, 1983)

——— *Al-Ahkam al-Shari'at wa alQanouniat fi Al-wasiat wa al-zawaj wa al-talaq I'nda al-dorous bialmoukaranat ma'a anzimat al-mazaheb wa al-tawaif al-'okhra fi loubnan*, (Beirut, Dar An-Nahar Lilnasher, 1989)

Al-Asa'ad, Naseeb *Kashf al-Sitar: bahthun mouathaqun fi mazhab al-tawheed–tarikhahou, falsafatehi, d'aqaidih, shkhsiatihi* (Dimashq, Mouasasat A'laa al-dine liltiba'ati was al-tawzi', 2004)

Al-Harshi, Asad *Al-talaq: asbabouhou al-ijtima'iyati wamobariratouhu al-Shari'ati* (Beirut, Dar al-ilm, 2002)

Al-Khoury, Fouad *Imamat Al-Shaheed walmamat al-Batal: al-tanzeem al-dini lada al-tawaif wa al-aqaliyat fi al-a'lam al-arabi* (Beirut, Markaz dar al-jamia't, 1988)

Al-Si'dawi, Nawal *Dirasat A'n al-marati wa al-rajoul fi al-moujtama' al-arabi* (Beirut, Al-mouasasa al-arabiati lildirasati wa al-nahri, 1990)

Al-Ghanem, Kolthoum Ali *Zahirat al-talaq fi al-moujtama' al-Qatari, dirasat maydania*, (Al-Dawha, Jamia't al–dawhat, 1998)

Ma'tou K, Fredirick *Mourtakazat Al-saytara al-gharbia: moukaraba socio-ma'arifiat* (Beirut, Dar al-Hadatha, 2008)

Nasr, Mirsil *Moujam al-halal wa al-haram inda al-mouahidin al-doruze* (Beirut, almoualif, 2004)

Sa'di, Sa'ad *Moujam al-sharq al-awsat: siyasat, tarykh, goqraphia, mazahib, wa tawaif*, (Beirut, Dar Al-jeel, 1998)

Taqii al-Dine, Adel Hamdan *Al-marati fi mogtama'a al-mouahidine al-dorouz bayna al-amsi wa al-yaoum* (Beirut, al-fourat lilnahser, 2004)

Taqii Al-Dine, Slieman and Abou Chakra, Nayel *Nizam al-Mowahedine Al-Dorouz Al-Ijtimaa': fi sijil al-ahkam al-mazhabiat lil qadi Ahmad Taqqi Al-Dine, 1866–1870* (Beirut: Dar Isharat lil Tiba'at Wa Al-Nashir Wa Al-Tawzee', 2000)

INDEX

Abduction (*see also* Kidnapping), 92
Abortion, 108, 154, 223
Abroad, 52, 100, 121, 122, 124, 126, 151, 166, 167, 170, 178, 182, 248
Abu Ali Al-Mansur Al-Azziz Bi-Allah, 18
Abu-Tourabi, 20, 24
Abuse, 60, 109, 140, 141, 147, 155, 187, 89, 280
Acceptance, 19, 27, 28, 87, 108, 149, 230, 271,
Actualization, 22
Ad-Darazi, 19, 20
Adjudicative, 33
Adjudicators (*see also Muhakkem*), 12, 101, 108–11, 121, 123, 163, 164, 173, 200, 202, 222, 231, 232, 263, 267, 278, 279
Admissible evidence, 161
Adultery (*see also* Infidelity), 102, 160, 221, 222
Africa, 154
Age,
  Average, 55
  of Custody, 226
  Difference, 179, 188, 189
  of Divorcing couples, 163
  Limitation in marriage, 214, 215
  of Marriage, 49, 54, 55, 59, 60–4, 66, 165, 175, 179, 180, 181, 185, 186, 197
  Young, 1, 35–7, 41, 42, 53, 57, 58, 60, 63, 65, 66, 70, 72, 80, 82, 85–7, 187–9, 203, 271, 273, 274, 276, 282
Agency, 7, 172
Agent, 33, 48, 95, 200, 202
Agreement, 11, 13, 48, 49, 85, 92, 99, 102, 104–8, 110, 113–5, 117, 119–22, 125, 126, 130, 133, 134, 136, 143, 145, 146, 149, 154, 155, 158, 159, 161, 163, 164, 168, 197, 200, 202, 217, 232, 236, 148, 155, 261, 264, 282
Agriculture, 36, 37, 587, 66, 81
Ajaweed, 16, 28–31, 66, 88, 140, 156, 170, 171, 197, 201, 256, 257, 262, 263, 268–70, 273, 281, 285
Alamuddine, 10, 35, 36, 73, 286
Alcohol, 29, 182, 257
  Alcoholic, 30, 181, 238
Aley (court), 266, 273
Aley (town), 64, 66, 67, 73, 120, 137, 138, 145, 167, 171, 178
Allegation, 132, 160, 164, 253
American Druze Association, 28
Anderson, 6, 266
Annulment, 49, 101
Anthropology, 7, 266, 268
Appeal, Court of, 10, 125, 229, 258
Appeal, to religion, 201, 284
Appeals,
  of a Husband, 132, 138
  of a Wife, 60, 118

Arab, 26, 53–6, 59, 68–70, 73, 171, 189, 226, 274, 275, 279, 280
Article (of law), 47, 49–51, 80, 100–3, 163, 166, 214–26, 220, 232, 265, 273, 274, 281
Aqida, 35, 262
'Aql, 101, 197, 214, 215, 262, 264, 267, 273, 283, 284
al-'Aql, Sheikh, 4, 48, 49, 214, 215–8, 264, 273
Asset, 81
Atashe, 18–20, 22
Attire, 98, 264, 276
Austere, 27, 29
Australia, 155, 169
Authority, 7, 22, 31–3, 36–8, 87, 154, 174, 199, 253, 167, 173, 178
Al-Awar, 4, 32, 48, 270, 291
Awareness, 36, 63, 64, 75, 126, 130
Azzam, 25, 26, 29, 35, 38, 140, 265, 266, 269, 280, 282

Baabda, 64
Baaqlin, 10, 178, 273
Babbie, 15
Bahauddin Al-Samuqi, 20, 24
Bailiff, 97, 259
Baklaweh, 46, 262
Banking, 37
Barakat, 68, 73
Bargains, 105, 133
Al-Bayada, 33, 262, 270, 272
Bayt byout, 186, 282
Beatings (*see also* Violence), 81, 83, 84, 86, 87, 89, 94, 99, 109, 112, 113, 136, 137, 139, 140, 151, 155–7, 182, 189, 245, 247
Bedroom (furniture), 124, 196, 275, 276
Beirut City Court, 10, 11, 36, 51, 52, 54, 60, 61, 64, 66, 67, 72, 89–92, 94, 102, 105, 114, 118, 119, 125, 127, 132, 136, 145, 149, 150, 155, 161, 165, 167, 177, 178, 180, 183, 188, 190, 194, 258, 265, 266, 267
Benefits, 76, 106, 130, 131, 133, 269
Betrothal (*see also* Engagement), 40, 168
Betts, 35, 62, 129, 131
Bint halal, 58
Bourdieu, 4, 5, 8, 21, 95, 201, 269
Books of Wisdom (*see also Kutub Al-Hikma*), 21, 26, 29, 203, 263, 268
Boycott, 30, 198
Bridal, 41, 42, 44, 45–7, 256, 273
Bride, 30, 39–47, 50, 52, 59, 63, 64, 68, 85, 89–91, 168–70, 256, 262–4, 271–5, 277, 282
  Search for a, 39, 68, 178
Bureaucratization, 5

Cairo, 18–20
Caliph, 18, 20, 268
Car, 40, 41, 44–7, 78–80, 110, 124, 141, 238, 254, 273
Carpet, 80, 87, 89
Celebration, 40, 44, 178, 262, 263, 271–3, 281
Chocolates, 40–2, 44, 46, 257, 272
Choice, 2–5, 16, 17, 23, 24, 35–7, 53, 71, 73–9, 95, 114, 120, 169, 189, 192, 197, 199, 200, 203, 225, 226, 274
Chouf, 10, 64, 167, 178, 226
Chouiefat, 64, 73, 120, 145, 226
Christians, 24
City residents, 64–7, 71–3, 76–8, 83, 86, 90, 94, 118–21, 145, 146, 148, 149
Civil marriage, 100
Civil war (*see also* War), 3, 26, 52, 55–8, 62, 75, 79, 84, 103, 115, 117, 128, 132, 137, 139, 178, 179, 181, 182, 194, 203, 237, 275, 281
Clan, 35, 279
Closet, 276
Clothes (*see also Jihaz*), 50, 81, 113, 134, 157, 169, 219, 236, 256, 262
Coercion, 23, 24, 48, 49, 197, 198
Cohabitation (*See also* Residence), 50, 274

Cohesion, 3, 27, 34, 35, 104, 200, 203, 266
Cohen, 6
Communalism, 37
Communication technology, 2, 5, 37, 95, 159
Community, 1–4, 6, 9, 10, 13–17, 21, 26–39, 52, 60, 66, 68, 76, 81, 91, 94, 95, 103, 104, 145, 150, 152, 162, 167, 169, 171, 172, 174, 194, 196, 197, 199–202, 239, 246, 247, 265, 271, 274, 276, 281
Commute, 36, 79
Comparative, 10, 11, 17, 56, 116, 175, 194, 282
Compensation, 101, 102, 124, 133, 154, 203, 274
Complaint, 97, 110, 187
Compromise, 11, 15, 85, 106, 164, 200, 267
Computer, 11, 84, 86, 88
Conciliatory, 31
Conference room, 98, 259
Confidentiality, 15
Conflict resolution (*see also* Mediation), 109, 110–2, 114, 116–20, 122, 127, 130, 163, 172, 173, 200, 231, 232, 241, 263, 279
  Mechanisms of, 2, 8, 158
Confrontation, 26, 51, 140, 255
Consanguinity, 36
Consent, 14, 25, 43, 47–49, 99, 104, 105, 115, 117, 119, 121, 126, 129, 155, 159, 160, 163, 164, 170, 172, 197, 217, 230, 238
Consummation, 13, 14, 16, 50, 102, 166, 219
Contemporary world, the, 5, 32, 114, 273
Contending parties, 88, 260
Contested, 14, 104, 1105, 114–116, 118, 119, 121, 125, 126, 129, 136, 147, 149, 155, 163
Contract, 4, 10–14, 16, 17, 33, 47–55, 60, 61, 64, 68, 69, 74, 80–89, 100, 101, 120, 155, 166–170, 176–180, 183, 185, 188,
Control, 5, 16, 86, 115, 198, 273
Cost, of the engagement and the wedding (*see also* Expenses; Financial demands), 47, 54, 58, 59, 66, 73, 110, 272, 273, 275
Court buildings, 10, 11, 36, 43, 51, 52, 54, 61, 64, 86, 89, 91, 94, 97, 190–3, 196, 201, 217, 218, 220–2, 223, 227, 229, 230, 236, 239, 245, 253, 258–259, 263, 266, 267, 272–7
Court intervention, 104, 117, 120, 172
Cousins, 36, 39, 43–5, 74, 80, 89, 113, 154, 155, 160, 165, 190, 192–4, 225, 237, 271
  Parallel cousins, 36
Custody, 7, 13, 38, 99, 103, 107, 108, 124, 125, 130, 131, 133–5, 138, 149, 152, 159, 160, 161, 173, 202, 203, 205, 223–6, 258, 278
  Denial of, 202
Custom(s), 3, 7, 8, 32, 33, 40, 66, 82, 85, 87, 90, 100, 150, 170, 190, 196, 264, 270, 274
Cyprus, 100

Dabkeh, 41, 262, 272
Al-Daher Ad-Din Allah, 20
Da'is, 19, 24
Dance, 44, 59, 262, 273
Dar Al-Hikma, 18
Data analysis, 11, 14, 103, 109, 129, 135, 136, 144, 162, 185, 233, 241–9, 282
Da'wa, 268
Decorations, 40, 41, 42, 44, 46, 47, 271, 273
Delays in marriage or divorce, 59, 63, 64, 66, 72, 73, 78, 142, 152, 164–6
Demographics, 51, 78, 175, 178
Devalue, 91
Diab, 10
Diffusive, 7
Disagreement, 101, 104, 114, 149, 154, 196, 193, 200, 231, 261

Disease, 102, 215, 221
Disharmony, 104
Disobedience, 125, 220, 261
Divorce,
By agreement, 102, 104, 117, 119, 120, 126, 163, 197
Non-fault, 124
Pseudo-divorce, 16, 166, 167, 278
Rate of, 175–8, 195
Type of, 103–5, 114, 115, 118–21, 125, 126, 163
Displacement, 137
Dispute, 101, 106, 115, 222
Dissent, 3
Document, 9, 11–13, 15, 49, 97, 104, 109, 118, 145, 155, 168, 184, 217, 231, 246, 258, 266, 267, 273, 281
Documentary research, 11, 14
Domestic violence (*see* Violence)
Dowry (*see also Mahr*), 112, 113, 120, 124, 196, 229, 238, 240, 245, 263
Drugs, 30, 181
Druze identity, 1, 14, 15, 24, 28, 40, 199, 201, 283,
Dupret, 7, 8, 33, 123, 135
Dyafeh, 41–44, 46, 47, 262, 273

Early marriage, 58, 67, 182
Economic productivity, 173
Economic rights, 3, 40, 43, 50, 66, 102, 106, 107, 109, 112, 113, 132–4, 142
Egypt, 18, 24, 74, 275
Elopement, 60, 66, 238
Emissaries, 20
Employment (*see also* Work), 37, 49
Engagement (*see also* Betrothal), 40–3, 44, 47, 59, 90, 167, 168, 171, 217, 219, 254, 272
Endogamy, 34–36, 76, 199, 204
Engle Merry, 6, 142, 172
Epistle, 21, 24, 25, 29, 203
Equal, 24, 28, 51, 100, 120, 136, 142, 181
Equality, 16, 24, 25, 28, 31, 32, 51, 100, 129, 130, 197, 198, 268, 278
ESCWA (Economic and Social Commission for Western Asia), 54, 55, 68
Esoteric, 26
Al-Estitar Bilma'louf, 26, 262
Ethics, 268
Ethical questions, 14
Ethnic, 34, 35, 203, 204, 270
Ethnic identity, 34, 35, 270
Ethno-religious identity, 34, 35, 203
Ethnographic, 9
Ethos, 6, 150
Evacuate, 137
Evaluate, 32, 91, 240, 248, 275, 276, 281
Evidence, 76, 97, 137, 155, 160–2, 197, 269, 281
Exchange, 42, 44, 45, 89, 91, 133, 271
Extended family, 37, 38, 40, 81, 118, 119, 144
Expenses (*see also* Cost; Financial demands), 54, 73, 124, 125, 132, 134–135, 169, 171, 279

Faith, 15, 16, 18, 19, 20, 22–29, 31, 34, 199, 203, 262–4, 267–8, 278
Family intervention, 104
Family life, 1, 3, 4, 9, 18, 37, 38, 64, 95, 103, 155, 158, 159, 175, 194, 196, 254
Family patterns, 4
Family, role of, 58
Father-in-law, 45
Fatimid, 18, 20, 268
Fault, 101, 111, 123, 124, 164, 185, 239
Fees, 47, 107, 108, 132, 184, 225, 226, 240, 255
Ferrie, 8
Feuds, 31
Fighter, 138, 284
Fitzpatrick, 7
Financial demands (*see also* Cost; Expenses), 73, 132
Flowers, 40, 42, 44, 46, 59
Forbearance, 27

Freedom, 16, 23, 24, 28, 32, 36, 37, 47–49, 85, 100, 129, 144, 170, 197, 199, 200, 268, 269, 275, 284
Free will, 23, 24
Funeral, 30, 198, 263, 264, 269, 272, 277, 281, 283

Gabon, 154
Gemeinschaft, 5, 6, 8, 265
Gender, 25, 31, 32, 51, 100, 114, 121, 129, 140, 150, 167, 173, 198, 269
Generation, 3, 30, 35, 36, 85, 87, 94, 117, 118, 122, 140, 141, 143, 158, 174, 198, 271
Germany, 122
Gesellschaft, 5, 6, 8, 265, 266
Al Ghaiba, 20, 262
Gharb, 10, 266
Globalization, 6
Goal, 2, 270
God, 21–4, 27, 156, 157, 230, 264, 267, 283
Gold (*see also Jihaz*), 42, 43, 80, 86, 88, 89, 90–4, 124, 141, 238, 240, 271, 277
Goode, 5, 148
Government, 195, 204, 270
Greek, 21
Groom, 30, 39, 40–7, 50, 59, 73, 90, 91, 168, 256, 262, 263, 271–5, 282
Group unity and solidarity, 16, 27, 173, 202, 203
Guardian, 31, 49, 178, 224, 273, 280
Guests, 40–44, 46, 59, 161, 256, 257, 262, 272, 273, 280
Gun, 109, 111, 137–9, 140, 261

Habitus, 95, 197, 200, 201
Al-Hakim Bi-Amr Allah, 18, 19, 20, 21, 25, 26, 268
Hamza Bin Ali, 19, 20
Hanafi, 32, 100
Haram, 100, 262
Harm, 20, 33, 99, 101, 102, 124, 125, 146, 154, 156, 160, 185, 222, 245, 278
Hasbaya, 24, 273
Heaven, 22
Heralds, 19, 20, 262
Historical, 9, 15, 18, 21, 198, 270, 284
History, 13, 16, 20, 24, 34, 95, 203, 228
Hodoud, 19, 262
Hofz al-Ikhwan, 34, 199, 262
Honeymoon, 47, 59
Honour, 40, 60, 118, 138, 140, 153, 170, 186, 264, 274, 275
Hospitalization, 133
Hostile, 26
Household, 12, 27, 37, 53, 59, 80, 81, 87, 89, 110, 124, 155, 173, 192, 237, 260, 269,
Humiliation, 147, 158, 172, 184, 237

Ibra' Zima, 30, 31, 262
Identity, 16, 16, 34, 35, 87, 95, 201, 203, 204
Ikhraj Qayd Fardi, 12, 262
Illegal, 25, 35, 157
Imam, 19
Immaturity (*see also* Psychology), 113, 184, 216
Immigrant (*see also* Migration), 28, 48, 52, 119, 150–153, 161, 167, 178
Impose, 104, 202
Inappropriate, 29, 125, 215, 248, 280
Income, 54, 67, 71, 81, 83, 110, 132, 134, 137, 254, 273, 275, 277
Indicator of change, 62, 171, 174
Individualism, 3, 30, 334, 36–8, 49, 53–5, 73, 90, 92, 95, 129, 152, 178, 197, 202, 245, 262, 263, 265, 268
Industrialization, 2, 5
Inferior, 25
Infidelity (*see also* Adultery), 136, 139, 142, 143, 145, 146, 148, 159, 261
Informal, 13, 14, 106, 122
Informant, 15, 59, 70, 81, 93, 142, 284

Inheritance, 7, 24, 31, 32, 33, 38, 218, 224, 258, 263, 269, 270, 278
Initiate, 29
Instrumentalize, 135
Insult, 116, 117, 133, 141, 184, 245, 247
Institution, 7, 9, 37, 95, 117, 232
Integrity, 123
Intellectual fervour, 18
Intercourse (*see also* Sex), 13, 50, 166, 223, 284
Internal cohesion, 3, 27, 34, 35, 104, 200, 266
Internal conflict, 26, 31, 103, 114, 130
Internet, 37, 205
Interviews, 9, 10, 13–15, 67
Investigation, court, 188
Invitation card, 44, 47
Iran, 19, 173
Irreconcilable differences, 147, 182, 200
Islam, 18, 21, 23, 25, 266, 268, 270, 274, 278
Ismael Ibn Muhammad, 19, 20

Jealousy, 151, 189, 190, 277, 279
Jewellery, 42, 59, 88, 89, 107, 140, 153, 182, 183, 187, 256
Jihaz (*see also* Clothes; Gold; Linen), 50, 169, 262
Jismani, 28, 29, 269
Jordan, 32, 204, 284
Judge (*see also Qadi*), 4, 8, 12, 13, 32, 33, 38, 43, 48, 60, 80, 82, 84–91, 95–102, 104–6, 108, 110, 112–4, 121–5, 127, 130, 132, 134, 140, 141, 143, 144, 146, 160–5, 173, 178, 182, 184, 197–200, 202, 214–23, 226, 231, 232, 233, 239, 246, 248, 258, 259, 263, 264, 267, 269, 272, 276–9, 281–3, 285
Junblatti family, 104
Jurisprudence, 32
Jurist, 33, 269
Just, 3, 7, 22, 24, 27, 32, 37, 50, 58, 86, 87, 98, 105, 111, 112, 133, 149, 154, 171, 179, 186, 187, 198, 199, 236, 253, 270, 271, 274, 285
Justice, 24, 27, 32, 33

Kalousah, 29, 263
Keesing, 6
Kelly, 9
Kennedy, 6
Khalieh, 41, 42, 44, 263
Khalweh, 29, 87, 263
Khuri, 18, 23, 24, 26, 30, 31, 33–35, 204
Kidnapping (*see also* Abduction), 60, 113, 139, 161, 183
Kin, 275
Knowledge, 12, 18, 21–4, 26, 29, 31, 146, 162, 197, 201, 203, 268, 269, 273
Kornhauser, 105
Kutub al-Hikma (*see also* Book of Wisdom), 21, 88, 263

Land, 34, 66, 203, 246
Lawful, 25
Lawyer, 8, 13, 105, 106, 108, 121
Legal, 4, 6–8, 6, 21, 25, 32, 38, 85, 100, 114, 119, 122, 127, 133, 161, 197, 276
Legitimate, 2, 51, 132, 140, 143, 146, 163, 164, 218, 230, 261
Lever, 92
Limit, 8, 22, 28, 31, 36, 48, 54, 60, 69, 162, 262, 277, 278
Lineage, 35
Linen (*see also Jihaz*), 50, 104, 276
Litigants, 8, 111, 135, 281
Love, 24, 39, 66, 68, 71, 159, 254

Mahr (*see also* Dowry), 43, 50, 80, 85, 87, 90–3, 102, 107, 144, 218, 221–3, 229, 260, 261
  Agreed upon, 28, 43, 88, 89, 114
Makarem, 19, 20–4, 267, 283
Maliki, 100
Mandeel, 29, 97, 256, 259, 263, 285
Maronites, 31, 204

Marriage contract, signing of, 14, 43, 53, 61, 85, 86, 89, 91, 95, 167, 168, 178, 272, 277, 282
Marriage proposal, 40
Marital house, 84, 108, 110, 125, 261
Maternal, 39, 40, 43, 80, 160, 194, 216, 224, 225, 236, 237
Matn, 10, 58, 64, 137, 167, 178, 266, 273
Maturity, 49
Maxwell, 2
Ma'zoun, 48, 263, 273
Media, 2, 6, 7, 78
  Mass media, 2, 6, 37, 78
Mediation (*see also* Conflict resolution), 9, 105, 116, 138, 238
Medical, 49, 60, 78, 108, 125, 134, 183, 187, 246
Melli, 106
Mentality, 37, 130, 158
Messick, 8, 269, 278
Methodology, 9, 11, 14, 35, 86, 106, 117, 155, 162, 167, 175–7, 179, 200, 266, 281
Migration (*see also* Immigrant), 3, 6, 36, 59
  Migrants, 28, 90, 150, 275
Military, 53, 137, 179
Minority, 32, 34, 91, 95, 202–4
Misconduct, 138
Misinform, 15
Missing cases, 120
Missionaries, 19
Mithaq; see also Vow of affirmation, 19, 263, 268
Mnookin, 105
Mu'ajjal, 50, 87, 91, 263
Money, 47, 54, 58, 59, 89
Morality, 31, 123, 173, 279
Mother-in-law, 122, 193
Muhakkem (*see also* Adjudicators), 12, 263
Mukasa, 26
Mukhtar, 49, 139, 217, 263, 273
Al-Muqattam, 20
Mutual consent (*see also Talaq bi al-taradi*), 104, 115, 129
Muwahhiddeen, 19, 20, 22, 23, 24, 101, 263

Nafaqa, 13, 123, 263
Nashez, 143, 144, 236, 264, 274
Nashtakine Ad-Darazi, 19
Negligence, 125
Nervous breakdown, 99, 133, 138
Nicolas, 2, 265
Non-supportive, 136
Normative, 7, 90, 96, 200, 202
Norms, 3, 7, 8, 9, 21, 82, 142, 246, 273
Noshouz, 102, 142–144, 148, 220, 261, 264, 280

Oaths, 20, 220
Observation, 9, 13, 14, 122, 126, 167, 267, 276
Oral, 118, 168
Organization, 15, 16, 32, 33, 198, 237
Orphanage, 99, 125
Osanloo, 135, 173
Ostracized, 198
Ottoman rule, 32, 268
Outcast, 19, 30
Out of court procedures, 105, 107, 143, 196, 278
Outsiders, 16, 27, 203
Ownership, 25

Palestine, 32, 33, 79, 204
Parents, 39, 40–3, 53, 57, 58, 60, 65, 66, 74–6, 89, 91, 92, 105, 110, 112, 113, 116, 117, 122, 123, 132, 143, 137–9, 142–4, 147, 151, 153, 154, 156, 159, 161, 162, 165–9, 171, 172, 182–4, 186–9, 193, 237, 238, 245–7, 253, 254, 261, 264, 272, 274, 277, 282, 282
  Paternal interference, 39, 40, 43, 44, 74, 139, 165, 191, 194, 216, 224–6, 236, 280
  Parental support, 66
Parliament, 32, 194, 195
Patience, 107, 137, 153, 156, 158, 182, 187, 189

Patriarchy, 3, 31, 36–8, 65, 74, 75, 77, 85, 140, 155, 164, 189, 191, 192, 271
Patrilineal, 36, 192
Patrilocal, 65
Persecution, 16, 20, 25, 26, 32, 34, 202, 203, 284
Personal particulars, 262
Personal status court, 2, 10, 36, 43, 258
Peripheral change, 17, 196, 197, 199, 200, 204
Petition, 6, 107, 108, 117, 121, 123, 133, 139, 141, 147, 153–6, 158, 159, 165, 169, 181–4, 186, 189, 196, 198, 236, 245, 247, 253
Philosopher, 5, 18
Photograph, 11, 42, 45, 169, 170, 267
Photographer, 42, 45
Pillars of religion, 23, 34, 262
Pious, 24, 123, 262
Private domain, 172
Pluralism, 7
Police, 97, 153, 280
Polygamy, 25, 50, 216, 270
Population census, 17, 175, 176, 179, 195
Power, 8, 12, 30, 32, 38, 49, 96, 230, 264, 369, 274
Power of attorney, 12, 49, 169, 217, 230
Practice(s), 2, 3, 5, 8, 9, 16, 21–6, 29, 31, 33–6, 50, 51, 53, 73, 74, 76, 81, 83, 86, 90, 94, 95, 100–5, 115, 117, 127, 150, 167, 171–174, 184, 192, 196–204, 256, 270–2, 275, 276, 278, 280, 281, 283, 284
Prayer, 23, 29, 31, 33, 43, 87, 197, 267, 268
Pregnancy, 134, 137, 154, 223, 277, 284
Privilege, 28, 35, 78
Progressive, 32, 57, 58, 102, 138, 280
Progressive Socialist Party, 5, 58, 138, 280
Proof, 97, 125, 126, 154, 159, 239, 281
Property, 25, 32, 85, 152, 273, 275, 279
Prothro, 10
Proximity, 6, 78, 79, 120, 278
Psychology (*see also* Immaturity Violence), 28, 108, 109, 112, 113, 117, 136, 138, 150, 173182, 183, 188, 245, 280
Puberty, 49
Public, 19, 23, 24, 35, 40, 89, 91, 104, 146, 147, 172, 173, 184, 229, 258, 263, 269, 272, 280

Qadi (*see also* Judge), 48, 49, 264
Qatar, 171
Qati'a, 121, 264, 279
Questionnaire, 9, 14, 15, 167, 170

Rahma, 30, 198, 264, 283
Ra'is al-Qalam, 128, 264
Ramification, 8, 13, 63, 104
Rape, 60
Rashaya, 10, 273
Ratification, 48, 217
Reason, 101–197
Recording, 159, 160, 161, 281
Reconcile, 101, 109, 111, 117
Registration, 4, 48, 217, 218, 229, 264, 273
Reincarnation, 16, 19, 22, 23, 27, 28, 31, 199, 264
  Previous lives, 3, 12, 13, 27, 28, 141, 179, 185, 245, 246, 260
Religious values, 7, 9, 26, 91, 202, 278
Remarriage, 100, 101, 123, 134, 158, 216, 221
Resilience to change, 82, 129
Report, 13, 16, 17, 49, 54, 61, 72, 109, 110–3, 138, 158, 163–5, 183, 184, 188, 232, 248, 263, 279
Repudiation, 101, 198, 278
Reputation, 92, 140, 157, 237
Resentment, 27
Residence, 79, 164, 218, 280
  Same residence (*see also* Cohabitation), 78, 79
Resort to court, 122, 126, 172
Retreat, 20, 262

Revocable, 25
Rice, 26, 45, 272
Rights,
 to assert, 129–31
 to forgo, 107, 173, 130–133
Rites, 23
Ritual, 23, 34
Ruling (*see also* Sentence), 4, 13, 32, 104, 114, 115, 124, 125, 130, 154, 168
Rural, 10, 34, 36, 37, 50, 74, 83

Sabotage, 97, 124
Sample, 10, 14, 54, 55, 61, 64, 68, 69, 74, 75, 77, 81, 82, 88, 90, 91, 106, 115, 118, 129, 145, 166, 167, 177, 179, 180, 186, 190, 227, 229, 267, 275
Sanctions, 8
Satr, 186
Saudi Arabia, 107, 184, 284
Al-Sayid Abdullah, 29
Schools, religious, 1, 6, 14, 21, 35, 63, 67, 81, 100, 108, 132, 135, 139, 156, 170, 184, 248, 254, 282
Scriptures, 20, 24–26, 29, 49, 270
Secrecy, 16, 25–27, 254
Secret, 26, 27, 151, 153, 160, 161, 285
Secrets of faith, 15, 26, 29, 87
Sect, 48, 51, 195, 204, 270, 273, 274
Sectarian, 3, 34, 90, 229, 276
Self perception, 42
Self realization, 22, 23, 67
Sentence (*see also* Ruling), 101, 110, 119, 123, 125, 132, 139, 154, 162, 163, 164–5, 169, 173–4, 202, 222, 239–40, 248, 255
Service sector, 37
Session, 9, 13, 49, 85, 97, 117, 122, 125, 139, 146, 160, 217, 239, 259, 277
Setback, 19
Sewing machine, 80–4, 86, 87, 94, 196, 199, 276
Sex (*see also* Intercourse), 102, 142, 151, 184, 186, 280, 282
Shame, 90, 104, 146, 280
Shari'a, 35, 100, 157, 232, 264, 278
Shi'a, 18, 32, 238, 265, 284
Shirwal, 29, 264
Shrines, 33, 201
Sin, 27, 43
Sitt Sara, 24
Smoke, 29
Social class, 218
Social position, 80
Social status, 269, 277
Social worker, 112, 173, 200, 202, 241, 243, 245, 247, 279
Solidarity, 3, 15, 16, 27, 28, 31, 34, 95, 104, 114, 115, 126, 155, 173, 174, 199, 200, 201–204
Sotra, 186, 264
Soul, 19, 22, 23, 27, 28, 30, 199, 264, 267
Spinster, 63
Spirit, 19, 269
Spiritual Committee, 33
Starr, 11, 36, 73, 74
State authority, 7
Statistics, 15, 118, 122, 131, 145, 195
Stewart, 85
Stigma, 11, 30, 147, 198
Strata, 16, 88, 140, 156, 170, 171, 174, 197, 201, 256, 263, 264, 267, 268
Strife, 104, 116
Structure, 3, 5, 15, 16, 21, 28, 33, 34, 75, 78, 81, 96, 194, 199, 200, 201
Support,13, 28, 57–59, 61, 66, 74, 81, 99, 106, 110, 113, 114, 123, 124, 132, 133, 135, 136, 138–140, 143, 147, 148, 152, 166, 172, 173, 181, 183, 187, 193, 194, 218–220, 222, 223, 225, 235, 240, 245, 267
Sweets, 40–2, 46, 257, 272
Syria, 32, 33, 73, 79, 118, 204, 246, 262, 266, 271, 275

Tailor, 81, 237, 238
Al tajruba, 20

Talaq bi al-taradi (*see also* Mutual consent), 104, 264
Taliq, 101, 118, 264
Taqlid (*see also* Tradition), 35, 264
Taqqi El-Dine, 10
Taqqiya, 25, 26, 32, 49, 264
Tawheed, 15, 18, 19, 21–26, 28, 48, 157, 203, 262–4
Telephone, 159
Television, 29, 266, 269
Theological, 21
Theoretical, 4, 8
Termination, 100, 215, 223
Territoriality, 33
Territories, 33, 270, 271
Testation, 32, 85, 269, 275
Threat, 60, 99, 109, 111, 114, 124, 132, 133, 139–41, 143, 153, 156, 157, 161, 189, 192, 198, 200, 202, 246, 247, 253, 261, 283, 284
Thursday prayer, 29, 31, 226, 267
Time, 51, 53, 54, 59, 69, 75, 78, 82, 83, 88
  Elapse of, 51, 53, 54, 59, 69, 75, 78, 82, 82, 88, 92
Tolbeh, 30, 39, 40, 157, 264, 271
Tonnies, 5, 265
Town residents, 64, 65, 71, 73, 77, 83, 94, 120, 146, 148, 149
Tradition (*see also Taqlid*), 3, 6, 7, 8, 18, 26, 32, 34, 36, 37, 52, 60, 66, 87, 89, 90, 91, 95, 118, 150, 168, 174, 200, 202, 203, 230, 273, 278
  Traditional, 3, 5, 15–41, 43, 44, 59, 64, 76, 81–5, 87, 91, 94–6, 142, 151, 155, 156, 158, 168–70, 199, 200, 201, 203, 262, 272
Training, 105, 135, 231, 276
Transportation, 135
Turban, 29
Turkey, 100
Turmoil, 20, 25, 281

Unemployment, 37
Unethical, 160
United Arab Emirates, 39, 125
United States, 122, 150–2, 161, 168, 265, 274
Unity, 16, 21, 22, 26, 27, 28, 31, 114, 115
Unobtrusive, 14
Urbanization, 1, 3, 5, 6, 36, 37, 53, 90, 226

Vacation, 167, 248
Variables (contractual), 5, 11, 16, 51, 54, 80, 103, 114, 118, 120, 131, 145, 162, 175, 176, 203
Venezuela, 122, 246
Verbal invitation, 44
Victim, 114, 142, 173, 188
Video, 42, 47, 59
Village community, 6, 30, 31, 35–7, 40, 41, 44, 45, 53, 58, 64–7, 71–3, 77–81, 83, 86, 90, 91, 94, 118–21, 126, 134, 137–9, 144–50, 167, 171, 176, 182, 183, 189–91, 203, 347
Village residents, 64, 67, 71–3, 78, 83, 86, 90, 94, 119, 120, 146–9
Violence (*see also* Beatings; Psychology), 136, 139, 145, 146, 155,
  Domestic, 116, 117, 136, 139, 140, 141, 142, 145, 146, 155, 173, 260–1, 280
  Marital, 146,
  Physical, 116, 140
  Psychological, 117, 280
  Visitation rights, 13, 120–32, 134, 135, 173, 197, 203
Vocational, 135
Vow, 19
Vow of affirmation (*see also Mithaq*), 19

Wadi Al-Taym, 24
Wages, 58
Wahab, Muhammad Ibn, 19
Al-Wahab, Salama ibn Abd, 19, 20
Waive, 92, 133, 134
Wakeel, 12, 264

War (*see also* Civil war), 26, 52, 55–8, 62, 75, 79, 83, 83, 95, 103, 115, 117, 127–9, 132, 137, 139, 177–9, 181, 182, 194, 203, 237, 247, 265, 275, 279, 282
Weddings, 14, 29, 30, 42–4, 46, 47, 58, 59, 66, 73, 83, 157, 168, 170, 190, 197, 227, 256, 262, 263, 271–5, 281
Westernization, 35
Wirth, 6
Wisdom, 18, 21, 26, 29, 197, 203, 262–4, 268
Woodman, 7
Worship, 23, 28, 263
Work (*see also* Employment), 6, 21, 33, 37, 54, 66–68, 78, 79, 93, 110–113, 116, 124, 155, 156, 170, 171, 182–183, 187, 190, 200, 232, 237, 238, 241, 246, 259, 275, 279

Yazbaki family, 104, 264
Youth, 5, 36, 37, 58, 174

Zayy, 199, 264

www.ingramcontent.com/pod-product-compliance
Ingram Content Group UK Ltd.
Pitfield, Milton Keynes, MK11 3LW, UK
UKHW021905150926
475560UK00003B/192

9 781780 765624